Developing for
Microsoft®
Agent

Microsoft® Press

PUBLISHED BY
Microsoft Press
A Division of Microsoft Corporation
One Microsoft Way
Redmond, Washington 98052-6399

Library of Congress Cataloging-in-Publication Data
Developing for Microsoft Agent / Microsoft Corporation.
     p.   cm.
  Includes index.
  ISBN 1-57231-720-5
   1. Computer software--Development. 2. Microsoft Agent.
  I. Microsoft Corporation.
  QA76.76.D4M488 1997
  006.6'768--DC21   97-38025
                                   CIP

Printed and bound in the United States of America.

1 2 3 4 5 6 7 8 9   QMQM 3 2 1 0 9 8

Distributed to the book trade in Canada by Macmillan of Canada, a division of Canada Publishing Corporation.

A CIP catalogue record for this book is available from the British Library.

Microsoft Press books are available through booksellers and distributors worldwide. For further information about international editions, contact your local Microsoft Corporation office. Or contact Microsoft Press International directly at fax (425) 936-7329. Visit our Web site at mspress.microsoft.com.

Acquisitions Editor: David Clark
Project Editor: Stuart J. Stuple

Contents

Introduction to Microsoft Agent

Microsoft Agent is a set of programmable software services that supports the presentation of interactive animated characters within the Microsoft Windows interface. Developers can use characters as interactive assistants to introduce, guide, entertain, or otherwise enhance their Web pages or applications in addition to the conventional use of windows, menus, and controls.

Microsoft Agent enables software developers and Web authors to incorporate a new form of user interaction, known as *conversational interfaces*, that leverages natural aspects of human social communication. In addition to mouse and keyboard input, Microsoft Agent includes optional support for speech recognition so applications can respond to voice commands. Characters can respond using synthesized speech, recorded audio, or text in a cartoon word balloon.

The conversational interface approach facilitated by the Microsoft Agent services does not replace conventional graphical user interface (GUI) design. Instead, character interaction can be easily blended with the conventional interface components such as windows, menus, and controls to extend and enhance your application's interface.

Microsoft Agent's programming interfaces make it easy to animate a character to respond to user input. Animated characters appear in their own window, providing maximum flexibility for where they can be displayed on the screen. Microsoft Agent includes an ActiveX control that makes its services accessible to programming languages that support ActiveX, including Web scripting languages such as Visual Basic Scripting Edition (VBScript). This means that character interaction can be programmed even from HTML pages using the <OBJECT> tag.

C H A P T E R   1

The Microsoft Agent User Interface

Microsoft Agent enables Web sites and conventional applications to include an enhanced form of user interaction. Included user interface components enable users to access and interact with the character, know the character's status, and change global settings (those that affect all characters). This chapter describes these basic elements of the Microsoft Agent user interface.

The Character Window

Microsoft Agent displays animated characters in their own windows that always appear at the top of the window z-order (that is, always on top). A user can move a character's window by dragging the character with the left mouse button. The character image moves with the pointer. In addition, an application can move a character using the **MoveTo** method.

When the user right-clicks a character, a pop-up menu appears that displays the following commands:

Open | Close Commands Window
Hide

_Command_*

...

OtherHostingApplicationCaption**

...

*Commands listed are based on the input-active client. For more information on defining commands that appear in the pop-up menu, see Chapter 3, "Microsoft Agent Programming Interface Overview."

**Entries listed are all other applications currently hosting the character. For more information on defining this entry, see Chapter 3, "Microsoft Agent Programming Interface Overview."

The Open | Close Commands Window command controls the display of the Commands Window of the current active character. If speech recognition services are disabled, this command is disabled. If speech recognition services are not installed, this command does not appear.

The Hide command hides the character. The animation assigned to the character's **Hiding** state plays and hides the character. The first letter of the character name becomes its access key (mnemonic).

The commands for the application(s) currently hosting the character follow the Hide command, preceded by a separator. Then the names of other applications using the character appear, also preceded by a separator.

The Taskbar Icon

When Microsoft Agent runs, its icon appears in the notification area of the taskbar. This icon provides access to Microsoft Agent's properties as well as user control of hiding and showing characters.

FIGURE 1-1. The Microsoft Agent Taskbar Icon

Moving the pointer over the taskbar icon displays a tip window that reflects the current state of Microsoft Agent. For example, during the normal operating state, the tip window might display "Say the name of a character to display it" or "Microsoft Agent is running."

Single-clicking the taskbar icon has no effect. However, double-clicking the icon displays the Microsoft Agent property sheet.

Right-clicking the icon displays a pop-up menu that has the following commands:

Hide | Show _CharacterName_

...

Hide _A_ll Characters

Open | Close _C_ommands Window

Microsoft Agent P_r_operties

E_x_it Microsoft Agent

The Hide | Show *CharacterName* command lists all characters that have been loaded. The command plays the character's **Hiding** state animation and hides the character. The Show *CharacterName* entry makes the character visible and plays the character's **Showing** state animation.

The Hide All Characters command hides all the characters, playing their associated **Hiding** animation.

Microsoft Agent Properties displays the Microsoft Agent property sheet. This command appears as bold text to indicate that this is the default command for the menu.

The Exit command quits the Microsoft Agent services. Because applications may depend on these services, the Exit command prompts for confirmation, informing the user that exiting Microsoft Agent can have unexpected results. If the user confirms the exit process, Microsoft Agent removes all characters and its taskbar icon and stops running. However, if another application starts up and requests Microsoft Agent's services, Microsoft Agent partially restarts, displaying its suspended icon in the taskbar notification area. It also displays a message that offers to resume full operation. If the user confirms restarting, Microsoft Agent resumes full operation. If the user declines, Microsoft Agent exits. The user can choose whether to be notified again through a check box in the message.

In the "suspended" state, right-clicking the taskbar displays the following menu items:

> Restart Microsoft Agent
> Exit Microsoft Agent

Restarting Microsoft Agent fully restores the server and displays the normal (non-suspended) Microsoft Agent icon. It also resets the notification message option to always prompt and resets the contents of the right-click pop-up menu for the taskbar icon to its normal configuration. Choosing Exit in the suspended state quits Microsoft Agent until another application requests its services.

The Commands Window

If a compatible speech engine is installed, Microsoft Agent supplies a special window called the Commands Window that displays the commands that have been voice-enabled for speech recognition. The Commands Window serves as a visual prompt for what can be spoken as input (commands cannot be selected with the mouse).

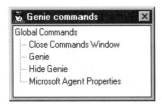

FIGURE 1-2. The Commands Window

The window appears when a user selects the Open Commands Window command, either by speaking the command or right-clicking the character and choosing the command from the character's pop-up menu. However, if the user disables speech input, the Commands Window is not accessible.

The Commands Window displays voice-enabled commands as a tree. If the current hosting application supplies voice commands, they appear expanded and at the top of the window. Entries also appear for other applications using the character. The window also includes the global voice commands supplied by Microsoft Agent. If the current hosting application has no voice commands, the global voice commands appear expanded and at the top of the window.

The user can size and move the Commands Window. Microsoft Agent remembers the last location of the window and redisplays it at that location if the user closes and re-opens the window. If the entries in the window exceed the current display size of the window, scroll bars appear.

The Word Balloon

In addition to spoken audio output, the Microsoft Agent interface also supports textual captioning in the form of text output in cartoon-style word balloons. Words appear in the balloon as they are spoken. The balloon hides when spoken output is completed. The Microsoft Agent property sheet provides options to disable the balloon's display as well as control attributes related to its appearance.

Hello, World!

FIGURE 1-3. The Word Balloon

The Listening Tip

If speech is enabled, a special tooltip window appears when the user presses the push-to-talk key to begin voice input. The Listening Tip displays contextual information related to the current input state of Microsoft Agent. If compatible speech recognition has not been installed or has been disabled, the Listening Tip does not appear.

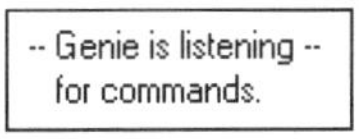

-- Genie is listening --
for commands.

FIGURE 1-4. The Listening Tip

The Agent Property Sheet

Selecting the Microsoft Agent Properties command displays the Microsoft Agent property sheet. This window provides access to configuration options that affect interaction with all characters. Microsoft Agent stores your settings and uses them when Microsoft Agent runs. Microsoft Agent remembers the last page viewed and displays that page when the property sheet appears.

The Output Page

This page includes properties that control character output. For example, the user can determine whether to display output in the word balloon, determine how balloon output should appear, play spoken output as audio, play character sound effects, display the restart prompt, and adjust the speaking speed.

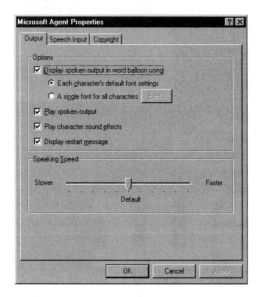

FIGURE 1-5. Output Property Page

The Speech Input Page

A user can adjust speech input options on this property page. The user can disable speech input, set the listening input key, choose whether to display the Listening Tip window, and choose to play a MIDI to indicate when you can speak. The user can also select a speech recognition engine, adjust sound-card and microphone settings, or access any advanced settings provided by the selected speech recognition. This page appears if a compatible (Microsoft Speech Application Programming Interface [SAPI]-compliant) speech recognition engine is installed.

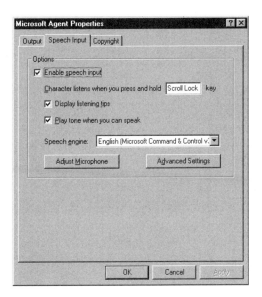

FIGURE 1-6. Speech Input Property Page

The Copyright Page

This page displays the copyright and version information for Microsoft Agent.

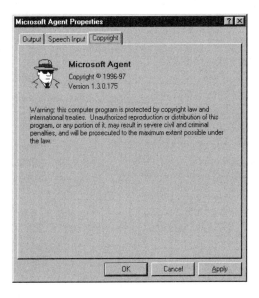

FIGURE 1-7. Copyright Page

C H A P T E R   2

Guidelines for Designing Character Interaction

This chapter outlines guidelines for designing user interfaces that incorporate interactive characters created with Microsoft Agent. For specific information on designing character animation, see Chapter 6, "Designing Characters for Microsoft Agent."

General Character Interaction Guidelines

Principles of good user interface design also apply to designing an interface using Microsoft Agent. You should understand your users and their goals as well as follow a good user interface design process. *The Windows Interface Guidelines for Software Design* (1995, Microsoft Press) provides an excellent overview of general design principles and methodology.

Be Non-Exclusive

Interactive characters can be employed in the user interface as assistants, guides, entertainers, storytellers, sales agents, or in a variety of other roles. The concept of a character performing or assisting should not be designed contrary to the design principle of keeping the user in control. When adding a character to the interface of a Web site or conventional application, use the character as an enhancement—rather than a replacement—of the primary interface. Avoid implementing any feature or operation that exclusively requires a character.

Similarly, let the user choose when they want to interact with your character. A user should be able to dismiss the character and have it return only with the user's permission. Forcing character interaction on users can have a serious negative effect. To support user control of character interaction, Microsoft Agent automatically includes Hide and Show commands. The Microsoft Agent API also supports these methods, so you can include support for these functions in your own interface. In addition, Microsoft Agent's user interface includes an Exit command that enables the user to suspend all character interaction as well as certain global properties that enable the user to override certain character output options. These properties cannot be overridden through the API to ensure that the user's perferences are maintained.

Provide Appropriate Feedback

Quality, appropriateness, and timing are important factors to consider when providing feedback in any interface design. When you incorporate interactive characters, the opportunity for natural forms of feedback increase, as does the user's expectation that the feedback conform to appropriate social interaction. A character can be designed to provide verbal and non-verbal conversational cues in addition to spoken audio output. Use gestures or facial expressions to convey information about its mood or intent. The face is especially important in communication so always consider the character's facial expression. Keep in mind that no facial expression is a facial expression.

We humans have an orienting reflex that causes us to attend to changes in our environment, especially changes in motion, volume, or contrast. Therefore, character animation and sound effects should be kept at a minimum to avoid distracting users when they aren't directly interacting with the character. This doesn't mean the character must freeze, but natural idling behavior such as breathing or looking around is preferable to greater movement. Idling behavior maintains the illusion of social context and availability of the character without distracting the user. You may also want to consider removing the character if the user hasn't interacted with it for a set time period, but make sure the user understands why the character is going away.

Conversely, large body motion, unusual body motion, or highly active animation is very effective if you want to capture the user's attention, particularly if the animation occurs outside the user's current focus. Note also that motion toward the user can effectively gain the user's attention.

Placement and movement of the character should be appropriate to its participation in the user's current task. If the current task involves the character, the character can be placed at the point of focus. When the user is not interacting with the character, move it to a consistent "standby" location or where it will not interfere with tasks or distract the user. Always provide a rationale for how the character gets from one location to another. Similarly, the user will feel most comfortable when the character appears from the same place it previously departed.

Use Natural Variation

While consistency of presentation in your application's conventional interface (such as menus and dialog boxes) makes the interface more predictable, it's recommended that you vary the animation and spoken ouput in the character's aspects of your interface. Appropriately varying the character's responses provides a more natural interface. If a character always addresses the user exactly the same way—always saying the same words for example—the user is likely to consider the character boring, disinterested, or even rude. Human communication rarely involves precise repetition. Even when repeating something in similar situations, we may change wording, gestures, or expression.

Microsoft Agent enables you to build in some variation for a character. When defining a character's animations, you can use branching probabilities on any animation frame to change an animation when it plays. You can also assign multiple animations to each state. Microsoft Agent randomly chooses one of the assigned animations each time it initiates a state. For speech output, you can also include vertical bar characters in your output text to automatically vary the text spoken. For example, Microsoft Agent will randomly select one of the following statements when processing this text as part of the **Speak** method:

"I can say this. | I can say that | I can say something else."

Social Interaction

Human communication is fundamentally social. From the time we are born, we begin reacting to the social cues in our environment and learning the appropriate rules for effective interaction, which include verbal behaviors such as intonation or word ordering, and also non-verbal behaviors such as posture, gestures, and facial expressions. These behaviors convey attitudes, identities, and emotions that color our communication. We often create substitute conventions for communication channels that don't naturally provide bandwidth for non-verbal cues, such as e-mail or online chat sessions.

Unfortunately, the majority of software interface design has focused primarily on the cognitive aspects of communication, overlooking most social aspects. However, recent research has demonstrated that human beings naturally react to social stimuli presented in an interactive context. Further, the reactions often follow the same conventions that people use with each other. Even the smallest cues, such as colors presented or word choice in messages, can trigger this automatic response. The presentation of an animated character with eyes and a mouth heightens the expectation of and strength of responses of social expectations. Never assume that users expect a character's behavior to be less socially appropriate because they know it is artificial. Knowing this, it is important to consider the social aspects of interaction when designing character interaction. *The Media Equation: How People Treat Computers, Televisions, and New Media as Real People and Places* by Byron Reeves and Clifford Nass (New York: Cambridge University Press, 1996) is an excellent reference on current research in this area.

Create Personality

We quickly classify the personality of people we meet based on the simplest of social cues, such as posture, gesture, appearance, word choice, and style. So the first impression a character makes is very important. Creating personality doesn't require artificial intelligence or realistic rendering. Great animators have known this for years and have used the simplest social cues to create rich personalities for normally inanimate objects. Consider, for example, the flying carpet in Disney's *Aladdin* and Lassitter's humorous animated video of a pair of desk lamps. Beginning animators at Disney were often given the challenge of drawing flour sacks that expressed emotion.

A character's name, how it introduces itself, how it speaks, how it moves, and how it responds to user input can all contribute to establishing its basic personality. For example, an authoritative or dominant style of personality can be established by a character making assertions, demonstrating confidence, and issuing commands, whereas a submissive personality may be characterized by phrasing things as questions or making suggestions. Similarly, personality can be conveyed in the sequence of interaction. Dominant personalities always go first. It is important to provide a distinct, well-defined personality type, regardless of which personality type you are creating. Everyone generally dislikes weakly defined or ambiguous personalities.

The kind of personality you choose for a character depends on your objective. If the character's purpose is to direct users toward specific goals, use a dominant, assertive personality. If the character's purpose is to respond to users' requests, use a more submissive personality.

Another approach is to adapt a character's personality to the user's. Studies have shown that users prefer interaction with personalities most like themselves. You might offer the user a choice of characters with different personalities or observe the user's style of interaction with the character and modify the character's interactive style. Research shows that when attempting to match a user's personality you don't always have to be 100% correct. Humans tend to show flexibility in their relationships and, because of the nature of social relationships, are also likely to modify their own behavior somewhat to working with a character.

Observe Appropriate Etiquette

All humans learn rules of social etiquette. Moreover, we come to judge others based on how well they conform to these rules. The presence of a character in your interface makes rules of etiquette directly applicable to your design.

We expect reciprocity in our interaction and when it doesn't happen we tend to view the behavior as incompetent or offensive. In new or formal situations, politeness is usually expected. Only after a relationship is established does familiarity allow for less formal interaction. So when in doubt, be polite.

For example, consider the appropriate protocol for starting and ending a social interaction. When engaging in a new social context, we generally greet each other and indicate our intent to leave before we depart. You can apply this model directly to character interaction; avoid the character appearing or disappearing without an appropriate indication.

A part of politeness is how we respond. We expect responses that are appropriate. For example, if you ask, "What day is it?" you don't expect the response to be "10 apples." However, accuracy and relevance are not enough; you may also need to determine the context. An accurate response could be "Monday" or "August 25th." Similarly, the wording of a response can be accurate but still be offensive, depending on intonation, facial expression, or other non-verbal behaviors.

In addition, we address each other while talking: we face the person, turning only to direct attention to something. Turning one's back, without some purpose, implies disinterest and is generally considered to be impolite.

Politeness also affects the way we respond to or perceive others. For example, social research indicates that we are more likely to be honest about our evaluation of others when asked by another person than when the people ask about themselves. Similarly, we accept positive evaluations of others more readily than positive self-evaluations. Immodest behavior is generally considered impolite. Therefore, unless intentionally trying to promote an impolite personality style, avoid having the character compliment its own performance.

Also consider the cultural impact on social etiquette. This may apply to the character's attire, gestures, or word choice. While polite behaviors may vary by culture, the concept of politeness is cross-cultural.

Use Praise

Humans respond better to praise than criticism, even when the praise may be unwarranted. Although most software interfaces strive to avoid evaluative feedback, praise is demonstrably more effective than providing no evaluation at all. Further, many interfaces designed as neutral are often perceived as critical by users, because they rarely get positive feedback when things are operating normally, and error messages when things go wrong. Similarly, wording that tells the user that there is a better way to perform a task implicitly criticizes the user.

Because characters create a social context, careful use of praise and criticism is even more important than in a traditional user interface. While few people enjoy sycophantic behavior, the limits of the liberal use of praise have yet to be demonstrated. Praise is especially effective in situations where users are less confident about their performance of a task. On the other hand, criticism should be used sparingly. Even when you think criticism is appropriate, be aware that humans have a tendency to dismiss it or redirect it back to its source.

However, avoid self-praise unless it is a humorous part of the personality the character projects. We tend to judge self-conceit with skepticism. If you want to direct approbation to a character, have it directed from another source, such as another character or descriptive explanation.

Create a Team Player

When a team is created, group dynamics have a powerful effect on the members in the group. First, people in a group or team context have a tendency to identify more with the other people on the team than they typically would in a non-team setting. As a result, they can also identify more with their teammates than those outside the team. But equally important, members of a team are more willing to cooperate and modify their attitudes and behavior. Because the social dynamics of a team affect its members' interaction, it can be useful to consider when designing interaction with characters.

Creating a sense of team involves two factors: identity and interdependence. You can create identity by creating a team name, color, symbol, or other identifier that the user and character share. For example, you could provide a sticker the user could affix to their computer or enable the user to pick a team name or icon that would appear with the character. Team identity may also be established by what the character says. For example, you could have the character verbally identify itself as a partner or to the user and itself as a team.

Interdependence may be harder to implement or take longer to establish, though it is important to consider because interdependence seems to have a stronger social impact than team identity. This is illustrated by the product brand loyalty that marketing organizations endeavor to establish. Creating a sense of interdependence involves demonstrating continuing usefulness and reliability for the user. Important questions to answer are "Does the character provide value?" and "Does the character operate predictably and reliably?" An important factor here is how the character's relationship is established with the user. To engender a sense of team interdependence, the character needs to be presented as a peer to the user. Although it may be useful in some scenarios to present the character as an expert or a servant, to leverage the collaborative benefits of team dynamics, there must be a sense of equality where the user can be dependent on the character without a sense of inferiority. This may be as simple as having the character refer to itself as a teammate or companion rather than as a wizard. It can also be influenced by how the character requests information from the user. For example, a character might say, "Let's work together to answer this question…"

Consider Gender Effects

Social responses can be affected by gender. For example, Nass and Reeves' work indicates that in the U.S., male personalities are stereotypically considered to understand more about technical subjects, while females are attributed to be better experts in interpersonal subjects like love and relationships. None of this suggest that you should perpetuate gender stereotypes, only that you be aware that they may exist and understand how they might affect interaction with your character.

Remember that a character's perceived gender isn't solely established by its name or appearance. Even a gender-neutral character may convey gender based on its voice characteristics, speech patterns, and movement.

Speech Recognition

Speech recognition provides a very natural and familiar interface for interacting with characters. However, speech input also presents many challenges. Currently, speech engines operate without substantial parts of the human speech communication repertoire, such as gestures, intonation, and facial expressions. Further, natural speech is typically unbounded. It is easy for the speaker to exceed the current vocabulary, or *grammar*, of the engine. Similarly, wording or word order can vary for any given request or response. In addition, speech recognition engines must often deal with large variations in the speaker's environment. For example, background noise, microphone quality, and location can affect input quality. Similarly, different speaker pronunciations or even same-speaker variations, such as when the speaker has a cold, make it a challenge to convert the acoustic data into representational understanding. Finally, speech engines must also deal with similar sounding words or phrases in a language, such as "new," "knew," and "gnu," or "wreck a nice beach" and "recognize speech."

Speech isn't always the best form of input for a task. Because of the turn-taking nature of speech, it can often be slower than other forms of input. Like the keyboard, speech input is a poor interface for pointing unless some type of mnemonic representation is provided. Therefore, always consider whether speech is the most appropriate input for a task. It is best to avoid using speech as the exclusive interface to any task. Provide other ways to access any basic functionality using other methods such as the mouse or keyboard. In addition, take advantage of the multimodal nature of using speech in the visual interface by combining speech input with visual information that helps specify the context and options.

Finally, the successful use of speech input is due only in part to the quality of the technology. Even human recognition, which exceeds any current recognition technology, sometimes fails. However, in human communication we use strategies that improve the probability of success and that provide error recovery when something goes wrong. Therefore, the effectiveness of speech input also depends on the quality of the user interface that presents it.

Often, studying human models of speech interaction can be useful in designing for more natural speech interfaces. Recording actual human speech dialogues for particular scenarios may help you better understand the constructs and patterns used, as well as effective forms of feedback and error recovery. It can also help determine the appropriate vocabulary to use (for input and output). It is better to design a speech interface based on how people actually speak than to simply derive it from the graphical interface in which it operates.

Note that Microsoft Agent uses the Microsoft Speech API (SAPI) to support speech recognition. This enables Microsoft Agent to be used with a variety of compatible engines. Although Microsoft Agent specifies certain basic interfaces, the performance requirements and quality of an engine may vary.

Speech is not the only means of supporting conversational interfaces. You can also use natural-language processing of keyboard input in place of or in addition to speech. In those situations, you can still generally apply guidelines for speech input.

Listen, Don't Just Recognize

Successful communication involves more than recognition of words. The process of dialogue implies exchanging cues to signal turn-taking and understanding. Characters can improve conversational interfaces by providing cues like head tilts, nods, or shakes to indicate when the speech engine is in the listening state and when something is recognized. For example, Microsoft Agent plays animations assigned to the **Listening** state when a user presses the push-to-talk listening key and animations assigned to the **Hearing** state when an utterance is detected. When defining your own character, make sure you create and assign appropriate animations to these states. For more information on designing characters, see Chapter 6, "Designing Characters for Microsoft Agent."

In addition to non-verbal cues, a conversation involves a common context between the conversing parties. Similarly, speech input scenarios with characters are more likely to succeed when the context is well established. Establishing the context enables you to better interpret similar-sounding phrases like "check's in the mail" and "check my mail." You may also want to enable the user to query the context by providing a command, such as "Help" or "Where am I," to which you respond by restating the current context, such as the last action your application performed.

Microsoft Agent provides interfaces that enable you to access the best match and the two next best alternatives returned by the speech recognition engine. In addition, you can access confidence scores for all matches. You can use this information to better determine what was spoken. For example, if the confidence scores of the best match and first alternative are close, it may indicate that the speech engine had difficulty discerning the difference between them. In such a case, you may want to ask the user to repeat or rephrase the request in an effort to improve performance. However, if the best match and first or second alternatives return the same command, it strengthens the indication of the correct recognition.

The nature of a conversation or dialogue implies that there should be a response to spoken input. Therefore, a user's input should always be responded to with verbal or visual feedback that indicates an action was performed or a problem was encountered, or provides an appropriate reply.

Clarify and Limit Choices

Speech recognition becomes more successful when the user learns the range of appropriate grammar. It also works better when the range of choices is limited. The less open-ended the input, the better the speech engine can analyze the acoustic information input.

Microsoft Agent includes several built-in provisions that increase the success of speech input. The first is the Commands Window displayed when the user says, "Open Commands Window," or "What can I say?" (or when the user chooses Open Commands Window from the character's pop-up menu). The Commands Window serves as a visual guide to the active grammar of the speech engine. It also reduces recognition errors by activating only the speech grammar of the input-active application and Microsoft Agent's global commands. Therefore, the active grammar of the speech engine applies to the immediate context. For more information on the Commands Window, see Chapter 1, "The Microsoft Agent User Interface."

When you create Microsoft Agent voice-enabled commands, you can author the caption text that appears in Commands Window as well as its voice text (grammar), the words that the engine should use for matching this command. Always try to make your commands as distinctive as possible. The greater the difference between the wording of commands, especially for the voice text, the more likely the speech engine will be able to discriminate between spoken commands and provide an accurate match. Also avoid single-word or very short commands. Generally, more acoustic information in a spoken utterance gives the engine a better chance to make an accurate match.

When defining the voice text for a command, provide a reasonable variety of wording. Requests that mean the same thing can be phrased very differently, as illustrated in the following example:

Add some pepperoni.

I'd like some pepperoni.

Could you add some pepperoni?

Pepperoni please.

Microsoft Agent enables you to easily specify alternatives or optional words for the voice grammar for your application. You enclose alternative words or phrases between parentheses, separated by a vertical bar character. You can define optional words by enclosing them between square bracket characters. You can also nest alternatives or optional words. You can also use an ellipsis (…) in voice text as a placeholder for any word. However, using ellipses too frequently may make it more difficult for the engine to distinguish between different voice commands. In any case, always make sure that your voice text includes at least one distinctive word for each command that is not optional. Typically, this should match a word or words in the caption text you define that appears in the Commands Window.

Although you can include symbols, punctuation, or abbreviations in your caption text, avoid them in your voice text. Many speech recognition engines cannot handle symbols and abbreviations or may use them to set special input parameters. In addition, spell out numbers. This also ensures more reliable recognition support.

You can also use directive prompts to avoid open-ended input. Directive prompts implicitly reference the choices or explicitly state them, as shown in the following examples:

What do you want?	Too general, an open-ended request
Choose a pizza style or ingredient.	Good, if choices are visible, but still general
Say "Hawaiian," "Chicago," or "The Works."	Better, an explicit directive with specific options

This guides the user toward issuing a valid command. By suggesting the words or phrase, you are more likely to elicit expected wording in return. To avoid unnatural repetitiveness, change the wording or shorten the original for subsequent presentation as the user becomes more experienced with the input style. Directive prompts can also be used in situations where the user fails to issue a command within a prescribed time or fails to provide an expected command. Directive prompts can be provided using speech output, your application interfaces, or both. The key is helping the user know the appropriate choices.

Wording influences the success of a prompt. For example, the prompt, "Would you like to order your pizza?" could generate either a "Yes" or "No" response, but it might also generate an order request. Define prompts to be non-ambiguous or be prepared to accept a larger variety of possible responses. In addition, note the tendency for people to mimic words and constructs they hear. This can often be used to help evoke an appropriate response as in the following example:

User: Show me all messages from Paul.

Character: Do you mean Paul Allen or Paul Maritz?

This is more likely to elicit the full name of one of the parties with the possible prefix of "I mean" or "I meant."

Because Microsoft Agent characters operate within the visual interface of Windows, you can use visual elements to provide directive prompts for speech input. For example, you can have the character gesture at a list of choices and request that the user select one, or display choices in a dialog box or message window. This has two benefits: it explicitly suggests the words you want the user to speak and it provides an alternate way for the user to reply.

You can also use other modes of interaction to subtly suggest to users the appropriate speech grammar, as shown in the following example:

User: (Clicks Hawaiian-style pizza option with the mouse)

Character: Hawaiian-style pizza.

User: (Clicks Extra Cheese option with the mouse)

Character: Add "Extra Cheese."

Another important factor in successful speech input is cueing the user when the engine is ready for input, because many speech engines allow only a single utterance at a time. Microsoft Agent provides support for this in two ways. First, if the sound card supports MIDI, Microsoft Agent generates a brief tone to signal when the speech-input channel is available. Second, the Listening Tip window displays an appropriate text prompt when the character (speech engine) is listening for input. In addition, this tip displays what the engine heard.

Provide Good Error Recovery

As with any well-designed interface, the interactive process should minimize the circumstances that lead to errors. However, it is rarely possible to eliminate all errors, so supporting good error recovery is essential to maintain the confidence and interest of the user. In general, error recovery involves detecting an error, determining the cause, and defining a way to resolve the error. Users respond better to interfaces that are cooperative, that work with the user to accomplish a task.

The first step in speech error recovery is detecting the failure condition. Speech recognition can fail due to a variety of errors. Error conditions can usually be detected as the result of invalid input, explicit user correction or cancellation, or user repetition.

A *rejection error* occurs when the recognition engine has no match for what the user has said. Background noise or early starts are also common causes of recognition failure, so asking the user to repeat a command is often a good initial solution. However, if the phrase is outside of the current active grammar, asking the user to rephrase the request may solve the problem. The difference in wording may result in a match with something in the current grammar. Listing or suggesting appropriate expected input options is another alternative.

A good strategy for rejection error recovery is to combine these techniques to get the user back on track, offering increasingly more assistance if the failure persists. For example, you can begin by responding to the initial failure with an interrogative like "Huh?" or "What?" or a hand-to-the-ear gesture. A short response increases the likelihood that the user's repeated statement will not fail because the user spoke too soon. Upon a repeated failure, the subsequent request to rephrase improves the chance of matching something within the given grammar. From here, providing explicit prompts of accepted commands further increases the chance of a match. This technique is illustrated in the following example:

User: I'd like a Chicago-style pizza with anchovies.

Character: (Hand to ear) Huh?

User: I want a Chicago pizza with anchovies.

Character: (Head shake) Please rephrase your request.

User: I said Chicago pizza, with anchovies.

Character: (Shrug) I'm sorry. Tell me the style of pizza you want.

User: Chicago, with anchovies.

Character: Still no luck. Here's what you can say: "Chicago," "Hawaiian," or "Combo."

To make the error handling feel more natural, make sure you provide a degree of random variation when responding to errors. In addition, a natural user reaction to any request to repeat a response is to exaggerate or increase the volume when repeating the statement. It may be useful to occasionally remind the user to speak normally and clearly, as the exaggeration or increased volume may make it harder for the speech engine to recognize the words.

Progressive assistance should do more than bring the error to the user's attention; it should guide the user toward speaking in the current grammar by successively providing more informative messages. Interfaces that appear to be trying to understand encourage a high degree of satisfaction and tolerance from the user.

Substitution errors, where the speech engine recognizes the input but matches the wrong command, are harder to resolve because the speech engine detects a matching utterance. A mismatch can also occur when the speech engine interprets extraneous sounds as valid input (also known as an *insertion error*). In these situations, the user's assistance is needed to identify the error condition. To do this, you can repeat what the speech engine returned and ask the user to confirm it before proceeding:

User: I'd like a Chicago-style pizza.

Character: Did you say you'd like a "Chicago-style pizza"?

User: Yes.

Character: What additional ingredients would you like on it?

User: Anchovies.

Character: Did you say "anchovies"?

User: Yes.

However, using this technique for every utterance becomes inefficient and tiresome. To handle this, restrict confirmation to situations that have significant negative consequences or increase the complexity of the immediate task. If it is easy for the user to make or reverse changes, you may be able to avoid requesting confirmation of their choices. Similarly, if you make choices visible you may not need to provide explicit correction. For example, choosing an item from a list may not require verification because the user can see the results and easily change them. You can also use confidence and alternative scores to provide a threshold for confirmation. You might adjust the threshold by keeping a history of the user's actions in a given situation and eliminating verification based on consistent user confirmation. Finally, consider the multi-modal nature of the interface. Confirmation from the mouse or keyboard may also be appropriate.

Carefully choose the wording of confirmations. For example, "Did you say…?" or "I think you said..." are better than "Do you really want to…?" because the former phrases imply that the accuracy of the character's listening (recognition) is being queried, not that the user may have misspoken.

Also consider the grammar for a response. For example, a negative response is likely to generate a rejection error, requiring an additional prompt as shown in the following example:

User: I'd like some pepperoni.

Character: Did you say "no ham"?

User: No, I said pepperoni.

Character: Huh?

User: Pepperoni.

Modifying your grammar to include prefixes to handle natural response variations increases the efficiency of the recovery process, especially when the user doesn't confirm the verification prompt. In this example, the confirmation could have been handled in a single step by modifying the grammar for the "pepperoni" by also including "no I said pepperoni", "I said pepperoni", and "no pepperoni".

You can also handle substitution errors using the alternative matches returned by the speech engine as the corrective confirmation:

User: I'd like some pepperoni.

Character: (Hears "no ham" as best match, "pepperoni" as first alternative) Did you say "no ham"?

User: No, pepperoni.

Character: (Still hears "no ham" as best match, but now offers first alternative) "Pepperoni"?

Similarly, you can keep a history of common substitution errors and if a particular error is frequent, offer the alternative the first time.

In any recognition error situation, avoid blaming the user. If the character suggests or even implies that the user is to blame, or the character seems indifferent to the error, the user may become offended. Here also, carefully choose wording that explicitly accepts responsibility, is appropriate to the situation, and uses variety to create a more natural response. When expressing an apology, avoid ambiguous words like "oops" or "uh oh" that could be interpreted as blaming the user. Instead, use phrases like "I'm sorry" or "My mistake." Repeated or more serious errors might use a more elaborate apology like "I am really sorry about that." Also consider the personality of the character when determining the type of response. Another option is to blame an external situation. Comments such as "Boy, it's noisy out there," takes the blame away from the user and the character. Also, reminding the user of the cooperative nature of the interaction may be helpful: consider phrases such as, "Let's see what we can do to make this work."

Microsoft Agent also supports some automatic feedback for recognition. When an utterance is detected, the Listening Tip displays the voice text of the best match heard. You can set your own text to display based on the confidence setting for a command you define.

Because of error potential, always require confirmation for any choices that have serious negative consequences and are irreversible. Naturally, you'll want to require confirmation when the results of an action could be destructive. However, consider also requiring confirmation for situations that abort any lengthy process or operation.

Speech Output

Like speech input, speech output is a familiar and natural form of communication, so it is also an appropriate complement in a character-based interface. However, speech output also has its liabilities. In some environments, speech output may not be preferred or audible. In addition, by itself, speech is invisible and has no persistent output, relying heavily on short-term memory. These factors limit its capacity and speed for processing large amounts of information. Similarly, speech output can also disrupt user input, particularly when speech is the input method. Speech engines generally have little support that enables the user to interrupt when speech or other audio has the output channel.

As a result, avoid using speech as the exclusive form of output. However, because Microsoft Agent presents characters as a part of the Windows interface, it provides several advantages over speech-only environments. Characters can be combined with other forms of input and output to make options and actions visible, enabling a more effective interface than one that is exclusively visual or speech-based.

In addition, to make speech output more visible, Microsoft Agent includes the option of authoring a character with a cartoon-style word balloon. Other settings enable you to determine how text appears in the balloon and when the balloon is removed. You can also determine what font to use. Although you can set a character's word balloon attributes, be aware that the user can override these settings.

Be Efficient and Natural

When accomplishing tasks, effective human conversations are typically exchanges of brief information. Often, elements in the discussion are established between the parties and then referred to indirectly using abbreviated responses. These forms of abbreviation are beneficial because they are efficient, and they also imply that the speaker and listener have a common context; that is, that they are communicating. Using appropriate forms of abbreviation also makes a dialogue more natural.

One form of conversational abbreviation is the use of contractions. When they are not used, they make a speaker seem more formal and rigid, and sometimes less human. Most human conversations demonstrate more freedom in the linguistic rules than written text.

Another common form of abbreviation in conversations is *anaphora*, the use of pronouns. For example, when someone asks, "Have you seen Bill today?" responses that substitute "him" for "Bill" are more natural than repeating the name again. The substitution is a cue that the parties in the dialogue share a common context of *who* "him" is. Keep in mind that the word "I" refers to the character when he or she says it.

Shared context is also communicated by the use of linguistic *ellipsis*, the truncation of many of the words in the original query. For example, the listener could respond, "Yes, I saw him," demonstrating the shared context of *when* or even respond with a simple "Yes" that demonstrates the shared context of *who* and *when*.

Implicit understanding can also be conveyed through other forms of abbreviated conversational style, where content is inferred without repetition, as shown in the following example:

User: I'd like a Chicago-style pizza.
Character: With "Extra Cheese"?

Similarly, if someone says, "It is hot in here," the phrase is understandable and requires no further detail if you know where the speaker is. However, if the context is not well-established or is ambiguous, eliminating all contextual references may leave the user confused.

When using abbreviated communication, always consider the user's context and the type of content. It is appropriate to use longer descriptions for new and unfamiliar information. However, even with long descriptive information, try to break it up into smaller chunks. This gives you the ability to change the animation as the character speaks. It also provides greater opportunity for the user to interrupt the character, especially when using speech input.

Consistency is important in speech output. Strange speech patterns or prosody may be interpreted as downgrading the intelligence of the character. Similarly, switching between TTS and recorded speech may cause users to interpret the character strangely or possessing different personalities. Lip-synced mouth movements can improve intelligibility of speech. Microsoft Agent automatically supports lip-syncing for TTS engines that comply with its required SAPI interfaces. However, lip-syncing is also supported for recorded speech. Sound files can also be enhanced using the Microsoft Linguisitc Sound Editing Tool.

Use the Active Voice

When using speech output to provide directive information or to elicit a user response, use the active voice and clearly specify the user's expected action. The following example illustrates the differences:

Let me repeat your number.	No user action
The number will be repeated.	Passive voice, no user action
Listen while the number is repeated.	Passive voice
Listen to the repetition.	Best choice

In addition, construct your output to unfold the key information at the end of the phrase as shown in the following examples:

Instead of: "Is three the next digit?"   **Use:** "Is the next digit three?"

Instead of: "Click OK to begin."   **Use:** "To begin, click OK."

Instead of: "Say 'Done' to complete your order."   **Use:** "To complete your order, say 'Done.'"

Use Appropriate Timing and Emphasis

Like all feedback, the effectiveness of speech output depends on timing and emphasis. A good deal of information can be communicated in the pace, volume, and pitch used when something is spoken. If you use a text-to-speech engine as your character's voice, most engines let you set the speed, pauses, pitch, and emphasis of words or phrases. You can use these attributes to indicate interest and understanding of the character as well as direct the user's attention or indicate your character's intent. For further information on how to set speech attributes, see Chapter 9, "Microsoft Agent Speech Output Tags." If you are using sound files as your character's output, consider these factors as well in your recorded audio.

C H A P T E R   3

Microsoft Agent Programming Interface Overview

The Microsoft Agent API provides services that support the display and animation of animated characters. Implemented as an OLE Automation/ Component Object Model (COM) server, Microsoft Agent enables multiple applications, called *clients* or *client applications*, to host and access its animation, input, and output services at the same time. A client can be any application that supports the Microsoft Agent's COM interfaces.

Although you can call Microsoft Agent's COM interfaces directly, Microsoft Agent also includes an ActiveX control. This control makes it easy to access Microsoft Agent's services from programming languages that support the ActiveX control interface. For information, see Chapter 4, "Programming the Microsoft Agent Control" and Chapter 5, "Programming the Microsoft Agent Server Interface."

As a COM server, Microsoft Agent starts up only when a client application requests to connect to it. It remains running until all clients close their connection. When no connected clients remain, Microsoft Agent automatically exits. Microsoft Agent also exits when a user explicitly chooses the Exit command on the pop-up menu of Microsoft Agent's taskbar icon and confirms exiting in the warning message box. This action causes the server to send a **Shutdown** event to all connected clients advising them that the server is exiting.

Licensing and Distribution

The Microsoft Agent self-extracting executable installs a number of system files and registry entries. Web developers can include the CLSID in the <OBJECT> tag of their HTML page, subject to the provisions of the license agreement displayed when the control is downloaded and installed. Application developers who want to add Microsoft Agent services and any of its components (including Microsoft Agent character files) to their application must obtain a redistribution license for Microsoft Agent. For more information on redistribution of Microsoft Agent, see Appendix E, "Microsoft Agent Licensing and Redistribution."

Animation Services

Microsoft Agent's animation services manage the animation and movement of a character's image in its own window on the screen. An animation is defined as a sequence of timed and optionally branched frames, composed of one or more images. Specifying the **Play** statement with the name of an animation plays that animation. Animation names are specific to a character definition. As an animation plays, the shape of its window changes to the match the image in the frame. This results in a movable graphic image, or *sprite*, displayed on top of the desktop and all windows.

Each client application can display and animate its own character. You can also share a character between multiple client applications. Microsoft Agent also supports clients using multiple characters displayed at the same time. The animation services enable you to animate characters independently or synchronize their animation.

To access a character, use the **Load** method to load the character's data. Microsoft Agent's services include a data provider that supports two formats for loading character and animation data: a single structured file and separate files. Typically, you would use the single file format (.ACS) when the data can be stored locally. The multiple file format (.ACF, .AAF) works best when you want to download animations individually, such as when accessing animations from a Web page script.

The *Developing with Microsoft Agent* CD-ROM provides a set of characters you can download and use, subject to the provisions of the license agreement.

You can define your own character and its animations using any rendering tool you prefer. To compile a character's animations for use with Microsoft Agent, use the Microsoft Agent Character Editor. This tool enables you to define a character's default properties as well as define animations for the character. The Microsoft Agent Character Editor also enables you to select the appropriate file format when you create a character. For alternative formats or rendering, you can supply your own animation data provider.

The animation services also play certain animations automatically. For example, when you call the **MoveTo** and **GestureAt** methods, the server determines what animation to play based on the character's current position. Similarly, the services play **Idling** animations when the user has not interacted with the character. These server-managed animations are called "states," and are defined when a character is created. For more information, see Chapter 7, "Using The Microsoft Agent Character Editor."

Client applications can directly hide or show a character by using the **Hide** or **Show** methods that play the animations assigned to the **Hiding** and **Showing** states and set the character's **Visible** property. This functionality enables you to display or hide a character using your own interface.

Although the server produces no output when a character is hidden, the server still queues and processes the animation request (plays the animation), but passes a request status back to the client. In the hidden state, the character cannot become input-active. However, if the user speaks the name of a hidden character (when speech input is enabled), the server automatically shows the character.

Microsoft Agent queues animation requests and processes them asynchronously. This enables your application's code to continue while character animations play. However, you can still monitor and manage your character's animation queue by creating an object reference to the request.

Input Services

A client application provides the primary user interface for interaction with a character. You can program a character to respond to any form of input, from button-clicks to typed-in text. In addition, Microsoft Agent provides events so you can program what happens when the user clicks, double-clicks, or drags the character. The server passes the coordinates of the pointer and any modifier key state for these events.

Speech Input Support

In addition to supporting mouse and keyboard interaction, Microsoft Agent includes support for speech input. You can use The Microsoft Command and Control Engine (included on the CD-ROM) for supporting speech recognition. The Command and Control speech engine enables users to speak naturally without pausing between words. Speech recognition is speaker-independent, but it can be trained for improved performance. Because Microsoft Agent's support for speech input is based on Microsoft SAPI (Speech Application Programming Interface), you can use Microsoft Agent with other engines that are SAPI-compliant.

The user can initiate speech input by pressing and holding the push-to-talk listening hot key. In this mode, if the speech engine receives the beginning of spoken input, it holds the audio channel open until it detects the end of the utterance. However, when not receiving input, it does not block audio output. This enables the user to issue multiple voice commands while holding down the key, and the character can respond when the user isn't speaking. If a character attempts to speak while the user is speaking, the character's audible output fails though text may still be displayed in its word balloon. If the character has the audio channel while listening key is pressed, the server automatically transfers control back to the user after processing the text in the **Speak** method. An optional MIDI tone is played to cue the user to begin speaking. This enables the user to provide input even if the application driving the character failed to provide logical pauses in its output.

Because multiple client applications can share the same character and because multiple clients can use different characters at the same time, the server designates one client as the *input-active* client and sends mouse and voice input only to that client application. This maintains the orderly management of user input, so that an appropriate client responds to the input. Typically, user interaction determines which client application becomes input-active. For example, if the user clicks a character, that character's client application becomes input-active; if a user speaks the name of a character, it becomes input-active. Also, when the server processes a character's **Show** method, the client of that character becomes input-active. In addition, you can call the **Activate** method to make your client input-active, but you should do so only when your client application is active. For example, if the user clicks your application's window, activating your application, you can call the **Activate** method to receive and process mouse and speech input.

If multiple clients use the same character, the server defines the last one shown or the last one input-active as the current input-active character. However, you can also use the **Activate** method to set your client to become input-active or remain non-input-active when the user selects that character.

The Commands Window

As described in Chapter 1, "The Microsoft Agent User Interface," when a speech engine is installed and enabled, Microsoft Agent also includes a special interface called the Commands Window. This window displays the voice-enabled commands defined by the client applications for a character.

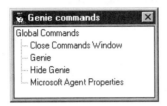

FIGURE 3-1. Commands Window

The Commands Window appears when the Open Commands Window command is chosen. Client commands appear in the Commands Window based on the Caption and Voice property settings of their Commands collection object.

The server creates a set of voice commands for general interaction and displays these under the Global Commands entry.

Caption	Voice Grammar
Open	Close Commands Window	((open | show) [the] commands [window]	what can I say [now]) toggles with: close [the] commands [window]
CharacterName	[show] *CharacterName*[*]
Hide All Characters	hide all [characters]
Hide *CharacterName*	hide *CharacterName*[**]
Microsoft Agent Properties	Close Microsoft Agent Property Sheet	[(open | show)] [microsoft] agent (properties | property sheet) toggles with: close [microsoft] agent (properties | property sheet)

* All loaded characters are listed.

** A character is listed here only if it is currently visible.

The server automatically displays the commands of the current input-active client and, if necessary, scrolls the window to display as many of the client's commands as possible, based on the size of the window. If the character has no client entries, the Global Commands entry is expanded. Non-input-active clients appear in the tree as single entries.

Speaking the voice command for a client's **Commands** collection switches to that client and the Commands Window displays the commands of that client. No other entries are expanded. Similarly, if the user switches characters, the Commands Window changes to display the commands of its input-active client. If the client is already input-active, speaking its voice command has no effect. (However, if the user collapses the active client's subtree with the mouse, speaking the client name redisplays the client's subtree.) If a client has voice commands, but no **Voice** setting for its **Commands** object (or no **Caption**), the tree displays "(command undefined)" as the parent entry, but only when that client is input-active and the client has commands in its collection that have **Caption** and **Voice** settings. The server includes voice commands in the Global Commands entry ([show] [me] global commands). If the user speaks "Global Commands," the Commands Window always displays its associated subtree entries. If they are already displayed, the command has no effect.

Although you can also display or hide the Commands Window from your application's code using the **Visible** property, you cannot change the Commands Window size or location. The server maintains the Commands Window's properties based on the user's interaction with the window. Its initial location is immediately adjacent to the Microsoft Agent taskbar icon.

The Commands Window is included in the ALT+TAB window order. This enables a user to switch to the window to scroll, resize, or reposition the window with the keyboard.

The Listening Tip

When speech input is installed, Microsoft Agent includes a special tooltip window that displays when the user presses the push-to-talk hot key. The following table summarizes the display of the Listening Tip when speech recognition is enabled.

Action	Result
User presses the listening mode hot key	The Listening Tip appears below the active client's character and displays: -- *CharacterName* is listening -- for "*InputActiveClientCaption*" commands. The first line identifying the character is centered. The second line is left justified and breaks to a third line when the text exceeds the Listening Tip's maximum width. If an input-active client of the character does not have a caption or defined voice parameters for its **Commands** object, the Listening Tip displays: -- *CharacterName* is listening -- for commands. If there are no visible characters, the Listening Tip appears adjacent to the Microsoft Agent taskbar icon and displays: -- All characters are hidden -- Say the name of a character to display it. If the speech recognition is still initializing, the Listening Tip displays: Say the name of a character to display it. If the audio channel is busy, as when the character is audibly speaking or some other application is using the audio channel, the Listening Tip displays: -- *CharacterName* is preparing to listen -- Please wait to speak.
User presses the listening mode hot key and speaks a voice command	The Listening Tip appears below the active client's character and displays: -- *CharacterName* heard -- "*CommandText*" The first line is centered. The second line is left justified and breaks to a third line when the text exceeds the Listening Tip's maximum width.

The Listening Tip automatically times out after being presented. If the "heard" text time-out completes when the user presses the hot key, the tip reverts to the "listening" text unless the server receives another matching utterance. In this case, the tip displays the new "heard" text and begins the time-out for that tip text. If the user releases the hot key and the server is displaying the "heard" text, the time-out continues. However, although the server displays the "listening" text, it immediately removes the Listening Tip when the user releases the hot key.

The Listening Tip does not appear when the pointer is over the Microsoft Agent taskbar icon. Instead, the standard notification tip window appears and displays "Press the *name of hot key* key to talk to *InputActiveCharacterName*" when the server is enabled. If all characters are hidden, the tip displays, "Press the *name of hot key* key and say the name of a character." However, if the user presses the speaking hot key, the tip reflects the same text as the listening tip. For example, it displays, "*CharacterName* is listening for *InputActiveClientCaption* commands," or, "*CharacterName* is listening for commands," if the input-active client has not defined its **Caption** property; and "*CharacterName* heard *CommandText,*" when the speech engine processes a recognition. When the user disables speech input (or speech recognition is not installed), the icon's tooltip displays, "Microsoft Agent is running." When the server is in its suspended state, the tip displays, "Microsoft Agent is suspended."

Clients cannot write directly to the Listening Tip, but you can specify alternative "heard" text that the server displays on recognition of a matching voice command. To do this, set the **Confidence** property and the new **ConfidenceText** property for the command. If spoken input matches the command, but the best match does not exceed the confidence setting, the server uses the text set in the **ConfidenceText** property in the tip window. If the client does not supply this value, the server displays the text (grammar) it matched.

Pop-up Menu Support

For each character, Microsoft Agent includes a pop-up menu (also known as a contextual menu) that the server displays automatically when a user right-clicks the character. This menu displays some standard commands managed by the server, but it also enables you to add and remove commands that your client application defines. The current input-active client's commands appear, provided that their **Caption** and **Visible** properties have been set. If the **Enabled** property has been set to **True**, the command appears enabled; if **False**, the command appears disabled (unavailable appearance). You define the access key for the entry by including an ampersand (&) before the text character of the **Caption** text setting. A separator appears before these commands. To create entries on a character's pop-up menu, define a **Commands** collection object and set the **Caption** and **Visible** properties of the commands. Note that menu entries do not change while the menu displays. If you add or remove commands or change their properties, the menu displays the changes when the user redisplays the menu.

The captions of any other clients (non-input-active) appear after another separator. To appear in the list, the **Caption** and **Visible** properties of their associated **Commands** object must be set. An ampersand in the text setting of the **Caption** property defines the access key for the entry. It is possible that access keys for menu items may be non-unique; this cannot be avoided. Separators appear only when there are items in the menu to separate. If no entries exist, the separator for that group does not appear.

Because the server provides the right-click pop-up menu as a standard service, avoid defining your own pop-up menu on the right-click event. However, if you define your own character, you can disable the server's pop-up menu by using the Microsoft Agent Character Editor. This enables you to support your own interface for the right-click action for your character. However, the pop-up menu cannot be disabled by a client application.

When the user selects a command from a character's pop-up menu or the Commands Window, the server triggers the **Command** event of the associated client and passes back the parameters of the input using the **UserInput** object.

The server also provides a pop-up menu for the Microsoft Agent taskbar icon. This menu provides the user access to all connected characters, and automatically assigns access keys for the characters based on the first letter of the character name. The menu also includes an entry that provides user access to the Microsoft Agent property sheet. You cannot modify the contents of the Microsoft Agent taskbar pop-up menu.

When the user chooses Exit from the Microsoft Agent taskbar icon pop-up menu, the server notifies the user that applications (clients with existing connections to the server) may not operate correctly and requests confirmation. If the user confirms shutting down the server, the server sends all client applications a **Shutdown** event. Your application becomes responsible for how it handles this state. Client applications cannot stop or cancel server shutdown.

If the server gets a request to restart after being shut down, for example, because a new client connects, the server partially reloads in suspended state, displaying the "suspended" Microsoft Agent icon in the taskbar notification area. Microsoft Agent also displays a message box indicating that the current application has requested to restart its services and offers to restart the server. (It also includes an option for the user not to be prompted again.) If the user chooses to restart, the server restores in its full operation and sends clients the **Restart** event. If the user chooses not to restart, the server remains its suspended state until all its clients close their connections or the user explicitly chooses to exit it again.

The Microsoft Agent Property Sheet

The Microsoft Agent property sheet provides options for users to adjust their interaction with all characters. For example, users can disable speech input or change input parameters. Users can also change the output settings for the word balloon. These settings override any that are set by a client application or set as part of the character definition. Your application cannot change or disable these options, because they apply to the general user preferences for operation of all characters. However, your application can display or close the property sheet and access the location of its window.

Output Services

Microsoft Agent also supports audio output for the character. This includes spoken output and sound effects. For spoken output, the server lip-syncs the character's defined mouth images to the output. You can choose text-to-speech (TTS) synthesis, recorded audio, or only word balloon text output.

Synthesized Speech Support

If you use synthesized speech, your character has the ability to say almost anything, which provides the greatest flexibility. With recorded audio, you can give the character a specific or unique voice. To specify output, provide the spoken text as a parameter of the **Speak** method.

Because Microsoft Agent's architecture uses Microsoft SAPI for synthesized speech output, you should be able to use any engine that conforms to this specification, and support International Phonetic Alphabet (IPA) output using the **Visual** method of the **ITTSNotifySinkW** interface. For further information on the SAPI interfaces, see the Microsoft Speech SDK at http://research .microsoft.com/research/srg.

Audio Output Support

Microsoft Agent enables you to use audio files for a character's spoken output. You can record audio files and use the **Speak** method to play that data. Microsoft Agent animation services automatically support lip-syncing the character mouth by using the audio characteristics of the audio file. Microsoft Agent also supports a special format for audio files, which includes additional phoneme and word-break information for more enhanced lip-sync support. You can generate this special format using the Microsoft Linguistic Information Sound Editing Tool discussed in Chapter 8.

Word Balloon Support

Spoken output can also appear as textual output in the form of a cartoon word balloon. This can be used to supplement the spoken output of a character or as an alternative to audio output.

FIGURE 3-2. The Word Balloon

Word balloons support only captioned communication from the character, not user input. Therefore, the word balloon does not support input controls. If you want to provide user input for a character, supply those interfaces from your application or the other input services provided by Microsoft Agent, such as the pop-up menu.

When you define a character, you can specify whether to include word balloon support. However, if you use a character that includes word balloon support, you cannot disable the support.

Animation Sound Effects

Microsoft Agent also enables you to include sound effects as a part of a character's animation. Using the Microsoft Agent Character Editor, you can specify the file name of standard Windows sound (.WAV) files to trigger on a given frame. Note that Microsoft Agent does not mix sound effects and spoken output, so spoken output does not begin until a sound effect completes. Therefore, avoid any long or looping sound effect as a part of a character's animation.

CHAPTER 4

Programming the Microsoft Agent Control

Although applications can write directly to the Microsoft Agent services using its automation server interfaces, Microsoft Agent also includes an ActiveX (OLE) control. The control supports easy programming using a scripting language such as Microsoft Visual Basic Scripting Edition (VBScript) or other languages that support the ActiveX control interface.

Notational Conventions

The code examples and command references presented here use the following typographical conventions:

Convention	Description
Sub, Visible, Caption	Words in bold with initial letter capitalized indicate keywords.
agent, String, Now	Italic words indicate placeholders for information you supply.
ENTER, F1	Words in all capital letters indicate file names, key names, and key sequences.
`Agent1.Commands.Enabled = True`	Words in this font indicate code samples.
`' This is a comment`	An apostrophe (') indicates a code comment.
`Agent1.Commands.Add "Test1", _` `"Test 1", "Lest one"`	A space and an underscore (_) continues a line of code.
`[words or expression]`	Items inside square brackets are optional.
`This	That`	A vertical bar indicates a choice between two or more items.
agent	The word "agent" in italics represents the name of the agent control you use.

The descriptions of programming interfaces in this document follow the conventions for Microsoft VBScript. However, they should be generally applicable to other languages as well.

Accessing the Control in Web Pages

To access the Microsoft Agent services from a Web page, use the HTML <OBJECT> tag within the <HEAD> or <BODY> element of the page, specifying the Microsoft CLSID (class identifier) for the control. In addition, use a CODEBASE parameter to specify the location of the Microsoft Agent installation file and its version number. The following example illustrates how to use the CODEBASE parameter to autodownload the English language version 1.5 of Microsoft Agent (which is also included on the CD-ROM). For information about the current location of the Microsoft Agent installation file for specific language versions and the current release number available, see the Microsoft Agent download page (http://www.microsoft.com/workshop/prog/agent/agentdl.htm).

```
<OBJECT
classid="clsid:F5BE8BD2-7DE6-11D0-91FE-00C04FD701A5"
CODEBASE = "http://activex.microsoft.com/controls/agent/
MSagent.exe#VERSION=1,5,0,0"
 id=Agent
>
</OBJECT>
```

Before any script on the page can access its services, Microsoft Agent must be installed on the system loading the page. If Microsoft Agent is not installed on the target system, Microsoft Internet Explorer will automatically download the Microsoft Agent server, data provider, and ActiveX control and ask the user whether to proceed with installation. Once installed, these three items do not have to be reinstalled unless the user uninstalls them. To begin using a character, you must also download its data using the **Load** and **Get** methods. For more information about the syntax for loading a character, see the **Load** method.

Note that you can also use the methods, properties, and events exposed by the browser to program the character; for example, to program its reaction to a button click. Consult the documentation for your browser to determine what features it exposes in its scripting model. For the Microsoft Internet Explorer, see the Scripting Object Model.

Supporting Microsoft Agent from a Web page requires installing Microsoft Internet Explorer version 3.0 or later to install the correct components. For other browsers, contact the supplier for information regarding their support for ActiveX.

Using VBScript

To program Microsoft Agent from VBScript, use the HTML <SCRIPT> tags. To access the programming interface, use the name of control you assign in the <OBJECT> tag, followed by the subobject (if any), the name of the method or property, and any parameters or values supported by the method or property:

```
agent[.object].Method parameter, [parameter]
agent[.object].Property = value
```

For events, include the name of the control followed by the name of the event and any parameters:

```
Sub agent_event (ByVal parameter[,ByVal parameter])
statements…
End Sub
```

You can also specify an event handler using the <SCRIPT> tag's **For…Event** syntax:

```
<SCRIPT LANGUAGE=VBScript For=agent
Event=event[(parameter[,parameter])]>
statements…
</SCRIPT>
```

Although Microsoft Internet Explorer supports this latter syntax, not all browsers do. For compatibility, use only the former syntax for events.

With VBScript 2.0, you can verify whether Microsoft Agent is installed by trying to create the object and checking to see if it exists. The following sample demonstrates how to check for the Agent control without triggering an auto-download of the control (as would happen if you included an <OBJECT> tag for the control on the page):

```
<!-- WARNING - This code requires VBScript 2.0.
It will always fail to detect the Agent control
in VbScript 1.x, because CreateObject doesn't work.
-->

<SCRIPT LANGUAGE=VBSCRIPT>
If HaveAgent() Then
        'Microsoft Agent control was found.
        document.write "<H2 align=center>Found</H2>"
Else
        'Microsoft Agent control was not found.
        document.write "<H2 align=center>Not Found</H2>"
End If
```

```
Function HaveAgent()
' This procedure attempts to create an Agent Control object.
' If it succeeds, it returns True.
'       This means the control is available on the client.
' If it fails, it returns False.
'       This means the control hasn't been installed on the client.

    Dim agent
    HaveAgent = False
    On Error Resume Next
    Set agent = CreateObject("Agent.Control.1")
    HaveAgent = IsObject(agent)

End Function

</SCRIPT>
```

You can download VBScript 2.0 and obtain further information on VBScript at the Microsoft VBScript site.

Using JavaScript and JScript

If you use JavaScript or Microsoft JScript to access Microsoft Agent's programming interface, follow the conventions for this language for specifying methods or properties:

```
agent.object.Method (parameter)
agent.object.Property = value
```

JavaScript does not currently have event syntax for non-HTML objects. However, with Internet Explorer you can use the <SCRIPT> tag's **For...Event** syntax:

```
SCRIPT LANGUAGE="JScript" FOR="object" EVENT="event()">
statements...
</SCRIPT>
```

Because not all browsers currently support this event syntax, you may want to use JavaScript only for pages that support Microsoft Internet Explorer or for code that does not require event handling.

The current release of JScript does not support collections. To access methods and properties of the Character object, use the Character method. Similarly, to access the properties of a Command object, use the Command method. For more information about using Microsoft Agent with Java, see Appendix B, "Microsoft Agent Technical FAQ."

Accessing Speech Support for Microsoft Agent

Although Microsoft Agent's services include support for speech recognition, a compatible speech engine must be installed to access Agent's speech recognition support. Your license for Microsoft Agent includes a license for the Microsoft Command and Control speech recognition engine when used as part of a Microsoft Agent client application.

To support automatic downloading and installation of Microsoft Command and Control from an HTML page, include a separate <OBJECT> tag specifying the CLSID of the engine. In addition, include a CODEBASE parameter to specify the location of the installation file as well as the version number, as shown in the following example. For the current location and version number to use for autodownloading the Microsoft Command and Control speech engine, consult the information posted on the Microsoft Agent download site at http://www.microsoft.com/workshop/prog/agent/agentdl.htm. A copy of the speech engine can also be found on the CD-ROM.

```
OBJECT
classid="clsid:161FA781-A52C-11d0-8D7C-00A0C9034A7E"
CODEBASE = http://www.research.microsoft.com/research/srg/
actcnc.exe#VERSION=3,0,0,1831
>
</OBJECT>
```

The license for Microsoft Command and Control does not permit redistribution of the speech engine independently. For information on licensing the engine separately from Microsoft Agent, contact the Microsoft Speech Research group e-mail alias: voicebug@microsoft.com. The Microsoft Command and Control engine is currently available only for English language input; however, other speech recognition vendors supporting the Microsoft Speech API may provide support for other languages. If you use another speech engine, contact its vendor for compatibility, installation, and licensing information.

Similarly, if you want to use Microsoft Agent's synthesized speech services, you must install a compatible text-to-speech (TTS) speech engine for your character's output. Your license for Microsoft Agent includes a license to use a special version of the Lernout & Hauspie TruVoice engine (included on the CD-ROM), but only when used with Microsoft Agent.

To support automatic downloading and installation of this engine from an HTML page, include the engine's CLSID in the <OBJECT> tag. In addition, include a CODEBASE parameter to specify the location of the installation file as well as the version number, such as shown in the following example. For the current location and version number to use for autodownloading the Lernout & Hauspie Text to Speech Engine for Microsoft Agent, consult the information posted on the Microsoft Agent download site at http:// www.microsoft.com/workshop/prog/agent.

```
<OBJECT
classid="clsid:B8F2846E-CE36-11D0-AC83-00C04FD97575"
CODEBASE = "http://activex.microsoft.com/controls/agent/
cgram.exe#VERSION=1,5,0,0"
>
</OBJECT>
```

This speech output engine supports only English language output. However, because Microsoft Agent uses the Microsoft Speech API, other languages may be available. If you want to use another compatible speech engine, contact its vendor for further information about their installation and licensing. Note that if you want to download sound (.WAV) files for your character's voice output, you do not have to install a TTS engine.

Accessing the Microsoft Agent Control from Visual Basic and Other Programming Languages

You can also use Microsoft Agent's control from Microsoft Visual Basic and other programming languages. Make sure that the language fully supports the ActiveX control interface, and follow its conventions for adding and accessing ActiveX controls.

Accessing Microsoft Agent's control from Visual Basic requires that you first create the control. The easiest way to do this is to place an instance of the control on a form. (You may have to add the control to your toolbox before adding it to your form.) Follow Visual Basic syntax for specifying methods, properties, or events. Using Microsoft Agent's control with Visual Basic is very similar to using the control with VBScript, except that events in Visual Basic must include the data type of passed parameters. However, adding the Microsoft Agent control to a form will automatically include Microsoft Agent's events with their appropriate parameters. For more advanced scenarios, such as creating an Agent control at run time, see the **Connected** property.

Most programming languages that support ActiveX controls follow conventions similar to Visual Basic. For programming languages that do not support object collections, you can use the **Character** method and **Command** method to access methods and properties of items in the collection.

Accessing Microsoft Agent Services Directly

If you are using C, C++, or Java, you can access the Microsoft Agent server directly using its ActiveX (OLE) interfaces. For more information on these interfaces, see Chapter 5, "Programming the Microsoft Agent Server Interface."

The Agent Object Model

The Microsoft Agent Object Model consists of the following objects:

- Request
- Agent (control)
- Characters (collection)
- Character
- Commands (collection)
- Command
- Balloon
- AudioOutput
- SpeechInput
- CommandsWindow
- PropertySheet

These objects are organized in the following hierarchy. (The dotted line following an object indicates that multiple objects can exist.)

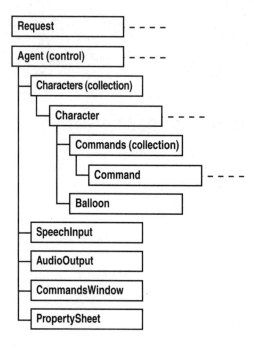

FIGURE 4-1. The Agent Object

The Request Object

The server processes some methods, such as **Load**, **Get**, **Play**, and **Speak**, asynchronously. This enables your application code to continue while the method is completing. When a client application calls one of these methods, the control creates and returns a **Request** object for the request. You can use the **Request** object to track the status of the method by assigning an object variable to the method. In VBScript and Visual Basic, first declare an object variable. In Visual Basic, you can use

```
Dim MyRequest as Object
```

In VBScript, you don't include the variable type in your declaration:

```
Dim MyRequest
```

And use Visual Basic's Set statement to assign the variable to the method call:

```
Set Request = agent.Characters("CharacterID").method (parameter)
```

This adds a reference to the **Request** object. The **Request** object will be destroyed when there are no more references to it. Where you declare the **Request** object and how you use it determines its lifetime. If the object is declared local to a subroutine or function, it will be destroyed when it goes out of scope; that is, when the subroutine or function is complete. If the object is declared globally, it will not be destroyed until either the program terminates or a new value (or a value set to "empty") is assigned to the object.

The **Request** object provides several properties you can query. For example, the **Status** property returns the current status of the request. You can use this property to check the status of your request:

```
Dim MyRequest

Set MyRequest = Agent1.Characters.Load ("Genie", _
    "http://agent.microsoft.com/characters/genie/genie.acf")

If (MyRequest.Status = Pending) Then
    'do something

Else If (MyRequest.Status = Complete) Then
    'do something right away

End If
```

The **Status** property returns the status of a **Request** object as a Long integer value.

Status	Definition
0	Request successfully completed.
1	Request failed.
2	Request pending (in the queue, but not complete).
3	Request interrupted.
4	Request in progress.

The **Request** object also includes a Long integer value in the **Number** property that returns the error or cause of the **Status** code. If none, this value is zero (0). The **Description** property contains a string value that corresponds to the error number. If the string doesn't exist, **Description** contains "Application-defined or object-defined error".

For the values and meaning returned by the **Number** property, see **Error Codes**.

The server places animation requests in the specified character's queue. This enables the server to play the animation on a separate thread, and your application's code can continue while animations play. If you create a **Request** object reference, the server automatically notifies you when an animation request has started or completed through the **RequestStart** and **Request-Complete** events. Because methods that return **Request** objects are asynchronous and may not complete during the scope of the calling function, declare your reference to the **Request** object globally.

The following methods can be used to return a **Request** object: **GestureAt**, **Get**, **Hide**, **Interrupt**, **Load**, **MoveTo**, **Play**, **Show**, **Speak**, **Wait**.

The Agent Control

Referencing the Agent control provides access to events and most other objects supported by Microsoft Agent. The Agent control also directly exposes its own set of properties.

Agent Control Properties

The following properties are directly accessed from the Agent control:

Connected   **Name**   **Suspended**

In addition, some programming environments may assign additional design-time or run-time properties. For example, Visual Basic adds **Left**, **Index**, **Tag**, and **Top** properties that define the location of the control on a form even though the control does not appear on the form's page at run time.

Connected Property

Description   Returns or sets whether the current control is connected to the Microsoft Agent server.

Syntax

*agent.***Connected** [= *boolean*]

Part	Description
boolean	A Boolean expression specifying whether the control is connected.
	True The control is connected.
	False The control is not connected.

Remarks

In many situations, specifying the control automatically creates a connection with the Microsoft Agent server. For example, specifying the Microsoft Agent control's CLSID in the <OBJECT> tag in a Web page automatically opens a server connection and exiting the page closes the connection. Similarly, for Visual Basic or other languages that enable you to drop a control on a form, running the program automatically opens a connection and exiting the program closes the connection. If the server isn't currently running, it automatically starts.

However, if you want to create an Agent control at run time, you may also need to explicitly open a new connection to the server using the **Connected** property. For example, in Visual Basic you can create an ActiveX object at run time using the Set statement with the **New** keyword (or **CreateObject** function). While this creates the object, it will not create the connection to the server, so you must use the **Connected** property before any code that calls into Microsoft Agent's programming interface, as shown in the following example:

```
' Declare a global variable for the control
Dim MyAgent as Agent

' Create an instance of the control using New
Set MyAgent = New Agent

' Open a connection to the server
MyAgent.Connected = True

' Load a character
MyAgent.Characters.Load "Genie", "C:\Some Directory\Genie.acs"

' Display the character
MyAgent.Characters("Genie").Show
```

Note that creating a control using this technique does not expose the Agent control's events. In Visual Basic 5.0, you can access the control's events by including the control in your project's references, and use the **WithEvents** keyword in your variable declaration:

```
Dim WithEvents agent as Agent

' Create an instance of the control using New
Set MyAgent = New Agent
```

Using **WithEvents** to create an instance of the Agent control at run time automatically opens the connection with the Microsoft Agent server. Therefore, you don't need to include a **Connected** statement.

You can close your control's connection to the server at run time by setting the **Connected** property to **False**. However, you must first release all references you defined to objects created by the server. In particular, you must release any references you created to character and command objects. In Visual Basic, you can disassociate a reference to an object by setting the reference to **Nothing**:

```
Dim Genie as IAgentCtlCharacter

Sub LoadCharacter

' Load the character into the Characters collection
Agent1.Characters.Load "Genie", _
"C:\Program Files\Microsoft Agent\Characters\Genie.acs"

' Create a reference to the character
Set Genie = Agent1.Characters("Genie")

End Sub

Sub CloseConnection

' Release the reference to the character object
Set Genie = Nothing

' Close the connection with the server
Agent1.Connected = False

End Sub
```

Although you can reopen your connection by resetting the **Connected** property to **True**, not all information established with the server in the original connection will be preserved. For example, if you loaded a character, you will have to reload it again before you can play any of its animations.

Setting the **Connected** property to **False** does not destroy your instance of the control. You must use the syntax supported by your programming language for releasing the object. For example, in Visual Basic, you set the control to **Nothing**:

```
Set Agent1 = Nothing
```

Attempting to query or set the **Connected** property before creating the control will raise an error.

Name Property

Description   Returns the name used in code to identify the control. This property is read-only at run time.

Syntax   *agent.***Name**

Remarks   In some programming environments such as Visual Basic, adding the control automatically generates a default name for the control that can be changed at design time. For HTML scripts, you can define the name in the <OBJECT> tag. If you define the name, follow the conventions of the programming language for defining object names.

Suspended Property

Description   Returns a Boolean indicating the Microsoft Agent server operational state.

Syntax   *agent.***Suspended**

Remarks   The **Suspended** property returns **False** when the server is in its normal running state. When the property returns **True**, the server is in its "suspended" state, which indicates that the user shut down the server and implies that no character interaction is desired. Client applications can only read this property, but you can display your own message box suggesting how to restart the server.

See also   **Restart** event, **Shutdown** event

Agent Control Events

The Microsoft Agent control provides several events that enable your client application to track the state of the server:

ActivateInput	**BalloonHide**	**BalloonShow**	**Bookmark**
Click	**Command**	**DblClick**	**DeactivateInput**
DragComplete	**DragStart**	**Hide**	**IdleComplete**
IdleStart	**Move**	**RequestComplete**	**RequestStart**
Restart	**Show**	**Shutdown**	**Size**

ActivateInput Event

Description   Occurs when a client becomes input-active.

Syntax   Sub *agent_***ActivateInput (ByVal** *CharacterID***)**

Value	Description
CharacterID	Returns the ID of the character through which the client becomes input-active.

Remarks   The input-active client receives mouse and speech input events supplied by the server. The server sends this event only to the client that becomes input-active.

This event can occur when the user switches to your **Commands** object, for example, by choosing your **Commands** object entry in the Commands Window or in the pop-up menu for a character. It can also occur when the user selects a character (by clicking or speaking its name), when a character becomes visible, and when the character of another client application becomes hidden. You can also call the **Activate** method (with **State** set to 2) to explicitly make the character topmost, which results in your client application becoming input-active and triggers this event. However, this event does not occur if you use the **Activate** method only to specify whether your client is the active client of the character.

See also   **DeactivateInput** event, **Activate** method

BalloonHide Event

Description   Occurs when a character's word balloon is hidden.

Syntax

Sub *agent_***BalloonHide** (**ByVal** *CharacterID*)

Value	Description
CharacterID	Returns the ID of the character associated with the word balloon.

Remarks

The server sends this event only to the clients of the character (applications that have loaded the character) that uses the word balloon.

See also

BalloonShow event

BalloonShow Event

Description

Occurs when a character's word balloon is shown.

Syntax

Sub *agent_***BalloonShow** (**ByVal** *CharacterID*)

Value	Description
CharacterID	Returns the ID of the character associated with the word balloon.

Remarks

The server sends this event only to the clients of the character (applications that have loaded the character) that uses the word balloon.

See also

BalloonHide event

Bookmark Event

Description

Occurs when a bookmark in a speech text string that your application defined is activated.

Syntax

Sub *agent_***Bookmark(ByVal** *BookmarkID*)

Value	Description
BookmarkID	A Long integer identifying the bookmark number.

Remarks

To specify a bookmark event, use the **Speak** method with a **Mrk** tag in your supplied text. For more information about tags, see Chapter 9, "Microsoft Agent Speech Output Tags."

Click Event

Description   Occurs when the user clicks a character.

Syntax   **Sub** *agent_***Click** (**ByVal** *CharacterID*, **ByVal** *Button*, **ByVal** *Shift*, **ByVal** *X*, **ByVal** *Y*)

Value	Description
CharacterID	Returns the ID of the clicked character as a string.
Button	Returns an integer that identifies the button that was pressed and released to cause the event. The button argument is a bit field with bits corresponding to the left button (bit 0), right button (bit 1), and middle button (bit 2). These bits correspond to the values 1, 2, and 4, respectively. Only one of the bits is set, indicating the button that caused the event.
Shift	Returns an integer that corresponds to the state of the SHIFT, CTRL, and ALT keys when the button specified in the button argument is pressed or released. A bit is set if the key is down. The shift argument is a bit field with the least-significant bits corresponding to the SHIFT key (bit 0), the CTRL key (bit 1), and the ALT key (bit 2). These bits correspond to the values 1, 2, and 4, respectively. The shift argument indicates the state of these keys. Some, all, or none of the bits can be set, indicating that some, all, or none of the keys are pressed. For example, if both CTRL and ALT were pressed, the value of shift would be 6.
X, Y	Returns an integer that specifies the current location of the mouse pointer. The X and Y values are always expressed in pixels, relative to the upper left corner of the screen.

Remarks   This event is sent only to the input-active client of a character. When the user clicks a character with no input-active client, the server sets its last input-active client as the current input-active client, sending the **ActivateInput** event to that client, and then sending the **Click** event.

Note Clicking a character does not disable all other character output (all characters). However, pressing the listening hot key does flush the input-active character's output and triggers the **RequestComplete** event, passing a **Request.Status** that indicates that the client's queue was interrupted.

Command Event

Description   Occurs when a (client's) command is chosen by the user.

Syntax   **Sub** *agent_***Command(ByVal** *UserInput***)**

Value	Description	
UserInput	Identifies the **Command** object returned by the server.	
	The following properties can be accessed from the **Command** object.	
	CharacterID	A string value identifying the name (ID) of the character that received the command.
	Name	A string value identifying the name (ID) of the command.
	Confidence	A Long integer value indicating the confidence scoring for the command.
	Voice	A string value identifying the voice text for the command.
	Alt1Name	A string value identifying the name of the next (second) best command.
	Alt1Confidence	A Long integer value indicating the confidence scoring for the next (second) best command.
	Alt1Voice	A string value identifying the voice text for the next best alternative command match.
	Alt2Name	A string value identifying the name of third best command match.
	Alt2Confidence	A Long integer identifying the confidence scoring for the third best command match.
	Alt2Voice	A string value identifying the voice text for the third best command match.
	Count	Long integer value indicating the number of alternatives returned.

Remarks   The server notifies you with this event when your application is input-active and the user chooses a command you defined to appear in the Commands

Window or a character's pop-up menu. The event passes back the number of possible matching commands in **Count** as well as the name, confidence scoring, and voice text for those matches.

If voice input triggers this event, the server returns a string that identifies the best match in the **Name** parameter, and the second- and third-best match in **Alt1Name** and **Alt2Name**. An empty string indicates that the input did not match any command your application defined; for example, it could be one of the server's defined commands. It is also possible that you may get the same command name returned in more than one entry. **Confidence**, **Alt1-Confidence**, and **Alt2Confidence** parameters return the relative scores, in the range of -100 to 100, that are returned by the speech recognition engine for each respective match. **Voice**, **Alt1Voice**, and **Alt2Voice** parameters return the voice text that the speech recognition engine matched for each alternative. If **Count** returns zero (0), the server detected spoken input, but determined that there was no matching command.

If voice input was not the source for the command, for example, if the user selected the command from the character's pop-up menu, the server returns the name (ID) of the command selected in the **Name** property. It also returns the value of the **Confidence** parameter as 100, and the value of the **Voice** parameters as the empty string (""). **Alt1Name** and **Alt2Name** also return empty strings. **Alt1Confidence** and **Alt2Confidence** return zero (0), and **Alt1Voice** and **Alt2Voice** return empty strings. **Count** returns 1.

Note The Microsoft Command and Control speech recognition engine supports returning values in the parameters of this event. If you use Microsoft Agent with another speech engine, check with the supplier to determine whether their engine supports the Microsoft Speech API interface for returning alternatives and confidence scores.

DblClick Event

Description   Occurs when the user double-clicks a character.

Syntax   **Sub** *agent_***DblClick** (**ByVal** *CharacterID*, **ByVal** *Button*, **ByVal** *Shift*, **ByVal** *X*, **ByVal** *Y*)

Value	Description
CharacterID	Returns the ID of the double-clicked character as a string.
Button	Returns an integer that identifies the button that was pressed and released to cause the event. The button argument is a bit field with bits corresponding to the left button (bit 0), right button (bit 1), and middle button (bit 2). These bits correspond to the values 1, 2, and 4, respectively. Only one of the bits is set, indicating the button that caused the event.
Shift	Returns an integer that corresponds to the state of the SHIFT, CTRL, and ALT keys when the button specified in the button argument is pressed or released. A bit is set if the key is down. The shift argument is a bit field with the least-significant bits corresponding to the SHIFT key (bit 0), the CTRL key (bit 1), and the ALT key (bit 2). These bits correspond to the values 1, 2, and 4, respectively. The shift argument indicates the state of these keys. Some, all, or none of the bits can be set, indicating that some, all, or none of the keys are pressed. For example, if both CTRL and ALT were pressed, the value of shift would be 6.
X,Y	Returns an integer that specifies the current location of the mouse pointer. The X and Y values are always expressed in pixels, relative to the upper left corner of the screen.

Remarks

This event is sent only to the input-active client of a character. When the user double-clicks a character with no input-active client, the server sets its last input-active client as the current input-active client, sending the **ActiveInput** event to that client, and then sending the **DblClick** event.

DeactivateInput Event

Description

Occurs when a client becomes non-input-active.

Syntax

Sub *agent_***DeactivateInput** (**ByVal** *CharacterID*)

Value	Description
CharacterID	Returns the ID of the character that makes the client become non-input-active.

Remarks

A non-input-active client no longer receives mouse or speech events from the server (unless it becomes input-active again). The server sends this event only to the client that becomes non-input-active. It does not occur when you use the **Activate** method and set the **State** parameter to 0.

This event occurs when your client application is input-active and the user chooses the caption of another client in a character's pop-up menu or the Commands Window. It may also occur when the user selects the name of another character by clicking or speaking. You also get this event when your character is hidden or another character becomes visible.

See also

ActivateInput event

DragComplete Event

Description

Occurs when the user completes dragging a character.

Syntax

Sub *agent*_**DragComplete (ByVal** *CharacterID*, **ByVal** *Button*, **ByVal** *Shift*, **ByVal** *X*, **ByVal** *Y*)

Value	Description
CharacterID	Returns the ID of the dragged character as a string.
Button	Returns an integer that identifies the button that was pressed and released to cause the event. The button argument is a bit field with bits corresponding to the left button (bit 0), right button (bit 1), and middle button (bit 2). These bits correspond to the values 1, 2, and 4, respectively. Only one of the bits is set, indicating the button that caused the event.
Shift	Returns an integer that corresponds to the state of the SHIFT, CTRL, and ALT keys when the button specified in the button argument is pressed or released. A bit is set if the key is down. The shift argument is a bit field with the least-significant bits corresponding to the SHIFT key (bit 0), the CTRL key (bit 1), and the ALT key (bit 2). These bits correspond to the values 1, 2, and 4, respectively. The shift argument indicates the state of these keys. Some, all, or none of the bits can be set, indicating that some, all, or none of the keys are pressed. For example, if both CTRL and ALT were pressed, the value of shift would be 6.
X,Y	Returns an integer that specifies the current location of the mouse pointer. The X and Y values are always expressed in pixels, relative to the upper left corner of the screen.

Remarks

This event is sent only to the input-active client of a character. When the user drags a character with no input-active client, the server sets its last input-active client as the current input-active client, sending the **ActivateInput** event to that client, and then sending the **DragStart** and **DragComplete** events.

See also

DragStart event

DragStart Event

Description

Occurs when the user begins dragging a character.

Syntax

Sub *agent*_**DragStart** (**ByVal** *CharacterID*, **ByVal** *Button*, **ByVal** *Shift*, **ByVal** *X*, **ByVal** *Y*)

Value	Description
CharacterID	Returns the ID of the clicked character as a string.
Button	Returns an integer that identifies the button that was pressed and released to cause the event. The button argument is a bit field with bits corresponding to the left button (bit 0), right button (bit 1), and middle button (bit 2). These bits correspond to the values 1, 2, and 4, respectively. Only one of the bits is set, indicating the button that caused the event.
Shift	Returns an integer that corresponds to the state of the SHIFT, CTRL, and ALT keys when the button specified in the button argument is pressed or released. A bit is set if the key is down. The shift argument is a bit field with the least-significant bits corresponding to the SHIFT key (bit 0), the CTRL key (bit 1), and the ALT key (bit 2). These bits correspond to the values 1, 2, and 4, respectively. The shift argument indicates the state of these keys. Some, all, or none of the bits can be set, indicating that some, all, or none of the keys are pressed. For example, if both CTRL and ALT were pressed, the value of shift would be 6.
X,Y	Returns an integer that specifies the current location of the mouse pointer. The X and Y values are always expressed in pixels, relative to the upper left corner of the screen.

Remarks

This event is sent only to the input-active client of a character. When the user drags a character with no input-active client, the server sets its last input-active client as the current input-active client, sending the **ActivateInput** event to that client, and then sending the **DragStart** event.

See also

DragComplete event

Hide Event

Description   Occurs when a character is hidden.

Syntax   **Sub** *agent_***Hide (ByVal** *CharacterID*, **ByVal** *Cause*)

Value	Description
CharacterID	Returns the ID of the hidden character as a string.
Cause	Returns a value that indicates what caused the character to hide.

    1   The user hid the character (using the menu or voice command).

    3   Your client application hid the character.

    5   Another client application hid the character.

Remarks   The server sends this event to all clients of the character. To query the current state of the character, use the **Visible** property.

See also   **Show** event, **VisibilityCause** property

IdleComplete Event

Description   Occurs when the server ends the **Idling** state of a character.

Syntax   **Sub** *agent_***IdleComplete (ByVal** *CharacterID*)

Value	Description
CharacterID	Returns the ID of the idling character as a string.

Remarks   The server sends this event to all clients of the character.

See also   **IdleStart** event

IdleStart Event

Description   Occurs when the server sets a character to the **Idling** state.

Syntax   **Sub** *agent_***IdleStart (ByVal** *CharacterID*)

Value	Description
CharacterID	Returns the ID of the idling character as a string.

Remarks

The server sends this event to all clients of the character.

See also

IdleComplete event

Move Event

Description

Occurs when a character is moved.

Syntax

Sub *agent_***Move** (**ByVal** *CharacterID*, **ByVal** *X*, **ByVal** *Y*, **ByVal** *Cause*)

Value	Description
CharacterID	Returns the ID of the character that moved.
X	Returns the x-coordinate (in pixels) of the top edge of character frame's new location as an integer.
Y	Returns the y-coordinate (in pixels) of the left edge of character frame's new location as an integer.
Cause	Returns a value that indicates what caused the character to move.
	1 The user dragged the character.
	2 Your client application moved the character.
	3 Another client application moved the character.

Remarks

This event occurs when the user or an application changes the character's position. Coordinates are relevant to the upper left corner of the screen. This event is sent only to the clients of the character (applications that have loaded the character).

See also

MoveCause property, **Size** event

RequestComplete Event

Description

Occurs when the server completes a queued request.

Syntax

Sub *agent_*__RequestComplete__ (**ByVal** *Request*)

Value	Description
Request	Returns the **Request** object.

Remarks

This event returns a **Request** object. Because requests are processed asynchronously, you can use this event to determine when the server completes processing a request (such as a **Get**, **Play**, or **Speak** method) to synchronize this event with other actions generated by your application. The server sends the event only to the client that created the reference to the **Request** object and only if you defined a global variable for the request reference:

```
Dim MyRequest
Dim Genie

Sub window_Onload

Agent1.Characters.Load "Genie", _
    "http://agent.microsoft.com/characters/genie/genie.acf"

Set Genie = Agent.Characters("Genie")

' This syntax will generate RequestStart and RequestComplete events.
Set MyRequest = Genie.Get("state", "Showing")
' This syntax will not generate RequestStart and RequestComplete events.
Genie.Get "state", "Hiding"

End Sub

Sub Agent1_RequestComplete(ByVal Request)

If Request = MyRequest Then
    Status = "Showing animation is now loaded"

End Sub
```

Note In VBScript 1.0, this event fires even if you don't define references to a **Request** object. This has been fixed in VBScript 2.0, which can be downloaded from http://microsoft.com/msdownload/scripting.htm.

See also

RequestStart event

RequestStart Event

Description

Occurs when the server begins a queued request.

Syntax

Sub *agent*_**RequestStart** (**ByVal** *Request*)

Value	Description
Request	Returns the **Request** object.

Remarks

The event returns a **Request** object. Because requests are processed asynchronously, you can use this event to determine when the server begins processing a request (such as a **Get**, **Play**, or **Speak** method) and thereby synchronize this with other actions generated by your application. The event is sent only to the client that created the reference to the **Request** object and only if you defined a global variable for the request reference:

```
Dim MyRequest
Dim Genie

Sub window_Onload

Agent1.Characters.Load "Genie", _
    "http://agent.microsoft.com/characters/genie/genie.acf"

Set Genie = Agent1.Characters("Genie")

' This syntax will generate RequestStart and RequestComplete events.
Set MyRequest = Genie.Get("state", "Showing")

' This syntax will not generate RequestStart and RequestComplete events.
Genie.Get ("state", "Hiding")

End Sub

Sub Agent1_RequestStart(ByVal Request)

If Request = MyRequest Then
    Status = "Loading the Showing animation"

End Sub
```

The **Status** returns 4 (request in progress) for the **Request** object returned.

Note In VBScript 1.0, this event fires even if you don't define references to a **Request** object. This has been fixed in VBScript 2.0, which can be downloaded from http://microsoft.com/msdownload/scripting.htm.

See also

RequestComplete event

Restart Event

Description

Occurs when the server restarts from its suspended state.

Syntax

Sub *agent_***Restart** ()

Remarks

The server sends this event to all client applications when the user chooses to restart the server from its suspended state. However, you will not get this event if you close your connection to the server when the server shuts down.

Show Event

Description

Occurs when a character is displayed.

Syntax

Sub *agent_***Show** (**ByVal** *CharacterID*, **ByVal** *Cause*)

Value	Description
CharacterID	Returns the ID of the character shown as a string.
Cause	Returns a value that indicates what caused the character to display.
	2 The user showed the character (using the menu or voice command).
	4 Your client application showed the character.
	6 Another client application showed the character.

Remarks

The server sends this event to all clients of the character. To query the current state of the character, use the **Visible** property.

See also

Hide event, **VisibilityCause** property

Shutdown Event

Description

Occurs when the user explicitly shuts down (exits) Microsoft Agent.

Syntax

Sub *agent_***Shutdown**()

Remarks

When the user explicitly chooses Exit on the pop-up menu on the Microsoft Agent taskbar icon and confirms the choice in the warning message box, the server sends this event to all connected clients and then exits. The server also sets the control's **Connected** property to **False**. Any subsequent calls you make to the server will fail. You may want to handle this error condition.

Size Event

Description   Occurs when a character's size changes.

Syntax   Sub *agent_*Size (**ByVal** *CharacterID*, **ByVal** *Width*, **ByVal** *Height*)

Value	Description
CharacterID	Returns the ID of the character that moved.
Width	Returns the character frame's new width (in pixels) as an integer.
Height	Returns the character frame's new height (in pixels) as an integer.

Remarks   This event occurs when an application changes the size of a character. This event is sent only to the clients of the character (applications that have loaded the character).

See also   **Move** event

The Characters Object

Your client application can support one or more characters. In addition, you can share a character among several applications. Microsoft Agent defines the **Characters** object as a collection of characters. To access a character, load the character's data into the **Characters** collection and specify that that item in the collection uses the methods and properties supported for that character.

Characters Object Methods

The **Characters** object supports methods for accessing, loading, and unloading characters into its collection:

Character   **Load**   **Unload**

Character Method

Description   Returns a **Character** object in a **Characters** collection.

Syntax   *agent.***Characters.Character** *"CharacterID"*

Remarks   You can use this method to access a **Character** object's methods and properties.

Note This method may be required for some programming languages that do not support collections. It is not required for VBScript or Visual Basic. For further information on specifying **Character** methods, see Character Object Methods.

Load Method

Description

Loads a character into the **Characters** collection.

Syntax

agent.**Characters.Load** *"CharacterID"*, *Provider*

Part	Description
CharacterID	Required. A string value that you will use to refer to the character data to be loaded.
Provider	Required. A variant data type that must be one of the following:

	Filespec	The local file location of the specified character's definition file.
	URL	The HTTP address for the character's definition file.
	Provider	An alternate character definition provider (object).

Remarks

The Microsoft Agent Data Provider supports loading character data stored either as a single structured file (.ACS) with character data and animation data together or as separate character data (.ACF) and animation (.AAF) files. Use the single structured .ACS file to load a character that is stored on a local disk or network and accessed using a conventional file protocol (such as UNC pathnames). Use the separate .ACF and .AAF files when you want to load the animation files individually from a remote site where they are accessed using the HTTP protocol.

For .ACS files, using the **Load** method provides access a character's animations. For .ACF files, you also use the **Get** method to load animation data. The **Load** method does not support downloading .ACS files from an HTTP site.

Loading a character does not automatically display the character. Use the **Show** method first to make the character visible.

If you create an object reference and assign it to this method, it returns a **Request** object. If you use HTTP protocol, assigning a **Request** object to the

Load method and checking its status in the **RequestComplete** event enables you to prevent your code from failing when the character data fails to load.

The *Provider* parameter also enables you to specify your own data provider (that would be loaded using a separate control) that can have its own methods for loading animation data. You only need to create a data provider object if you supply character data in special formats.

To load a character from the Microsoft Agent site, consult the character data page at http://www.microsoft.com/workshop/prog/agent/characterdata.htm for the latest information on the location of the character files.

Unload Method

Description

Unloads the character data for the specified character.

Syntax

agent.**Characters.Unload** *"CharacterID"*

Remarks

Use this method when you no longer need a character, to free up memory used to store information about the character. If you access the character again, use the **Load** method.

This method does not return a **Request** object.

Character Object Methods

The server also exposes methods for each character in a **Characters** collection. The following methods are supported:

Activate	**GestureAt**	**Get**	**Hide**
Interrupt	**MoveTo**	**Play**	**Show**
Speak	**Stop**	**StopAll**	**Wait**

To use a method, reference the character in the collection. In VBScript and Visual Basic, you do this by specifying the ID for a character:

```
Sub FormLoad

'Load the genie character into the Characters collection
Agent1.Characters.Load "Genie", _
    "C:\Program Files\Microsoft Agent\Characters\Genie.acs"

'Display the character
Agent1.Characters("Genie").Show
Agent1.Characters("Genie").Play "Greet"
Agent1.Characters("Genie").Speak "Hello. "

End Sub
```

To simplify the syntax of your code, you can define an object variable and set it to reference a character object in the **Characters** collection; then you can use your variable to reference methods or properties of the character. The following example demonstrates how you can do this using the Visual Basic Set statement:

```
'Define a global object variable
Dim Genie as Object

Sub FormLoad

'Load the genie character into the Characters collection
Agent1.Characters.Load "Genie", _
    "C:\Program Files\Microsoft Agent\Characters\Genie.acs"

'Create a reference to the character
Set Genie = Agent1.Characters("Genie")

'Display the character
Genie.Show

'Get the Restpose animation
Genie.Get "animation", "RestPose"

'Make the character say Hello
Genie.Speak "Hello."

End Sub
```

In Visual Basic 5.0, you can also create your reference by declaring your variable as a **Character** object:

```
Dim Genie as IAgentCtlCharacter

Sub FormLoad

'Load the genie character into the Characters collection
Agent1.Characters.Load "Genie", _
    "C:\Program Files\Microsoft Agent\Characters\Genie.acs"

'Create a reference to the character
Set Genie = Agent1.Characters("Genie")

'Display the character
Genie.Show

End Sub
```

Declaring your object of type **IAgentCtlCharacter** enables early binding on the object, which results in better performance.

In VBScript, you cannot declare a reference as a particular type. However, you can simply declare the variable reference:

```
<OBJECT
classid="clsid:F5BE8BD2-7DE6-11D0-91FE-00C04FD701A5"
CODEBASE = "http://activex.microsoft.com/controls/agent/
MSagent.exe#VERSION=1,5,0,0"
id=AgentCtl>

</OBJECT>

<SCRIPT LANGUAGE = VBScript>

<!--

    Dim Genie

    SUB window_OnLoad

    'Load the character
    AgentCtl.Characters.Load "Genie", _
     "http://agent.microsoft.com/characters/genie/genie.acf"

    'Create an object reference to the character in the collection
    set Genie= AgentCtl.Characters ("Genie")

    'Get the Showing state animation
    Genie.Get "state", "Showing"

    'Display the character
    Genie.Show

    'Get the RestPose animation
    Genie.Get "animation", "RestPose"

    'Make the character say Hello
    Genie.Speak "Hello."

    End Sub

-->

</SCRIPT>
```

Some programming languages do not support collections. However, you can access a **Character** object's methods with the **Character** method:

```
agent.Characters.Character("CharacterID").method
```

In addition, you can also create a reference to the **Character** object to make your script code easier to follow:

```
<OBJECT
classid = "clsid:F5BE8BD2-7DE6-11D0-91FE-00C04FD701A5"
CODEBASE = "http://activex.microsoft.com/controls/agent/
MSagent.exe#VERSION=1,5,0,0"
id=AgentCtl>

</OBJECT>

<SCRIPT LANGUAGE="JScript" FOR="window" EVENT="onLoad()">
<!--

    //Load the character's data
    AgentCtl.Characters.Load ("Genie", _
        "http://agent.microsoft.com/characters/genie/genie.acf");

    //Create a reference to this object
    Genie = AgentCtl.Characters.Character("Genie");

    //Get the Showing state animation
    Genie.Get("state", "Showing");

    //Display the character
    Genie.Show();

-->
</SCRIPT>
```

Activate Method

Description   Sets the active client or character.

Syntax   *agent*.**Characters** (*"CharacterID"*).**Activate** [*State*]

Part	Description
State	Optional. You can specify the following values for this parameter:
	0 Not the active client.
	1 The active client.
	2 (Default) The topmost character.

Remarks   When multiple characters are visible, only one of the characters receives speech input at a time. Similarly, when multiple client applications share the same character, only one of the clients receives mouse input (for example, Microsoft Agent control click or drag events). The character set to receive mouse and speech input is the topmost character and the client that receives the input is the active client of that character. (The topmost character's window also appears at the top of the character windows z-order.) Typically, the user determines the topmost character by explicitly selecting the character. However, topmost activation also changes when a character is shown or hidden (the character becomes or is no longer topmost, respectively.)

You can also use this method to explicitly manage when your client receives input directed to the character such as when your application itself becomes active. For example, setting **State** to 2 makes the character topmost and your client receives all mouse and speech input events generated from user interaction with the character. Therefore, it also makes your client the input-active client of the character.

However, you can also set yourself to be the active client for a character without making the character topmost, by setting **State** to 1. This enables your client to receive input directed to that character when the character becomes topmost. Similarly, you can set your client to not be the active client (not to receive input) when the character becomes topmost, by setting **State** to 0.

Avoid calling this method directly after a **Show** method. **Show** automatically sets the input-active client. When the character is hidden, the **Activate** call may fail if it gets processed before the **Show** method completes.

If you call this method to a function, it returns a Boolean value that indicates whether the method succeeded. Attempting to call this method with the **State** parameter set to 2 when the specified character is hidden will fail. Similarly, if you set **State** to 0 and your application is the only client, this call fails because a character must always have a topmost client.

```
Dim Genie as Object

Sub FormLoad()

Agent1.Characters.Load "Genie", _
    "C:\Program Files\Microsoft Agent\Characters\Genie.acs"

Set Genie = Agent1.Characters ("Genie")

If (Genie. Activate = True) Then
    'I'm active

Else
    'I must be hidden or something

End If

End Sub
```

See also   **ActivateInput** event, **DeactivateInput** event

GestureAt Method

Description   Plays the gesturing animation for the specified character at the specified location.

Syntax   *agent***.Characters (***"CharacterID"***).GestureAt** *X,Y*

Part	Description
X,Y	Required. An integer value that indicates the horizontal (X) screen coordinate and vertical (Y) screen coordinate to which the character will gesture. These coordinates must be specified in pixels.

Remarks   The server automatically plays the appropriate animation to gesture toward the specified location. The coordinates are always relative to the screen origin (upper left).

If you declare an object reference and set it to this method, it returns a **Request** object. In addition, if the associated animation has not been loaded on the local machine, the server sets the **Request** object's **Status** property to "failed" with an appropriate error number. Therefore, if you are using the HTTP protocol to access character animation data, use the **Get** method to load the **Gesturing** state animations before calling the **GestureAt** method.

Get Method

Description   Retrieves specified animation data for the specified character.

Syntax   *agent***.Characters (***"CharacterID"***).Get** *Type, Name, [Queue]*

Part	Description
Type	Required. A string value that indicates the animation data type to load.
	"Animation" A character's animation data.
	"State" A character's state data.
	"WaveFile" A character's audio (for spoken output) file.
Name	Required. A string that indicates the name of the animation type.
	"name" The name of the animation or state.
	For animations, the name is based on that defined for the character when saved using the Microsoft Agent Character Editor.

Part	Description
	For states, the following values can be used:

"Gesturing"	To get all **Gesturing** state animations.
"GesturingDown"	To get the **GesturingDown** animation.
"GesturingLeft"	To get the **GesturingLeft** animation.
"GesturingRight"	To get the **GesturingRight** animation.
"GesturingUp"	To get the **GesturingUp** animation.
"Hiding"	To get the **Hiding** state animation.
"Hearing"	To get the **Hearing** state animation.
"Idling"	To get all **Idling** state animations.
"IdlingLevel1"	To get all **IdlingLevel1** animations.
"IdlingLevel2"	To get all **IdlingLevel2** animations.
"IdlingLevel3"	To get all **IdlingLevel3** animations.
"Listening"	To get the **Listening** state animation.
"Moving"	To get all **Moving** state animations.
"MovingDown"	To get the **MovingDown** animation.
"MovingLeft"	To get the **MovingLeft** animation.
"MovingRight"	To get the **MovingRight** animation.
"MovingUp"	To get the **MovingUp** animation.
"Showing"	To get the **Showing** state animation.
"Speaking"	To get the **Speaking** state animation.

You can specify multiple animations and states by separating them with commas. However, you cannot mix types in the same **Get** statement.

"URL or filespec"	The specification for the sound (.WAV or .LWV) file. If the specification is not complete, it is interpreted as being relative to the specification used in the **Load** method.

Queue	Optional. A Boolean expression specifying whether the server queues the **Get** request.

True (Default) Queues the **Get** request. Any animation request that follows the **Get** request (for the same character) waits until the animation data is loaded.

False Does not queue the **Get** request.

Remarks

You need to use the **Get** method only to retrieve animation data using the HTTP protocol.

If you declare an object reference and set it to this method, it returns a **Request** object. If the associated animation fails to load, the server sets the **Request** object's **Status** property to "failed" with an appropriate error number. You can use the **RequestComplete** event to check the status and determine what action to take.

Animation or sound data retrieved with the **Get** method is stored in the browser's cache. Subsequent calls will check the cache, and if the animation data is already there, the control loads the data directly from the cache. Once loaded, the animation or sound data can be played with the **Play** or **Speak** methods.

See also

Load method

Hide Method

Description

Hides the specified character.

Syntax

agent.**Characters** (*"CharacterID"*).**Hide** [*Fast*]

Part	Description
Fast	Optional. A Boolean value that indicates whether to skip the animation associated with the character's Hiding state

	True	Does not play the **Hiding** animation.
	False	(Default) Plays the **Hiding** animation.

Remarks

The server queues the actions of the **Hide** method in the character's queue, so you can use it to hide the character after a sequence of other animations. You can play the action immediately by using the **Stop** method before calling this method.

If you declare an object reference and set it to this method, it returns a **Request** object. In addition, if the associated **Hiding** animation has not been loaded and you have not specified the **Fast** parameter as **True**, the server sets the **Request** object **Status** property to "failed" with an appropriate error number. Therefore, if you are using the HTTP protocol to access character or animation data, use the **Get** method and specify the **Hiding** state to load the animation before calling the **Hide** method.

Hiding a character can also result in triggering the **ActivateInput** event of another client.

Note Hidden characters cannot access the audio channel. The server will pass back a failure status in the **RequestComplete** event if you generate an animation request and the character is hidden.

See also

Show method

Interrupt Method

Description

Interrupts the animation for the specified character.

Syntax

agent.**Characters** (*"CharacterID"*).**Interrupt** *Request*

Remarks

You can use this to sync up animation between characters. For example, if another character is in a looping animation, this method will stop the loop and move to the next animation in the character's queue. You cannot interrupt a character animation that you are not using (that you have not loaded).

To specify the request parameter, you must create a variable and assign the animation request you want to interrupt:

```
Dim GenieRequest as Object
Dim RobbyRequest as Object
Dim Genie as Object
Dim Robby as Object

Sub FormLoad()

    MyAgent1.Characters.Load "Genie", _
        "C:\Program Files\Microsoft Agent\Characters\Genie.acs"

    MyAgent1.Characters.Load "Robby", _
        "C:\Program Files\Microsoft Agent\Characters\Robby.acs"


    Set Genie = MyAgent1.Characters ("Genie")
    Set Robby = MyAgent1.Characters ("Robby")

    Genie.Show

    Genie.Speak "Just a moment"

    Set GenieRequest = Genie.Play ("Processing")
```

(continued)

(continued)

```
        Robby.Show
        Robby.Play "confused"
        Robby.Speak "Hey, Genie. What are you doing?"
        Robby.Interrupt GenieRequest

        Genie.Speak "I was just checking on something."

    End Sub
```

You cannot interrupt the animation of the same character you specify in this method because the server queues the **Interrupt** method in that character's animation queue. Therefore, you can only use **Interrupt** to halt the animation of another character you have loaded.

If you declare an object reference and set it to this method, it returns a **Request** object.

Note **Interrupt** does not flush the character's queue; it halts the existing animation and moves on to the next animation in the character's queue. To halt and flush a character's queue, use the **Stop** method.

See also

Stop method

MoveTo Method

Description

Moves the specified character to the specified location.

Syntax

agent.**Characters ("***CharacterID***").MoveTo** *X,Y,* [*Speed*]

Part	Description
X,Y	Required. An integer value that indicates the left edge (X) and top edge (Y) of the animation frame. Express these coordinates in pixels.
Speed	Optional. A Long integer value specifying in milliseconds how quickly the character's frame moves. The default value is 1000. Specifying zero (0) moves the frame without playing an animation.

Remarks

The server automatically plays the appropriate animation assigned to the **Moving** states. The location of a character is based on the upper left corner of its frame.

If you declare an object variable and set it to this method, it returns a **Request** object. In addition, if the associated animation has not been loaded on the local machine, the server sets the **Request** object's **Status** property to "failed" with an appropriate error number. Therefore, if you are using the HTTP protocol to access character or animation data, use the **Get** method to load the **Moving** state animations before calling the **MoveTo** method.

Even if the animation is not loaded, the server still moves the frame.

Note If you call **MoveTo** with a non-zero value before the character is shown, it will return a failure status if you assigned it a **Request** object, because the non-zero value indicates that you are attempting to play an animation when the character is not visible.

Play Method

Description

Plays the specified animation for the specified character.

Syntax

agent.**Characters** (*"CharacterID"*).**Play** *"AnimationName"*

Part	Description
AnimationName	Required. A string that specifies the name of an animation sequence.

Remarks

An animation's name is defined when the character is compiled with the Microsoft Agent Character Editor. Before playing the specified animation, the server attempts to play the **Return** animation for the previous animation, if one has been assigned.

When accessing a character's animations using a conventional file protocol, you can simply use the **Play** method specifying the name of the animation. However, if you are using the HTTP protocol to access character animation data, use the **Get** method to load the animation before calling the **Play** method.

For more information, see the **Get** method.

To simplify your syntax, you can declare an object reference and set it to reference the **Character** object in the **Characters** collection and use the reference as part of your **Play** statements:

```
Dim Genie
Agent1.Characters.Load "Genie", _
    "http://agent.microsoft.com/characters/genie/genie.acf"

Set Genie = Agent1.Characters ("Genie")
```

(continued)

(continued)

```
Genie.Get "state", "Showing"
Genie.Show

Genie.Get "animation", "Greet, GreetReturn"
Genie.Play "Greet"
Genie.Speak "Hello."
```

If you declare an object reference and set it to this method, it returns a **Request** object. In addition, if you specify an animation that is not loaded or if the character has not been successfully loaded, the server sets the **Status** property of **Request** object to "failed" with an appropriate error number. However, if the animation does not exist and the character's data has already been successfully loaded, the server raises an error.

The **Play** method does not make the character visible. If the character is not visible, the server plays the animation invisibly, and sets the **Status** property of the **Request** object.

Show Method

Description

Makes the specified character visible and plays its associated **Showing** animation.

Syntax

agent.**Characters** (*"CharacterID"*).**Show** [*Fast*]

Part	Description
Fast	Optional. A Boolean expression specifying whether the server plays the **Showing** animation.
	True Skips the **Showing** state animation.
	False (Default) Does not skip the **Showing** state animation.

Remarks

If you declare an object reference and set it to this method, it returns a **Request** object. In addition, if the associated **Showing** animation has not been loaded and you have not specified the **Fast** parameter as **True**, the server sets the **Request** object's **Status** property to "failed" with an appropriate error number. Therefore, if you are using the HTTP protocol to access character animation data, use the **Get** method to load the **Showing** state animation before calling the **Show** method.

Avoid setting the **Fast** parameter to **True** without first playing an animation beforehand; otherwise, the character frame may display with no image. In particular, note that if you call **MoveTo** when the character is not visible, it does not play any animation. Therefore, if you call the **Show** method with **Fast** set to **True**, no image will display. Similarly, if you call **Hide** then **Show** with **Fast** set to **True**, there will be no visible image.

See also   **Hide** method

Speak Method

Description   Speaks the specified text for the specified character.

Syntax   *agent*.**Characters** (*"CharacterID"*).**Speak** [*Text*] [, *Url*]

Part	Description
Text	Optional. A string that specifies what the character says.
Url	Optional. A string expression specifying the specification for an audio file. The specification can be a file specification or URL.

Remarks   Although the *Text* and *Url* parameters are optional, one of them must be supplied. To use this method with a character configured to speak only in its word balloon or using a text-to-speech (TTS) engine, simply provide the *Text* parameter. Include a space between words to define appropriate word breaks in the word balloon, even for languages that do not traditionally include spaces.

You can also include vertical bar characters (|) in the *Text* parameter to designate alternative strings, so that the server randomly chooses a different string each time it processes the method.

Character support of TTS output is defined when the character is compiled using the Microsoft Agent Character Editor. To generate TTS output, a compatible TTS engine must already be installed before calling this method. For further information, see Accessing Speech Support for Microsoft Agent.

If you use recorded sound-file output for the character, specify the file's location in the *Url* parameter. However, if you are using the HTTP protocol to access character or animation data, use the **Get** method to load the animation before calling the **Speak** method. When doing so, you still use the *Text* parameter to specify the words that appear in the character's word balloon. However, if you specify a linguistically enhanced sound file (.LWV) for the *Url* parameter and do not specify text for the word balloon, the *Text* parameter uses the text stored in the file.

You can also vary parameters of the speech output with special tags that you include in the *Text* parameter. For more information, see Chapter 9, "Microsoft Agent Speech Output Tags." If you declare an object reference and set it to this method, it returns a **Request** object. In addition, if the file has not been loaded, the server sets the **Request** object's **Status** property to "failed" with an appropriate error code number.

The **Speak** method uses the last action played to determine which speaking animation to play. For example, if you preceded the **Speak** command with a **Play** "**GestureRight**", the server will play **GestureRight** and then the **GestureRight** speaking animation.

If you call **Speak** and the audio channel is busy, the character's audio output will not be heard, but the text will display in the word balloon.

Note The word balloon's **Enabled** property must also be **True** for text to display.

Note If you are using a character that you did not compile, check the balloon **FontName** and **CharSet** properties for the character to determine whether they are appropriate for your locale. You may need to set these values before using the **Speak** method to ensure appropriate text display within the word balloon.

Stop Method

Description

Stops the animation for the specified character.

Syntax

agent.**Characters** ("*CharacterID*").**Stop** [*Request*]

Part	Description
Request	Optional. To use this parameter, set the **Request** object in your code.

Remarks

If you don't set the **Request** parameter, the server stops all animations for the character, including queued **Get** calls, and clears its animation queue unless the character is currently playing its **Hiding** or **Showing** animation. This method does not stop non-queued **Get** calls.

To stop a specific animation or **Get** call, declare an object variable and assign your animation request to that variable:

```
Dim MyRequest
Dim Genie

Agent1.Characters.Load "Genie", _
    "http://agent.microsoft.com/characters/genie/genie.acf"

Set Genie = Agent1.Characters ("Genie")

Genie.Get "state", "Showing"
Genie.Get "animation", "Greet, GreetReturn"

Genie.Show

'This animation will never play
Set MyRequest = Genie.Play ("Greet")

Genie.Stop MyRequest
```

This method will not generate a **Request** object.

See also   **StopAll** method

StopAll Method

Description   Stops all animation requests or specified types of requests for the specified character.

Syntax   *agent*.**Characters** (*"CharacterID"*).**StopAll** [*Type*]

Part	Description
Type	Optional. To use this parameter you can use any of the following values. You can also specify multiple types by separating them with commas.

"Get"	To stop all queued **Get** requests.
"NonQueuedGet"	To stop all non-queued **Get** requests (**Get** method with **Queue** parameter set to **False**).
"Move"	To stop all queued **MoveTo** requests.
"Play"	To stop all queued **Play** requests.
"Speak"	To stop all queued **Speak** requests.

Remarks

If you don't set the **Type** parameter, the server stops all animations for the character, including queued and non-queued **Get** requests, and clears its animation queue. It also stops playing a character's Hiding or Showing animation.

This method will not generate a **Request** object.

See also

Stop method

Wait Method

Description

Causes the animation queue for the specified character to wait until the specified animation request completes.

Syntax

agent.**Characters** (*"CharacterID"*).**Wait** *Request*

Part	Description
Request	A **Request** object specifying a particular animation. To set this parameter you must assign the **Request** object variable in your code.

Remarks

Use this method only when you support multiple (simultaneous) characters and are trying to sequence the interaction of characters (as a single client). (For a single character, each animation request is played sequentially—after the previous request completes.) If you have two characters and you want a character's animation request to wait until the other character's animation completes, set the **Wait** method to the other character's animation **Request** object, as shown in the following example:

```
Dim GenieRequest
Dim RobbyRequest
Dim Genie
Dim Robby

Sub window_Onload

Agent1.Characters.Load "Genie", _
    "http://agent.microsoft.com/characters/genie/genie.acf"
Agent1.Characters.Load "Robby", _
    "http://agent.microsoft.com/characters/robby/robby.acf"

Set Genie = Agent1.Characters("Genie")
Set Robby = Agent1.Characters("Robby")
```

```
Genie.Get "State", "Showing"
Robby.Get "State", "Showing"

Genie.Get "Animation", "Announce, AnnounceReturn, Pleased, _
    PleasedReturn"

Robby.Get "Animation", "Confused, ConfusedReturn, Sad, SadReturn"

Set Genie = Agent1.Characters ("Genie")
Set Robby = Agent1.Characters ("Robby")

Genie.MoveTo 100,100
Genie.Show

Robby.MoveTo 250,100
Robby.Show

Genie.Play "Announce"
Set GenieRequest = Genie.Speak ("Why did the chicken cross the _
    road?")

Robby.Wait GenieRequest
Robby.Play "Confused"
Set RobbyRequest = Robby.Speak ("I don't know. Why did the chicken _
    cross the road?")

Genie.Wait RobbyRequest
Genie.Play "Pleased"
Set GenieRequest = Genie.Speak ("To get to the other side.")

Robby.Wait GenieRequest
Robby.Play "Sad"
Robby.Speak "I never should have asked."

End Sub
```

Character Object Properties

The **Character** object exposes the following read-only properties:

Description	ExtraData	HasOtherClients	Height	IdleOn
Left	MoveCause	Name	Pitch	SoundEffectsOn
Speed	Top	VisibilityCause	Visible	Width

Note that the **Height**, **Left**, **Top**, and **Width** properties of a character differ from those that may be supported by the programming environment for the placement of the control. The **Character** properties apply to the visible presentation of a character, not the location of the Microsoft Agent control.

As with **Character** object methods, you can access a character's properties using the **Characters** collection, or simplify your syntax by declaring an object variable and setting it to a character in the collection. In the following example, Test1 and Test2 will be set to the same value:

```
Dim Genie
Dim MyRequest

Sub window_Onload

Agent.Characters.Load "Genie", _
  "http://agent.microsoft.com/characters/genie/genie.acf"

Set Genie = Agent.Characters("Genie")

Genie.MoveTo 15,15
MyRequest = Genie.Show()

End Sub

Sub Agent_RequestComplete(ByVal Request)

If Request = MyRequest Then
  Test1 = Agent.Characters("Genie").Top
  Test2 = Genie.Top
  MsgBox "Test 1 is " + cstr(Test1) + "and Test 2 is " + cstr(Test2)
End If

End Sub
```

Because the server loads a character asynchronously, ensure that the character has been loaded before querying its properties, for example, using the **RequestComplete** event. Otherwise, the properties may return incorrect values.

Description Property

Description

Returns or sets a string that specifies the description for the specified character.

Syntax

agent.**Characters("***CharacterID***").Description**

Remarks

The default value for the **Description** property for a character is defined when the character is compiled with the Microsoft Agent Character Editor.

Note The **Description** property setting is optional and may not be supplied for all characters.

ExtraData Property

Description   Returns a string that specifies additional data stored as part of the character.

Syntax   *agent*.**Characters(**"*CharacterID*"**).ExtraData**

Remarks   The default value for the **ExtraData** property for a character is defined when the character is compiled with the Microsoft Agent Character Editor. It cannot be changed or specified at run time.

Note The **ExtraData** property setting is optional and may not be supplied for all characters.

HasOtherClients Property

Description   Returns whether the specified character is in use by other applications.

Syntax   *agent*.**Characters(**"*CharacterID*"**).HasOtherClients**

Value	Description
True	The character has other clients.
False	The character does not have other clients.

Remarks   You can use this property to determine whether your application is the only or last client of the character, when more than one application is sharing (has loaded) the same character.

Height Property

Description   Returns or sets the height of the specified character's frame.

Syntax   *agent*.**Characters (**"*CharacterID*"**).Height** [= *value*]

Part	Description
value	A Long integer that specifies the character's frame height.

Remarks   The **Height** property is always expressed in pixels, relative to screen coordinates (upper left).

Even though the character appears in an irregularly shaped region window, the height of the character is based on the external dimensions of the rectangular animation frame used when the character was compiled with the Microsoft Agent Character Editor.

IdleOn Property

Description   Returns or sets a Boolean value that determines whether the server manages the specified character's **Idling** state animations.

Syntax   *agent*.**Characters** (*"CharacterID"*).**IdleOn** [=*boolean*]

Part	Description
True	Server idle processing is enabled. The character's Idling animations are automatically played.
False	Server idle processing is disabled. The character's Idling animations are not automatically played.

Remarks   The server automatically sets a time-out after the last animation played for a character. When this timer's interval is complete, the server begins the **Idling** state for a character, playing its associated **Idling** animations at regular intervals. The default value for the **IdleOn** property is **True**, meaning that the server manages the character's **Idling** state. If you want to manage the **Idling** state animations yourself, set the property to **False**.

Left Property

Description   Returns or sets the left edge of the specified character's frame.

Syntax   *agent*.**Characters** (*"CharacterID"*).**Left** [= *value*]

Part	Description
value	A Long integer that specifies the left edge of the character's frame.

Remarks   The **Left** property is always expressed in pixels, relative to screen origin (upper left).

Even though the character appears in an irregularly shaped region window, the location of the character is based on the external dimensions of the rectangular animation frame used when the character was compiled with the Microsoft Agent Character Editor.

MoveCause Property

Description   Returns an integer value that specifies what caused the character's last move.

Syntax   *agent*.**Characters("***CharacterID***").MoveCause**

Value	Description
0	The character has not been moved.
1	The user moved the character.
2	Your application moved the character.
3	Another client application moved the character.

Remarks   You can use this property to determine what caused the character to move, when more than one application is sharing (has loaded) the same character. These values are the same as those returned by the **Move** event.

See also   **Move** event, **MoveTo** method

Name Property

Description   Returns or sets a string that specifies the default name of the specified character.

Syntax   *agent*.**Characters ("***CharacterID***").Name**

Remarks   The default value for the **Name** property for a character is defined when the character is compiled with the Microsoft Agent Character Editor. The server uses the **Name** property to automatically create commands for hiding and showing a character.

Pitch Property

Description   Returns a Long integer for the specified character's current speech output (TTS) pitch setting.

Syntax   *agent*.**Characters ("***CharacterID***").Pitch**

Remarks   This property applies only to characters configured for TTS output. If the speech synthesis (TTS) engine is not enabled or installed, or the character does not support TTS output, this property returns zero (0).

Although your application cannot write this value, you can include **Pit** (pitch) tags in your output text that will temporarily increase the pitch for a particular utterance. For further information, see Chapter 9, "Microsoft Agent Speech Output Tags."

SoundEffectsOn Property

Description

Returns or sets whether sound effects are enabled for your character.

Syntax

*agent.***Characters(***"CharacterID"***).SoundEffectsOn** [=*boolean*]

Value	Description
Boolean	A Boolean expression specifying whether sound effects are enabled.
	True Sound effects are enabled.
	False Sound effects are disabled.

Remarks

This property determines whether sound effects included as a part of a character's animations will play when an animation plays.

See also

SoundEffects property

Speed Property

Description

Returns a Long integer that specifies the speed of the character's speech output.

Syntax

*agent.***Characters (***"CharacterID"***).Speed**

Remarks

This property returns the current speaking output speed setting for the character. For characters using TTS output, the property returns the actual TTS output for the character. If TTS is not enabled or the character does not support TTS output, the setting reflects the user setting for output speed.

Although your application cannot write this value, you can include **Spd** (speed) tags in your output text that will temporarily speed up the output for a particular utterance. For further information, see Chapter 9, "Microsoft Agent Speech Output Tags."

Top Property

Description   Returns or sets the top edge of the specified character's frame.

Syntax   *agent.***Characters** (*"CharacterID"*).**Top** [= *value*]

Part	Description
value	A Long integer that specifies the character's top edge.

Remarks   The **Top** property is always expressed in pixels, relative to screen origin (upper left).

Even though the character appears in an irregularly shaped region window, the location of the character is based on the external dimensions of the rectangular animation frame used when the character was compiled with the Microsoft Agent Character Editor.

Use the **MoveTo** method to change the character's location.

VisibilityCause Property

Description   Returns an integer value that specifies what caused the character's visible state.

Syntax   *agent.***Characters(***"CharacterID"***).VisibilityCause**

Value	Description
0	The character has not been shown.
1	The user hid the character.
2	The user showed the character.
3	Your application hid the character.
4	Your application showed the character.
5	Another client application hid the character.
6	Another client application showed the character.

Remarks   You can use this property to determine what caused the character to move when more than one application is sharing (has loaded) the same character. These values are the same as those returned by the **Show** and **Hide** events.

See also   **Hide** event, **Show** event, **Hide** method, **Show** method

Visible Property

Description

Returns a Boolean indicating whether the character is visible.

Syntax

*agent.***Characters** (*"CharacterID"*)**.Visible**

Return	Description
True	The character is displayed.
False	The character is hidden (not visible).

Remarks

To make a character visible or hidden, use the **Show** or **Hide** methods.

Width Property

Description

Returns or sets the width of the frame for the specified character.

Syntax

*agent.***Characters** (*"CharacterID"*)**.Width** [= *value*]

Part	Description
value	A Long integer that specifies the character's frame width.

Remarks

The **Width** property is always expressed in pixels.

Even though the character appears in an irregularly shaped region window, the location of the character is based on the external dimensions of the rectangular animation frame used when the character was compiled with the Microsoft Agent Character Editor.

The Commands Collection Object

The Microsoft Agent server maintains a list of commands that are currently available to the user. This list includes commands that the server defines for general interaction (such as Hide and Microsoft Agent Properties), the list of available (but non-input-active) clients, and the commands defined by the current active client. The first two sets of commands are global commands; that is, they are available at any time, regardless of the input-active client. Client-defined commands are available only when that client is input-active.

Each client application can define a collection of commands called the **Commands** collection. To add a command to the collection, use the **Add** or **Insert** method. Although you can specify a command's properties with separate statements, for optimum code performance, specify all of a command's properties in the **Add** or **Insert** method statement. For each command in the collection, you can determine whether user access to the command appears in the character's pop-up menu, in the Commands Window, in both, or in neither. For example, if you want a command to appear on the pop-up menu for the character, set the command's **Caption** and **Visible** properties. To display the command in the Commands Window, set the command's **Caption** and **Voice** properties.

A user can access the individual commands in your **Commands** collection only when your client application is input-active. Therefore, you'll typically want to set the **Caption** and **Voice** properties for the **Commands** collection object as well as for the commands in the collection, which places an entry for your **Commands** collection in a character's pop-up menu and in the Commands Window. When the user switches to your client by choosing its entry, the server automatically makes your client input-active and makes the commands in its collection available. This enables the server to present and accept only the commands that apply to the current input-active client's context. It also serves to avoid command-name collisions between clients.

When a character's pop-up menu displays, changes to the properties of a **Commands** collection or the commands in its collection do not appear until the user redisplays the menu. However, the Commands Window does display changes as they happen.

Commands Object Methods

The server supports the following methods for the **Commands** collection object:

Add   **Command**   **Insert**   **Remove**   **RemoveAll**

Add Method

Description   Adds a **Command** object to the **Commands** collection.

Syntax   *agent*.**Characters** (*"CharacterID"*).**Commands.Add** *Name, Caption, Voice,_Enabled, Visible*

Part	Description
Name	Required. A string value corresponding to the ID you assign for the command.
Caption	Optional. A string value corresponding to the name that will appear in the character's pop-up menu and in the Commands Window when the client application is input-active. For more information, see the **Command** object's **Caption** property.
Voice	Optional. A string value corresponding to the words or phrase to be used by the speech engine for recognizing this command. For more information on formatting alternatives for the string, see the **Command** object's **Voice** property.
Enabled	Optional. A Boolean value indicating whether the command is enabled. The default value is **True**. For more information, see the **Command** object's **Enabled** property.
Visible	Optional. A Boolean value indicating whether the command is visible in the character's pop-up menu for the character when the client application is input-active. The default value is **True**. For more information, see the **Command** object's **Visible** property.

Remarks

The value of a **Command** object's **Name** property must be unique within its **Commands** collection. You must remove a **Command** before you can create a new **Command** with the same **Name** property setting. Attempting to create a **Command** with a **Name** property that already exists raises an error.

See also

Insert method, **Remove** method, **RemoveAll** method

Command Method

Description

Returns a **Command** object in a **Commands** collection.

Syntax

agent.**Characters** (*"CharacterID"*).**Commands.Command** *"Name"*

Remarks

You can use this method to access a **Command** object's properties.

Note This method may be required for some programming languages. It is not required for VBScript or Visual Basic. For further information on specifying **Command** methods, see Command Object Properties.

Insert Method

Description   Inserts a **Command** object in the **Commands** collection.

Syntax   *agent*.**Characters** (*"CharacterID"*).**Commands.Insert** *Name, RefName, Before, _Caption, Voice, Enabled, Visible*

Part	Description
Name	Required. A string value corresponding to the ID you assign to the **Command**.
RefName	Required. A string value corresponding to the name (ID) of the command just above or below where you want to insert the new command.
Before	Optional. A Boolean value indicating whether to insert the new command before the command specified by RefName.
	True (Default). The new command will be inserted before the referenced command.
	False The new command will be inserted after the referenced command.
Caption	Optional. A string value corresponding to the name that will appear in the character's pop-up menu and in the Commands Window when the client application is input-active. For more information, see the **Command** object's **Caption** property.
Voice	Optional. A string value corresponding to the words or phrase to be used by the speech engine for recognizing this command. For more information on formatting alternatives for the string, see the **Command** object's **Voice** property.
Enabled	Optional. A Boolean value indicating whether the command is enabled. The default value is **True**. For more information, see the **Command** object's **Enabled** property.
Visible	Optional. A Boolean value indicating whether the command is visible in the Commands Window when the client application is input-active. The default value is **True**. For more information, see the **Command** object's **Visible** property.

Remarks   The value of a **Command** object's **Name** property must be unique within its **Commands** collection. You must remove a **Command** before you can create a new **Command** with the same **Name** property setting. Attempting to create a **Command** with a **Name** property that already exists raises an error.

See also   **Add** method, **Remove** method, **RemoveAll** method

Remove Method

Description   Removes a **Command** object from the **Commands** collection.

Syntax   *agent*.**Characters** (*"CharacterID"*).**Commands.Remove** *Name*

Part	Description
Name	Required. A string value corresponding to the ID for the command.

Remarks   When a **Command** object is removed from the collection, it no longer appears when the character's pop-up menu is displayed or in the Commands Window when your client application is input-active.

See also   **RemoveAll** method

RemoveAll Method

Description   Removes all **Command** objects from the **Commands** collection.

Syntax   *agent*.**Characters** (*"CharacterID"*).**Commands.RemoveAll**

Remarks   When a **Command** object is removed from the collection, it no longer appears when the character's pop-up menu is displayed or in the Commands Window when your client application is input-active.

See also   **Remove** method

Commands Object Properties

The server supports the following properties for the **Commands** collection:

Caption   **Count**   **Visible**   **Voice**

An entry for the **Commands** collection can appear in both the pop-up menu and the Commands Window for a character. To make this entry appear, set its **Caption** property. The following table summarizes how the properties of a **Commands** object affect the entry's presentation:

Caption Property	Voice Property	Visible Property	Appears in Character's Pop-up Menu	Appears in Commands Window
Yes	Yes	True	Yes	Yes
Yes	No	True	Yes	No
Yes	Yes	False	No	Yes
Yes	No	False	No	No
No	Yes	True	No	No*
No	Yes	False	No	No*
No	No	True	No	No
No	No	False	No	No

The command is still voice-accessible. If the client is input-active and has commands in its collection, "(command undefined)" appears in the Commands Window.

Caption Property

Description

Determines the text displayed for the **Commands** object in the character's pop-up menu and in the Commands Window.

Syntax

agent.**Characters** (*"CharacterID"*).**Commands.Caption** [=*string*]

Part	Description
string	A string expression that evaluates to the text displayed as the caption.

Remarks

If you define commands for a **Commands** collection that have their **Caption**, **Enabled**, and **Voice** properties set, you would typically also define **Caption** and **Voice** settings for the associated **Commands** collection. If the **Commands** collection has no **Voice** or no **Caption** setting and is currently input-active, but the commands in its collection have **Caption** and **Voice** settings, the commands appear in the Commands Window tree view under "(undefined command)" when your client application becomes input-active.

Count Property

Description Returns a Long integer (read-only property) that specifies the count of **Command** objects in the **Commands** collection.

Syntax *agent*.**Characters** (*"CharacterID"*).**Commands.Count**

Remarks **Count** includes only the number of **Command** objects you define in your **Commands** collection. Server or other client entries are not included.

Visible Property

Description Returns or sets a value that determines whether your **Commands** collection's caption appears in the character's pop-up menu.

Syntax *agent*.**Characters** (*"CharacterID"*).**Commands.Visible** [= *boolean*]

Part	Description
boolean	A Boolean expression specifying whether your **Commands** object appears in the character's pop-up menu.
	True The **Caption** for your **Commands** collection appears.
	False The **Caption** for your **Commands** collection does not appear.

Remarks This property must be set to **True** for commands in your collection to appear in the pop-up menu when your application is input-active.

Voice Property

Description Returns or sets the text that is passed to the speech engine (for recognition).

Syntax *agent*.**Characters** (*"CharacterID"*).**Commands.Voice** [= *string*]

Part	Description
string	A string value corresponding to the words or phrase to be used by the speech engine for recognizing this command.

Remarks If you do not supply this parameter, the caption for your **Commands** object will not appear in the Commands Window.

The string expression you supply can include square bracket characters ([ ]) to indicate optional words and vertical bar characters, (|) to indicate alternative strings. Alternates must be enclosed in parentheses. For example, "(hello [there] | hi)" tells the speech engine to accept "hello," "hello there," or "hi" for the command. Remember to include appropriate spaces between the text that's in brackets or parentheses and the text that's not in brackets or parentheses.

You can also use an ellipsis (...) to support *word spotting*, that is, telling the speech recognition engine to ignore words spoken in this position in the phrase (sometimes called *garbage* words). When you use ellipses, the speech engine recognizes only specific words in the string regardless of when spoken with adjacent words or phrases. For example, if you set this property to "...check mail...", the speech recognition engine will match phrases like "please check mail" or "check mail please" to this command. Ellipses can be used anywhere within a string. However, be careful using this technique as voice settings with ellipses may increase the potential of unwanted matches.

When defining the word grammar for your command, always make sure that you include at least one word that is required; that is, avoid supplying only optional words. In addition, make sure that the word includes only pro-nounceable words and letters. For numbers, it is better to spell out the word than use the numeric representation. Also, omit any punctuation or symbols. For example, instead of "the #1 $10 pizza!", use "the number one ten dollar pizza". Including non-pronounceable characters or symbols for one command may cause the speech engine to fail to compile the grammar for all your com-mands. Finally, make your voice parameter as distinct as reasonably possible from other voice commands you define. The greater the similarity between the voice grammar for commands, the more likely the speech engine will make a recognition error. You can also use the confidence scores to better distinguish between two commands that may have similar or similar-sounding voice grammar.

Note The operation of this property depends on the state of the server's speech recognition property. For example, if speech recognition is disabled or not installed, this parameter has no effect. If speech recognition is enabled during a session, however, the command will become accessible when its client application is input-active.

The Command Object

A **Command** object is an item in a **Commands** collection. The server pro-vides the user access to your **Command** objects when your client application becomes input-active.

To access the property of a **Command** object, you reference it in its collection using its **Name** property. In VBScript and Visual Basic you can use the **Name** property directly:

```
agent.Characters("CharacterID").Commands("Name").property [= value]
```

For programming languages that don't support collections, use the **Command** method:

```
agent.Characters("CharacterID").Commands.Command("Name").property
    [= value]
```

You can also reference a Command object by creating a reference to it. In Visual Basic, declare an object variable and use the Set statement to create the reference:

```
Dim Cmd1 as Object
...
Set Cmd1 = Agent.Characters("MyCharacterID").Commands("SampleCommand")
...
Cmd1.Enabled = True
```

In Visual Basic 5.0, you can also declare the object as type **IAgentCtl-Command** and create the reference. This convention enables early binding, which results in better performance:

```
Dim Cmd1 as IAgentCtlCommand
...
Set Cmd1 = Agent.Characters("MyCharacterID").Commands("SampleCommand")
...
Cmd1.Enabled = True
```

In VBScript, you can declare a reference as a particular type, but you can still declare the variable and set it to the **Command** in the collection:

```
Dim Cmd1
...
Set Cmd1 = Agent.Characters("MyCharacterID").Commands("SampleCommand")
...
Cmd1.Enabled = True
```

A command may appear in either the character's pop-up menu and the Commands Window, or in both. To appear in the pop-up menu it must have a caption and have the **Visible** property set to **True**. In addition, its Commands collection object **Visible** property must also be set to **True**. To appear in the Commands Window, a **Command** must have its **Caption** and **Voice** properties set. Note that a character's pop-up menu entries do not change while the menu displays. If you add or remove commands or change their properties while the character's pop-up menu is displayed, the menu displays those changes whenever the user next displays it. However, the Commands Window dynamically reflects any changes you make.

The following table summarizes how the properties of a **Command** affect its presentation:

Caption Property	Voice Property	Visible Property	Enabled Property	Appears in Character's Pop-up Menu	Appears in Commands Window
Yes	Yes	True	True	Normal	Yes
Yes	Yes	True	False	Disabled	No
Yes	Yes	False	True	Does not appear	Yes
Yes	Yes	False	False	Does not appear	No
Yes	No	True	True	Normal	No
Yes	No	True	False	Disabled	No
Yes	No	False	True	Does not appear	No
Yes	No	False	False	Does not appear	No
No	Yes	True	True	Does not appear	No*
No	Yes	True	False	Does not appear	No
No	Yes	False	True	Does not appear	No*
No	Yes	False	False	Does not appear	No
No	No	True	True	Does not appear	No
No	No	True	False	Does not appear	No
No	No	False	True	Does not appear	No
No	No	False	False	Does not appear	No

The command is still voice-accessible.

Generally, if you define commands with **Voice** settings, you also define **Caption** and **Voice** settings for its associated **Commands** collection. If a **Commands** collection has no **Voice** or no **Caption** setting and is currently input-active, but its **Command** objects do have **Caption** and **Voice** settings and their **Enabled** properties are **True**, the **Command** objects appear in the Commands Window tree view under "(undefined command)" when your client application becomes input-active.

When the server receives input for one of your commands, it sends a **Command** event, and passes back the name of the **Command** as an attribute of the **UserInput** object. You can then use conditional statements to match and process the **Command**.

Command Object Properties

The following **Command** properties are supported:

Caption	Confidence	ConfidenceText
Enabled	Visible	Voice

Caption Property

Description

Determines the text displayed for a **Command** in the specified character's pop-up menu and the Commands Window.

Syntax

agent.**Characters** (*"CharacterID"*).**Commands**(*"name"*).**Caption** [= *string*]

Part	Description
string	A string expression that evaluates to the text displayed as the caption for the **Command**.

Confidence Property

Description

Returns or sets whether the client's **ConfidenceText** appears in the Listening Tip.

Description

agent.**Characters** (*"CharacterID"*).**Commands**(*"name"*).**Confidence** [= *number*]

Part	Description
number	A numeric expression that evaluates to a Long integer that identifies confidence value for the **Command**.

Remarks

If the returned confidence value of the best match (**UserInput.Confidence**) does not exceed value you set for the **Confidence** property, the text supplied in **ConfidenceText** is displayed in the Listening Tip.

ConfidenceText Property

Description

Returns or sets the client's **ConfidenceText** that appears in the Listening Tip.

Syntax

agent.**Characters** (*"CharacterID"*).**Commands**(*"name"*).**ConfidenceText** [= *string*]

Part	Description
string	A string expression that evaluates to the text for the **ConfidenceText** for the **Command**.

Remarks

When the returned confidence value of the best match (**UserInput.Confidence**) does not exceed the **Confidence** setting, the server displays the text supplied in **ConfidenceText** in the Listening Tip.

Enabled Property

Description

Returns or sets whether the **Command** is enabled in the specified character's pop-up menu.

Syntax

agent.**Characters** (*"CharacterID"*).**Commands**(*"name"*).**Enabled** [= *boolean*]

Part	Description
boolean	A Boolean expression specifying whether the **Command** is enabled.
	True The **Command** is enabled.
	False The **Command** is disabled.

Remarks   If the **Enabled** property is set to **True**, the **Command** object's caption appears as normal text in the character's pop-up menu when the client application is input-active. If the **Enabled** property is **False**, the caption appears as unavailable (disabled) text. A disabled **Command** is also not accessible for voice input.

Visible Property

Description   Returns or sets whether the **Command** is visible in the character's pop-up menu.

Syntax   *agent*.**Characters** (*"CharacterID"*).**Commands**(*"name"*).**Visible**
[= *boolean*]

Part	Description
boolean	A Boolean expression specifying whether the **Command**'s caption appears in the character's pop-up menu.
	True (Default) The caption appears.
	False The caption does not appear.

Remarks   Set this property to **False** when you want to include voice input for your own interfaces without having them appear in the pop-up menu for the character. If you set a **Command** object's **Caption** property to the empty string (" "), the caption text will not appear in the pop-up menu (for example, as a blank line), regardless of its **Visible** property setting.

The **Visible** property setting of a **Command** object's parent **Commands** collection does not affect the **Visible** property setting of the **Command**.

Voice Property

Description   Returns or sets the text that is passed to the speech engine grammar (for recognition) for matching this **Command** for the character.

Syntax   *agent*.**Characters** (*"CharacterID"*).**Commands** (*"name"*).**Voice** [= *string*]

Part	Description
string	A string value corresponding to the words or phrase to be used by the speech engine for recognizing this **Command**.

Remarks

If you do not supply this parameter, the caption for your **Commands** object will not appear in the Commands Window. If you specify a **Voice** parameter but not a **Caption**, the command will not appear in the Commands Window, but it will be voice-accessible when the client application becomes input-active.

Your string expression can include square bracket characters ([ ]) to indicate optional words and vertical bar characters (|) to indicate alternative strings. Alternates must be enclosed in parentheses. For example, "(hello [there] | hi)" tells the speech engine to accept "hello," "hello there," or "hi" for the command. Remember to include appropriate spaces between the text that's in brackets or parentheses and the text that's not in brackets or parentheses.

You can also use an ellipsis (...) to support *word spotting*, that is, telling the speech recognition engine to ignore words spoken in this position in the phrase (sometimes called *garbage* words). Therefore, the speech engine recognizes only specific words in the string regardless of when spoken with adjacent words or phrases. For example, if you set this property to "...check mail...", the speech recognition engine will match phrases like "please check mail" or "check mail please" to this command. Ellipses can be used anywhere within a string. However, be careful using this technique as it may increase the potential of unwanted matches.

When defining the word grammar for your command, always make sure that you include at least one word that is required; that is, avoid supplying only optional words. In addition, make sure that the word includes only pronounceable words and letters. For numbers, it is better to spell out the word rather than using the numeric representation. Also, omit any punctuation or symbols. For example, instead of "the #1 $10 pizza!", use "the number one ten dollar pizza". Including non-pronounceable characters or symbols for one command may cause the speech engine to fail to compile the grammar for all your commands. Finally, make your voice parameter as distinct as reasonably possible from other voice commands you define. The greater the similarity between the voice grammar for commands, the more likely the speech engine will make a recognition error. You can also use the confidence scores to better distinguish between two commands that may have similar or similar-sounding voice grammar.

Note The operation of this property depends on the state of the server's speech recognition property. For example, if speech recognition is disabled or not installed, this property has no effect.

The Balloon Object

Microsoft Agent supports textual captioning of spoken output using a cartoon word balloon. A character's initial word balloon window defaults are defined and compiled in the Microsoft Agent Character Editor.

Balloon Object Properties

Once running, the word balloon's **Enabled** and **Font** properties may be over-ridden by the user. If a user changes the word balloon's properties, they affect all characters. You can access the properties for a character's word balloon through the **Balloon** object, which is a child of the **Characters** collection.

The **Balloon** object supports the following properties:

BackColor	**BorderColor**	**CharSet**	**CharsPerLine**	**Enabled**
FontName	**FontBold**	**FontItalic**	**FontSize**	**FontStrikeThru**
FontUnderline	**ForeColor**	**NumberOfLines**	**Visible**	

BackColor Property

Description

Returns the background color currently displayed in the word balloon window for the specified character.

Syntax

agent.**Characters (**"*CharacterID*"**).Balloon.BackColor**

Remarks

The valid range for a normal RGB color is 0 to 16,777,215 (&HFFFFFF). The high byte of a number in this range equals 0; the lower 3 bytes, from least to most significant byte, determine the amount of red, green, and blue, respectively. The red, green, and blue components are each represented by a number between 0 and 255 (&HFF).

BorderColor Property

Description

Returns the border color currently displayed for the word balloon window for the specified character.

Syntax

agent.**Characters (**"*CharacterID*"**).Balloon.BorderColor**

Remarks

The valid range for a normal RGB color is 0 to 16,777,215 (&HFFFFFF). The high byte of a number in this range equals 0; the lower 3 bytes, from least to most significant byte, determine the amount of red, green, and blue, respectively. The red, green, and blue components are each represented by a number between 0 and 255 (&HFF).

CharSet Property

Description

Returns or sets the character set used for the font displayed in the specified character's word balloon.

Syntax

agent.**Characters** (*"CharacterID"*).**Balloon.CharSet** [= *value*]

Part	Description
value	A integer value that specifies the character set used by the font. The following are some common settings for value:

0	Standard Windows® characters (ANSI).
1	Default character set.
2	The symbol character set.
128	Double-byte character set (DBCS) unique to the Japanese version of Windows.
129	Double-byte character set (DBCS) unique to the Korean version of Windows.
134	Double-byte character set (DBCS) unique to the Simplified Chinese version of Windows.
136	Double-byte character set (DBCS) unique to the Traditional Chinese version of Windows.
255	Extended characters normally displayed by DOS applications.

For other character set values, consult the Microsoft Win32® documentation.

Remarks

The default value for the character set of a character's word balloon is set in the Microsoft Agent Character Editor. In addition, the user can override the character-set settings for all characters in the Microsoft Agent property sheet.

Note If you are using a character that you did not compile, check the **FontName** and **CharSet** properties for the character to determine whether they are appropriate for your locale. You may need to set these values before using the **Speak** method to ensure appropriate text display within the word balloon.

See also

FontName property

CharsPerLine Property

Description

Returns the characters per line supported for the word balloon for the specified character.

Syntax

agent.**Characters** (*"CharacterID"*).**Balloon.CharsPerLine**

Remarks

The **CharsPerLine** property returns the average number of characters (letters) being displayed in the word balloon as a Long integer value.

Enabled Property

Description

Returns whether the word balloon is enabled for the specified character.

Syntax

agent.**Characters** (*"CharacterID"*).**Balloon.Enabled**

Remarks

The **Enabled** property returns a Boolean value specifying whether the balloon is enabled by the user. **True** indicates the **Balloon** is enabled. **False** indicates it is not enabled (displayed).

The word balloon can also be disabled as part of a character's definition when the character is compiled in the Microsoft Agent Character Editor. If a character is defined to not support the word balloon, this property will always be **False** for the character.

FontName Property

Description

Returns or sets the font used in the word balloon for the specified character.

Syntax

agent.**Characters** (*"CharacterID"*).**Balloon.FontName** [= *font*]

Part	Description
font	A string value corresponding to the font's name.

Remarks

The **FontName** property defines the font used to display text in the word balloon window as a string. The default value for the font settings of a character's word balloon are set in the Microsoft Agent Character Editor. In addition, the user can override font settings for all characters in the Microsoft Agent property sheet.

Note If you are using a character that you did not compile, check the **FontName** and **CharSet** properties for the character to determine whether they are appropriate for your locale. You may need to set these values before using the **Speak** method to ensure appropriate text display within the word balloon.

See also   **CharSet** property

FontBold Property

Description   Returns the font style currently displayed in the word balloon window for the specified character.

Syntax   *agent*.**Characters** (*"CharacterID"*).**Balloon.FontBold**

Remarks   The **FontBold** property returns a Boolean value specifying whether the font is bold. **True** indicates the font is bold. **False** indicates the font is not bold.

The default value for the font settings of a character's word balloon are set in the Microsoft Agent Character Editor. In addition, the user can override font settings for all characters in the Microsoft Agent property sheet.

FontItalic Property

Description   Returns the font style currently displayed in the word balloon window for the specified character.

Syntax   *agent*.**Characters** (*"CharacterID"*).**Balloon.FontItalic**

Remarks   The **FontItalic** property returns a Boolean value specifying whether the font is italic. **True** indicates the font is italic. **False** indicates the font is not italic.

The default value for the font settings of a character's word balloon are set in the Microsoft Agent Character Editor. In addition, the user can override font settings for all characters in the Microsoft Agent property sheet.

FontSize Property

Description   Returns or sets the font size supported for the word balloon for the specified character.

Syntax   *agent*.**Characters** (*"CharacterID"*).**Balloon.FontSize** [= *points*]

Part	Description
points	A Long integer value specifying the font size in points.

Remarks   The **FontSize** property returns a Long integer value specifying the current font size in points.The maximum value for **FontSize** is 2160 points.

The default value for the font settings of a character's word balloon are set in the Microsoft Agent Character Editor. In addition, the user can override font settings for all characters in the Microsoft Agent property sheet.

FontStrikeThru Property

Description   Returns the font style currently displayed in the word balloon window for the specified character.

Syntax   *agent*.**Characters** (*"CharacterID"*).**Balloon.FontStrikeThru**

Remarks   The **FontStrikeThru** property returns a Boolean value specifying whether the font uses the strikethrough effect. **True** indicates the font uses the strikethrough effect. **False** indicates the font does not use the strikethrough effect.

The default value for the font settings of a character's word balloon are set in the Microsoft Agent Character Editor. In addition, the user can override font settings for all characters in the Microsoft Agent property sheet.

FontUnderline Property

Description   Returns the font style currently displayed in the word balloon window for the specified character.

Syntax   *agent*.**Characters** (*"CharacterID"*).**Balloon.FontUnderline**

Remarks   The **FontUnderline** property returns a Boolean value specifying whether the font is underlined. **True** indicates the font is underlined. **False** indicates the font is not underlined.

The default value for the font settings of a character's word balloon are set in the Microsoft Agent Character Editor. In addition, the user can override font settings for all characters in the Microsoft Agent property sheet.

ForeColor Property

Description

Returns the foreground color currently displayed in the word balloon window for the specified character.

Syntax

agent.**Characters** (*"CharacterID"*).**Balloon.ForeColor**

Remarks

The **ForeColor** property returns a value that specifies the color of text in the word balloon. The valid range for a normal RGB color is 0 to 16,777,215 (&HFFFFFF). The high byte of a number in this range equals 0; the lower 3 bytes, from least to most significant byte, determine the amount of red, green, and blue, respectively. The red, green, and blue components are each represented by a number between 0 and 255 (&HFF).

NumberOfLines Property

Description

Returns the number of lines supported for the word balloon for the specified character.

Syntax

agent.**Characters** (*"CharacterID"*).**Balloon.NumberOfLines**

Remarks

The NumberOfLines property returns the number of lines of text as a Long integer value.

Visible Property

Description

Returns or sets the visible setting for the word balloon for the specified character.

Syntax

agent.**Characters** (*"CharacterID"*).**Balloon.Visible** [*=boolean*]

Part	Description
boolean	A Boolean expression specifying whether the word balloon is visible.
	True The balloon is visible.
	False The balloon is hidden.

Remarks

If you attempt to set this property while the character is speaking, moving, or being dragged, the property setting does not take effect until the preceding operation is completed. Calling the **Speak** method automatically makes the balloon visible, setting the **Visible** property to **True**. If the character's balloon AutoHide property is enabled, the balloon is automatically hidden after the output text is spoken. Clicking or dragging a character that is not currently speaking also automatically hides the balloon even if its AutoHide property is disabled. (A character's word-balloon AutoHide property can only be set in the Microsoft Agent Character Editor. The property is not exposed in the API.)

The AudioOutput Object

The **AudioOutput** object provides access to audio output properties maintained by the server.

AudioOutput Properties

The properties are read-only, but the user can change them in the Microsoft Agent property sheet.

Enabled   **SoundEffects**

Enabled Property

Description   Returns a Boolean indicating whether audio (spoken) output is enabled.

Syntax   *agent*.**AudioOutput.Enabled**

Remarks   When the **Enabled** property returns **True**, the **Speak** method produces audio output. When it returns **False**, it means that speech output is not installed or has been disabled by the user. Only the user can set this property value.

SoundEffects Property

Description   Returns a Boolean indicating whether sound effects (.WAV) files configured as part of a character's actions will play.

Syntax   *agent*.**AudioOutput.SoundEffects**

Remarks   When the **SoundEffects** property returns **True**, sound effects included in a character's definition will be played. When **False**, the sound effects will not be played. Only the user can set this property value.

The SpeechInput Object

The **SpeechInput** object provides access to the speech input properties maintained by the server. The properties are read-only for client applications, but the user can change them in the Microsoft Agent property sheet. The server returns values only if a compatible speech engine has been installed and is enabled.

SpeechInput Properties

If a speech recognition engine is installed and enabled, accessing these properties will start the speech engine:

Enabled	**Engine**	**HotKey**
Installed	**Language**	**ListeningTip**

Enabled Property

Description   Returns a Boolean value indicating whether speech input is enabled.

Syntax   *agent*.**SpeechInput.Enabled**

Remarks   The **Enabled** property reflects the state of the speech recognition engine set in the **Engine** property. Values for other **SpeechInput** properties do not change when **Enabled** is set to **False**. Querying this property raises an error if no speech engine has been installed.

Note The user can override this property.

Engine Property

Description   Returns or sets the speech recognition engine that is currently selected for input.

Syntax   *agent*.**SpeechInput.Engine** [*=modeID*]

Part	Description
modeID	A string expression specifying the mode ID of the speech engine.

Remarks   The **Engine** property takes a string value specifying the mode ID of the speech engine. Querying this property raises an error if **Installed** or **Enabled** is **False**.

Note The user can override this property.

HotKey Property

Description   Returns a string that specifies the user's current setting for the push-to-talk hot key.

Syntax   *agent*.**SpeechInput.HotKey**

Remarks   Querying this property raises an error if **Installed** or **Enabled** is **False**.

Installed Property

Description   Returns a Boolean that indicates whether a compatible speech engine is installed.

Syntax   *agent*.**SpeechInput.Installed**

Remarks   If no compatible speech engine has been installed, this property returns **False**. However, querying any other **SpeechInput** properties raises an error. Therefore, check this property before checking the values of the **SpeechInput** or **CommandsWindow** objects.

Language Property

Description   Returns a string that specifies what language is configured for speech input.

Syntax   *agent*.**SpeechInput.Language**

Remarks   This property value is set based on the selected speech recognition engine set in the **Engine** property. Querying this property raises an error if **Installed** or **Enabled** is **False**.

ListeningTip Property

Description   Returns a Boolean indicating whether the server displays the Listening Tip.

Syntax   *agent*.**SpeechInput.ListeningTip**

Remarks   When **ListeningTip** returns **True**, the server displays the tip window when the user presses the push-to-talk hot key. Querying this property raises an error if **Installed** or **Enabled** is **False**.

The CommandsWindow Object

The **CommandsWindow** object provides access to properties of the Commands Window. The Commands Window is a shared resource primarily designed to enable users to view voice-enabled commands. If speech recognition is disabled, the Commands Window is also disabled, but you can still read its property settings. If no speech engine is installed or if speech is disabled, querying for the **CommandsWindow** properties raises an error.

CommandsWindow Properties

Height   **Left**   **Top**   **Visible**   **Width**

Height Property

Description   Returns an integer value specifying the current height, in pixels, of the Commands Window.

Syntax   *agent*.**CommandsWindow.Height**

Remarks   The server displays the Commands Window based on the position and size set by the user. Querying this property raises an error if no speech engine has been installed.

Left Property

Description   Returns an integer value specifying the left edge, in pixels, of the Commands Window.

Syntax   *agent*.**CommandsWindow.Left**

Remarks   The server displays the Commands Window based on the position and size set by the user. Querying this property raises an error if no speech engine has been installed.

Top Property

Description   Returns an integer value specifying the top edge, in pixels, of the Commands Window.

Syntax   *agent*.**CommandsWindow.Top**

Remarks   The server displays the Commands Window based on the position and size set by the user. Querying this property raises an error if no speech engine has been installed.

Visible Property

Description   Returns or sets whether the Commands Window is visible (open).

Syntax   *agent*.**CommandsWindow.Visible** [*=boolean*]

Part	Description
boolean	A Boolean expression specifying whether the Commands Window is visible.
	True The window is visible.
	False The window is hidden (closed).

Remarks   The server displays the window based on the position and size set by the user. Querying this property raises an error if no speech engine has been installed.

Note The user can override this property.

Width Property

Description   Returns an integer value specifying the width, in pixels, of the Commands Window.

Syntax   *agent*.**CommandsWindow.Width**

Remarks   The server displays the Commands Window based on the position and size set by the user. Querying this property raises an error if no speech engine has been installed.

The PropertySheet Object

The **PropertySheet** object provides several properties you can use if you want to manipulate the character relative to the Microsoft Agent property sheet.

PropertySheet Properties

Height   Left   Page   Top   Visible   Width

If you query **Height**, **Left**, **Top**, and **Width** properties before the property sheet has ever been shown, their values return as zero (0). Once shown, these properties return the last position and size of the window (relative to your current screen resolution).

Height Property

Description   Returns an integer value specifying the current height, in pixels, of the Microsoft Agent property sheet window.

Syntax   *agent*.**PropertySheet.Height**

Remarks   The server displays the window based on the location set by the user.

Left Property

Description   Returns an integer value specifying the current left edge, in pixels, of the Microsoft Agent property sheet window.

Syntax   *agent*.**PropertySheet.Left**

Remarks   The server displays the window based on the location set by the user.

Page Property

Description   Returns or sets the page displayed in the Microsoft Agent property sheet window.

Syntax   *agent*.**PropertySheet.Page** [= *string*]

Part	Description
string	A string expression with one of the following values.
	"Speech" Displays the Speech Recognition page.
	"Output" Displays the Output page.
	"Copyright" Displays the Copyright page.

Remarks   If no speech engine is installed, setting **Page** to "**Speech**" has no effect. Also, the window's **Visible** property must be set to **True** for the user to see the page.

Note The user can override this property.

Top Property

Description   Returns an integer value specifying the current top edge, in pixels, of the Microsoft Agent property sheet window.

Syntax   *agent*.**PropertySheet.Top**

Remarks   The server displays the window based on the location set by the user.

Visible Property

Description   Returns or sets whether the Microsoft Agent property sheet window is visible (open).

Syntax   *agent*.**PropertySheet.Visible** [=*boolean*]

Part	Description
Boolean	A Boolean expression specifying whether the window is visible.
	True The window is visible.
	False The window is hidden (closed).

Remarks   The server displays the window based on the location and size set by the user.

Note The user can override this property.

Width Property

Description   Returns an integer value specifying the current width, in pixels, of the Microsoft Agent property sheet window.

Syntax   *agent*.**PropertySheet.Width**

Remarks   The server displays the window based on the location set by the user.

CHAPTER 5

Programming the Microsoft Agent Server Interface

Microsoft Agent provides services that enable you to program animated characters from an application. These services are implemented as an OLE Automation server. OLE Automation enables an application to control another application's object programmatically. This document assumes an understanding of the Component Object Model (COM) and OLE. For an introduction of these services, see the Programming Interface Overview. Sample programs are available on the CD-ROM.

Adding Microsoft Agent Functionality to Your Application

To access Microsoft Agent services, create an instance of the server and request a pointer to a specific interface that the server supports using the standard COM convention. In particular, the COM library provides an API function, **CoCreateInstance**, that creates an instance of the object and returns a pointer to the requested interface of the object. Request a pointer to the **IAgent** interface in your **CoCreateInstance** call or in a subsequent call to **QueryInterface**.

The following code illustrates this in C/C++:

```
hRes = CoCreateInstance(CLSID_AgentServer,
                        NULL,
                        CLSCTX_SERVER,
                        IID_IAgent,
                        (LPVOID *)&pAgent);
```

If the Microsoft Agent server is running, this function connects to the server; otherwise, it starts up the server.

Functions that take pointers to BSTRs allocate memory using **SysAllocString**. It is the caller's responsibility to free this memory using **SysFreeString**.

Loading Character and Animation Data

Once you have a pointer to the **IAgent** interface, you can use the **Load** method to load a character and retrieve its **IDispatch** interface:

```
// Create a variant to store the full path of the character to load
VariantInit(&vPath);
vPath.vt = VT_BSTR;
vPath.bstrVal = SysAllocString(kpwszCharacter);
// Load the character
hRes = pAgent->Load(vPath, &lCharID, &lRequestID);
// Get its IDispatch interface
hRes = pAgent->GetCharacter(lCharID, &pdCharacter);
```

You can then use this information to request a pointer to the **IAgentCharacter**:

```
// Query for IAgentCharacter

hRes = pdCharacter->QueryInterface(IID_IAgentCharacter, (LPVOID
*)&pCharacter);

// Release the IDispatch

pdCharacter->Release();
```

You can use this interface to access the character's methods:

```
// Show the character.  The first parameter tells Microsoft
// Agent to show the character by playing an animation.

hRes = pCharacter->Show(FALSE, &lRequestID);

// Make the character speak
```

```
bszSpeak = SysAllocString(L"Hello World!");

hRes = pCharacter->Speak(bszSpeak, NULL, &lRequestID);

SysFreeString(bszSpeak);
```

When you no longer need Microsoft Agent services, such as when your client application shuts down, release its interfaces. Note that releasing the character interface does not unload the character. Call the **Unload** method to do this before releasing the **IAgent** interface:

```
// Clean up

if (pCharacter) {

    // Release the character interface

    pCharacter->Release();

    // Unload the character.  NOTE:  releasing the character
    // interface does NOT make the character go away.  You must
    // call Unload.

    pAgent->Unload(lCharID);
}

// Release the Agent

pAgent->Release();

VariantClear(&vPath);
```

Creating a Notification Sink

To be notified of events by Microsoft Agent, you must implement the **IAgentNotifySink** interface, and create and register an object of that type following COM conventions:

```
// Create a notification sink

pSink = new AgentNotifySink;

pSink->AddRef();

// And register it with Microsoft Agent

hRes = pAgent->Register((IUnknown *)pSink, &lNotifySinkID);
```

Remember to unregister your notification sink when your application shuts down and releases Microsoft Agent's interfaces.

Accessing Services Using Java

You can also access Microsoft Agent services from a Java applet. Many of the functions accessible through the Microsoft Agent interfaces return values through parameters passed by reference. In order to pass these parameters from Java, it is necessary to create single-element arrays in your code and pass them as parameters to the appropriate function. If you're using Microsoft Visual J++ and have run the Java Type Library Wizard on the Microsoft Agent server, refer to the summary.txt file to review which functions require array arguments. The procedure is similar to that in C; you use the **IAgent** interface to create an instance of the server, then load the character:

```
private IAgent            m_Agent = null;
private IAgentCharacter    m_Merlin[] = {null};
private int               m_MerlinID[] = {-1};
private int               m_RequestID[] = {0};
private final String      m_CharacterPath =
"c:\\agentx\\agtchared\\merlin.acs";

public void start()
{
        // Start the Microsoft Agent Server

        m_Agent = (IAgent) new AgentServer();

        try
        {
            // The filespec parameter of the Load method is a
            // COM variant to accept alternate Agent data providers.
            // We want a standard provider so we can just specify
            // the filespec for our character.

            Variant characterPath = new Variant();
            characterPath.putString(m_CharacterPath);

            // Load the character

            m_Agent.Load(characterPath,
                    m_MerlinID,
                    m_RequestID);
        }
```

The procedure is slightly different when loading characters from an HTTP remote location such as a Web site. In this case the Load method is asynchronous and will raise a com exception of E_PENDING (0x8000000a). You will need to catch this exception and handle it correctly as is done in the following functions:

```java
// Constants used in asynchronous character loads

private final int E_PENDING = 0x8000000a;
private final int NOERROR = 0;


// This function loads a character from the specified path.
// It correctly handles the loading of characters from
// remote sites.

// This sample doesn't care about the request id returned
// from the Load call.  Real production code might use the
// request id and the RequestComplete callback to check for
// a successful character load before proceeding.

public int LoadCharacter(Variant path, int[] id)
{
    int requestid[] = {-1};
    int hRes = 0;

    try
    {
        // Load the character

        m_Agent.Load(path, id, requestid);
    }
    catch(com.ms.com.ComException e)
    {
        // Get the HRESULT

        hRes = e.getHResult();

        // If the error code is E_PENDING, we return NOERROR

        if (hRes == E_PENDING)
            hRes = NOERROR;
    }

    return hRes;
}

public void start()
{
    if (LoadCharacter(characterPath, m_MerlinID) != NOERROR)
    {
        stop();
        return;
    }

    // Other initialization code here

    .
    .
    .

}
```

Then get the **IAgentCharacter** interface that enables you to access its methods:

```
// Get the IAgentCharacter interface for the loaded
// character by passing its ID to the Agent server.

m_Agent.GetCharacter(m_MerlinID[0], m_Merlin);

// Show the character

m_Merlin[0].Show(FALSE, m_RequestID);

// And speak hello

m_Merlin[0].Speak("Hello World!", "", m_RequestID);
```

Similarly, to be notified of events, you must implement the **IAgentNotifySink** interface, creating and registering an object of that type:

```
...
// Declare an Agent Notify Sink so that we can get
// notification callbacks from the Agent server.

private AgentNotifySink m_Sink = null;
private int             m_SinkID[] = {-1};

public void start()
    {
    ...
    // Create and register a notify sink

    m_Sink = new AgentNotifySink();

    m_Agent.Register(m_Sink, m_SinkID);
    ...
    // Give our notify sink access to the character

    m_Sink.SetCharacter(m_Merlin[0]);
    ...
    }
```

In order to access Microsoft Agent from a Java applet, you must generate Java classes that you then install with the applet. You can use the Visual J++ Java Type Library Wizard, for example, to generate these files. If you plan to host the applet on a Web page, you build a signed Java CAB that includes the generated class files and that downloads with the page. The class files are necessary to access the Microsoft Agent Server because it is a COM object that executes outside of the Java sandbox. To learn more about Trust-Based Security for Java, see http://www.microsoft.com/java/security/.

Microsoft Agent Server Reference

This reference contains the following sections:

- Interfaces
- Functions
- Events

For information about the notational system used, see the table on page 39.

Interfaces

Microsoft Agent defines interfaces that allow applications to access its services, enabling an application to control the animation of a character, support user input events, and specify output.

All the Microsoft Agent interfaces are defined in header (.h) files.

IAgent

IAgent defines an interface that allows applications to load characters, receive events, and check the current state of the Microsoft Agent Server.

IAgent Methods in Vtable Order	Description
Load	Loads a character's data file.
Unload	Unloads a character's data file.
Register	Registers a notification sink for the client.
Unregister	Unregisters a client's notification sink.
GetCharacter	Returns the IAgentCharacter interface for a loaded character.
GetSuspended	Returns whether the server is currently suspended.

IAgent::GetCharacter

```
HRESULT GetCharacter(
    long dwCharID  // character ID
);
```

Retrieves the **IAgentCharacter** for a loaded character.

- Returns S_OK to indicate that the operation was successful.

DwCharID   The character's ID.

IAgent::GetSuspended

```
HRESULT GetSuspended(
    long * pbSuspended  // address of variable for suspended flag
);
```

Retrieves whether the Microsoft Agent server is currently suspended.

- Returns S_OK to indicate that the operation was successful.

pbSuspended   Address of a variable that receives TRUE if the Microsoft Agent server is in the suspended state and FALSE if not.

Microsoft Agent loads in a suspended state when a client application attempts to start it up after the user has previously quit (by choosing the Exit command on the Microsoft Agent taskbar icon). In the suspended state Microsoft Agent handles connection requests, but returns failure on any animation methods. Therefore, a character cannot be displayed in this state. Client applications can advise users to restart the server (by choosing Restart on the taskbar pop-up menu), but cannot restart the server directly.

IAgent::Load

```
HRESULT Load(
    VARIANT vLoadKey,  // data provider
    long * pdwCharID,  // address of a variable for character ID
    long * pdwReqID    // address of a variable for request ID
);
```

Loads a character into the **Characters** collection.

- Returns S_OK to indicate that the operation was successful.

vLoadKey   A variant datatype that must be one of the following:

      filespec   The local file location of the specified character's defini-
               tion file.

      URL   The HTTP address for the character's definition file.

      provider   An alternate character definition provider.

pdwCharID   Address of a variable that receives the character's ID.

pdwReqID   Address of a variable that receives the **Load** request ID.

Microsoft Agent's data provider supports loading character data stored as a single structured file (.ACS) with character data and animation data together, or as separate character data (.ACF) and animation (.AAF) files. Generally, use the single structured .ACS file to load a character that is stored on a local disk drive or network and accessed using conventional file protocol (such as UNC pathnames). Use the separate .ACF and .AAF files when you want to load the animation files individually from a remote site where they are accessed using HTTP protocol.

For .ACS files, using the **Load** method provides access a character's animations. For .ACF files, you also use the **Prepare** method to load animation data. The **Load** method does not support downloading .ACS files from an HTTP site.

Loading a character does not automatically display the character. Use the **Show** method first to make the character visible.

The *vLoadKey* parameter also enables you specify your own data provider (that would be loaded separately) that can have its own methods for loading animation data. You need to create a data provider object only if you supply character data in special formats.

IAgent::Register

```
HRESULT Register(
    IUnknown * punkNotifySink    // address of IUnknown for client
                                 // notification sink
    long * pdwSinkID             // address of the notification sink ID
);
```

Registers a notification sink for the client application and returns the notification sink ID.

- Returns S_OK to indicate that the operation was successful.

IUnknown   Address of **IUnknown** for your notification sink interface.

pdwSinkID   Address of notification sink ID (used to unregister the notification sink).

You need to register your notification sink (also known as a notify sink or event sink) to receive events from the Microsoft Agent server.

See also   **IAgent::Unregister**

IAgent::UnLoad

```
HRESULT UnLoad(
    long * dwCharID  //character ID
);
```

Unloads the character data for the specified character from the **Characters** collection.

- Returns S_OK to indicate that the operation was successful.

dwCharID   The character's ID.

Use this method when you no longer need a character, to free up memory used to store information about the character. If you access the character again, use the **Load** method.

See also   **IAgent::Load**

IAgent::Unregister

```
HRESULT Unregister(
    long dwSinkID  //notification sink ID
);
```

Unloads the character data for the specified character from the **Characters** collection.

- Returns S_OK to indicate that the operation was successful.

dwSinkID   The notification sink ID.

Use this method when you no longer need Microsoft Agent services, such as when your application shuts down.

See also   **IAgent::Register**

IAgentCharacter

IAgentCharacter defines an interface that allows applications to query character properties and play animations.

IagentCharacter Methods in Vtable Order	Description
GetVisible	Returns whether the character (frame) is currently visible.
SetPosition	Sets the position of the character frame.
GetPosition	Returns the position of the character frame.
SetSize	Sets the size of the character frame.
GetSize	Returns the size of the character frame.
GetName	Returns the name of the character.
GetDescription	Returns the description for the character.
GetTTSSpeed	Returns the current TTS output speed setting for the character.
GetTTSPitch	Returns the current TTS pitch setting for the character.
Activate	Sets whether a client is active or a character is topmost.
SetIdleOn	Sets the server's idle processing.
GetIdleOn	Returns the setting of the server's idle processing.
Prepare	Retrieves animation data for the character.
Play	Plays a specified animation.
Stop	Stops an animation for a character.
StopAll	Stops all animations for a character.
Wait	Holds the character's animation queue.
Interrupt	Interrupts a character's animation.
Show	Displays the character and plays the character's **Showing** state animation.
Hide	Plays the character's **Hiding** state animation and hides the character's frame.
Speak	Plays spoken output for the character.
MoveTo	Moves the character frame to the specified location.

IagentCharacter Methods in Vtable Order	Description
GestureAt	Plays a gesturing animation based on the specified location.
GetMoveCause	Retrieves the cause of the character's last move.
GetVisibilityCause	Retrieves the cause of the last change to the character's visibility state.
HasOtherClients	Retrieves whether the character has other current clients.
SetSoundEffectsOn	Determines whether a character animation's sound effects play.
GetSoundEffectsOn	Retrieves whether a character's sound effects setting is enabled.
SetName	Sets the character's name.
SetDescription	Sets the character's description.
GetExtraData	Retrieves additional data stored with the character.

IAgentCharacter::Activate

```
HRESULT Activate(
    short sState, // topmost character or client setting
);
```

Sets whether a client is active or a character is topmost.

- Returns S_OK to indicate that the operation was successful.

- Returns S_FALSE to indicate that the operation was not successful.

sState   You can specify the following values for this parameter:

   0   Set as not the active client.
   1   Set as the active client.
   2   Make the topmost character.

When multiple characters are visible, only one of the characters receives speech input at a time. Similarly, when multiple client applications share the same character, only one of the clients receives mouse input (for example, Microsoft Agent control click or drag events) at a time. The character set to receive mouse and speech input is the topmost character and the client that receives input is the character's active client. (The topmost character's window also appears at the top of the character window's z-order.) Typically, the user determines which character is topmost by explicitly selecting it. However, topmost activation also changes when a character is shown or hidden (the character becomes or is no longer topmost, respectively.)

You can also use this method to explicitly manage when your client receives input directed to the character, such as when your application itself becomes active. For example, setting **State** to 2 makes the character topmost, and your client receives all mouse and speech input events generated from user interaction with the character. Therefore, it also makes your client the input-active client of the character. However, you can also set the active client for a character without making the character topmost, by setting **State** to 1. This enables your client to receive input directed to that character when the character becomes topmost. Similarly, you can set your client to not be the active client (to not receive input) when the character becomes topmost, by setting **State** to 0. You can determine if a character has other current clients using **IAgentCharacter::HasOtherClients**.

Avoid calling this method directly after a **Show** method. **Show** automatically sets the input-active client. When the character is hidden, the **Activate** call may fail if it gets processed before the **Show** method completes.

If you call this method to a function, it returns a Boolean value that indicates whether the method succeeded. Attempting to call this method with the **State** parameter set to 2 when the specified character is hidden will fail. Similarly, if you set **State** to 0 and your application is the only client, this call fails because a character must always have a topmost client.

See also   **IAgentCharacter::HasOtherClients**

IAgentCharacter::GestureAt

```
HRESULT GestureAt(
    short x,           // x-coordinate of specified location
    short y,           // y-coordinate of specified location
    long * pdwReqID    // address of a request ID
);
```

Plays the associated **Gesturing** state animation based on the specified location.

- Returns S_OK to indicate that the operation was successful. When the function returns, *pdwReqID* contains the ID of the request.

x	The x-coordinate of the specified location in pixels, relative to the screen origin (upper left).
y	The y-coordinate of the specified location in pixels, relative to the screen origin (upper left).
pdwReqID	Address of a variable that receives the **GestureAt** request ID.

The server automatically determines and plays the appropriate gesturing animation based on the character's current position and the specified location. When using the HTTP protocol to access character and animation data, use the **Prepare** method to ensure that the animations are available before calling this method.

IAgentCharacter::GetDescription

```
HRESULT GetDescription(
    BSTR * pbszDescription    // address of buffer for character
);                           // description
```

Retrieves the description of the character.

- Returns S_OK to indicate that the operation was successful.

pbszDescription	The address of a BSTR that receives the value of the description for the character. A character's description is defined when it is compiled with the Microsoft Agent Character Editor. The description setting is optional and may not be supplied for all characters.

IAgentCharacter::GetExtraData

```
HRESULT GetExtraData(
    BSTR * pbszExtraData    // address of buffer for additional character
);                         // data
```

Retrieves additional data stored as part of the character.

- Returns S_OK to indicate that the operation was successful.

pbszExtraData   The address of a BSTR that receives the value of the additional data for the character. A character's additional data is defined when it is compiled with the Microsoft Agent Character Editor. A character developer can supply this string by editing the .ACD file for a character. The setting is optional and may not be supplied for all characters, nor can the data be defined or changed at run time. In addition, the meaning of the data supplied is defined by the character developer.

IAgentCharacter::GetIdleOn

```
HRESULT GetIdleOn(
   long * pbOn  // address of idle processing flag
);
```

Indicates the automatic idle processing state for a character.

- Returns S_OK to indicate that the operation was successful.

pbOn   Address of a variable that receives TRUE if the Microsoft Agent server automatically plays **Idling** state animations for a character and FALSE if not.

See also   **IAgentCharacter::SetIdleOn**

IAgentCharacter::GetMoveCause

```
HRESULT GetMoveCause(
   long * pdwCause  // address of variable for cause of character move
);
```

Retrieves the cause of the character's last move.

- Returns S_OK to indicate that the operation was successful.

pdwCause   Address of a variable that receives the cause of the character's last move and will be one of the following:

const unsigned short NeverMoved = 0;	Character has not been moved.
const unsigned short UserMoved = 1;	User dragged the character.
const unsigned short ProgramMoved = 2;	Your application moved the character.
const unsigned short OtherProgramMoved = 3;	Another application moved the character.

See also   **IAgentNotifySink::Move**

IAgentCharacter::GetName

```
HRESULT GetName(
   BSTR * pbszName    // address of buffer for character name
);
```

Retrieves the name of the character.

- Returns S_OK to indicate that the operation was successful.

pbszName   The address of a BSTR that receives the value of the name for the character. A character's default name is defined when it is compiled with the Microsoft Agent Character Editor. The name setting is optional and may not be supported for all characters. You can also set the character's name using **IAgentCharacter:-SetName**; however, this changes the name for all current clients of the character.

See also   **IAgentCharacter::SetName**

IAgentCharacter::GetPosition

```
HRESULT GetPosition(
   long * plLeft,  // address of variable for left edge of character
   long * plTop    // address of variable for top edge of character
);
```

Retrieves the character's animation frame position.

- Returns S_OK to indicate that the operation was successful.

plLeft   Address of a variable that receives the screen coordinate of the character animation frame's left edge in pixels, relative to the screen origin (upper left).

plTop   Address of a variable that receives the screen coordinate of the character animation frame's top edge in pixels, relative to the screen origin (upper left).

Even though the character appears in an irregularly shaped region window, the location of the character is based on its rectangular animation frame.

See also   **IAgentCharacter::SetPosition, IAgentCharacter::GetSize**

IAgentCharacter::GetSize

```
HRESULT GetSize(
    long * plWidth,  // address of variable for character width
    long * plHeight  // address of variable for character height
);
```

Retrieves the size of the character's animation frame.

- Returns S_OK to indicate that the operation was successful.

plWidth   Address of a variable that receives the width of the character animation frame in pixels, relative to the screen origin (upper left).

plHeight   Address of a variable that receives the height of the character animation frame in pixels, relative to the screen origin (upper left).

Even though the character appears in an irregularly shaped region window, the location of the character is based on its rectangular animation frame.

See also   **IAgent::SetSize**

IAgentCharacter::GetSoundEffectsOn

```
HRESULT GetSoundEffectsOn(
    long * pbOn  // address of variable for sound effects setting
);
```

Retrieves whether the character's sound effects setting is enabled.

- Returns S_OK to indicate that the operation was successful.

pbOn   Address of a variable that receives TRUE if the character's sound effects setting is enabled, FALSE if disabled.

The character's sound effects setting determines whether sound effects compiled as a part of the character are played when you play an associated animation. The setting is subject to the user's global sound effects setting in **IAgentAudioOutputProperties::GetUsingSoundEffects**.

See also   **IAgentCharacter::SetSoundEffectsOn**,
IAgentAudioOutputProperties::GetUsingSoundEffects

IAgentCharacter::GetTTSPitch

```
HRESULT GetTTSPitch(
   long * pdwPitch  // address of variable for character TTS pitch
);
```

Retrieves the character's TTS output pitch setting.

- Returns S_OK to indicate that the operation was successful.

pdwPitch   Address of a variable that receives the character's current TTS pitch setting in Hertz.

Although your application cannot write this value, you can include pitch tags in your output text that will temporarily increase the pitch for a particular utterance. This method applies only to characters configured for TTS output. If the speech synthesis (TTS) engine is not enabled (or installed) or the character does not support TTS output, this method returns zero (0).

IAgentCharacter::GetTTSSpeed

```
HRESULT GetTTSSpeed(
   long * pdwSpeed  // address of variable for character TTS output
);                 // speed
```

Retrieves the character's TTS output speed setting.

- Returns S_OK to indicate that the operation was successful.

pdwSpeed   Address of a variable that receives the output speed of the character in words per minute.

Although your application cannot write this value, you can include speed tags in your output text that will temporarily speed up the output for a particular utterance.

This property returns the current speaking output speed setting for the character. For characters using TTS output, the property returns the actual TTS output for the character. If TTS is not enabled or the character does not support TTS output, the setting reflects the user setting for output speed.

IAgentCharacter::GetVisibilityCause

```
HRESULT GetVisibilityCause(
    long * pdwCause  // address of variable for cause of character
);                   // visible state
```

Retrieves the cause of the character's visible state.

- Returns S_OK to indicate that the operation was successful.

pdwCause   Address of a variable that receives the cause of the character's last visibility state change and will be one of the following:

const unsigned short NeverShown = 0;	Character has not been shown.
const unsigned short UserHid = 1;	User hid the character.
const unsigned short UserShowed = 2;	User showed the character.
const unsigned short ProgramHid = 3;	Your application hid the character.
const unsigned short ProgramShowed = 4;	Your application showed the character.
const unsigned short OtherProgramHid = 5;	Another application hid the character.
const unsigned short OtherProgramShowed = 6;	Another application showed the character.

See also   **IAgentNotifySink::Hide**, **IAgentNotifySink::Show**

IAgentCharacter::GetVisible

```
HRESULT GetVisible(
    long * pbVisible  // address of variable for character Visible
);                    // setting
```

Determines whether the character's animation frame is currently visible.

- Returns S_OK to indicate that the operation was successful.

pbVisible   Address of a variable that receives TRUE if the character's frame is visible and FALSE if hidden.

You can use this method to determine whether the character's frame is currently visible. To make a character visible, use the **Show** method. To hide a character, use the **Hide** method.

IAgentCharacter::HasOtherClients

```
HRESULT HasOtherClients(
    long * pbHasOtherClients  // address of variable for whether
);                            // character has other clients
```

Retrieves whether a character has other clients.

- Returns S_OK to indicate that the operation was successful.

pbHasOtherClients   Address of a variable that receives TRUE if the character has other clients and FALSE if not.

IAgentCharacter::Hide

```
HRESULT Hide(
    long bFast,      // play Hiding state animation flag
    long * pdwReqID  // address of request ID
);
```

Hides the character.

- Returns S_OK to indicate that the operation was successful. When the function returns, *pdwReqID* contains the ID of the request.

bFast   **Hiding** state animation flag. If this parameter is TRUE, the **Hiding** animation does not play before the character frame is hidden; if FALSE, the animation plays.

pdwReqID   Address of a variable that receives the **Hide** request ID.

The server queues the animation associated with the **Hide** method in the character's queue. This allows you to use it to hide the character after a sequence of other animations. You can play the action immediately by using the **Stop** method before calling the **Hide** method.

When using the HTTP protocol to access character and animation data, use the **Prepare** method to ensure the availability of the **Hiding** state animation before calling this method.

Hiding a character can also result in triggering the **ActivateInput** event of another visible character.

Hidden characters cannot access the audio channel. The server will pass back a failure status in the **RequestComplete** event if you generate an animation request and the character is hidden.

See also   **IAgentCharacter::Show**

IAgentCharacter::Interrupt

```
HRESULT Interrupt(
    long dwReqID,       // request ID to interrupt
    long * pdwReqID     // address of request ID
);
```

Interrupts the specified animation (request) of another character.

- Returns S_OK to indicate that the operation was successful. When the function returns, *pdwReqID* contains the ID of the request.

dwReqID   An ID of the request to interrupt.

pdwReqID   Address of a variable that receives the **Interrupt** request ID.

You can use this method to sync up animation between characters. For example, if another character is in a looping animation, this method will stop the looping animation and start the next animation in the character's queue.

Interrupt halts the existing animation, but does not flush the character's animation queue. It starts the next animation in the character's queue. To halt and flush a character's queue, use the **Stop** method.

You cannot use this method to have a character interrupt itself because the Microsoft Agent server queues the **Interrupt** method in the character's animation queue. Therefore, you can only use **Interrupt** to halt the animation of another character you have loaded.

IAgentCharacter::MoveTo

```
HRESULT MoveTo(
    short x,            // x-coordinate of new location
    short y,            // y-coordinate of new location
    long lSpeed,        // speed to move the character
    long * pdwReqID     // address of request ID
);
```

Plays the associated **Moving** state animation and moves the character frame to the specified location.

- Returns S_OK to indicate that the operation was successful. When the function returns, this variable contains the ID of the request.

x   The x-coordinate of the new position in pixels, relative to the screen origin (upper left). The location of a character is based on the upper left corner of its animation frame.

y   The y-coordinate of the new position in pixels, relative to the screen origin (upper left). The location of a character is based on the upper left corner of its animation frame.

lSpeed   A parameter specifying in milliseconds how quickly the character's frame moves. The recommended value is 1000. Specifying zero (0) moves the frame without playing an animation.

pdwReqID   Address of a variable that receives the **MoveTo** request ID.

When using the HTTP protocol to access character and animation data, use the **Prepare** method to ensure the availability of the **Moving** state animations before calling this method. Even if the animation is not loaded, the server still moves the frame.

See also   **IAgentCharacter::SetPosition**

IAgentCharacter::Play

```
HRESULT Play(
   BSTR bszAnimation,   // name of an animation
   long * pdwReqID      // address of request ID
);
```

Plays the specified animation.

- Returns S_OK to indicate that the operation was successful. When the function returns, *pdwReqID* contains the ID of the request.

bszAnimation   The name of an animation.

pdwReqID   Address of a variable that receives the **Play** request ID.

An animation's name is defined when the character is compiled with the Microsoft Agent Character Editor. Before playing the specified animation, the server attempts to play the **Return** animation for the previous animation (if one has been assigned).

When a character's animation data is stored on the user's local machine, you can use the **Play** method and specify the name of the animation. When using the HTTP protocol to access animation data, use the **Prepare** method to ensure the availability of the animation before calling this method.

See also   **IAgentCharacter::Prepare**

IAgentCharacter::Prepare

```
HRESULT Prepare(
    long dwType,        // type of animation data to load
    BSTR bszName,       // name of the animation
    long bQueue,        // queue the request
    long * pdwReqID     // address of request ID
);
```

Retrieves animation data for a character.

- Returns S_OK to indicate that the operation was successful. When the function returns, *pdwReqID* contains the ID of the request.

dwType   A value that indicates the animation data type to load that must be one of the following:

const unsigned short PREPARE_ANIMATION = 0;	A character's animation data.
const unsigned short PREPARE_STATE = 1;	A character's state data.
const unsigned short PREPARE_WAVE = 2	A character's sound file (.WAV or .LWV) for spoken output.

bszName   The name of the animation or state.

The animation name is based on that defined for the character when it was saved using the Microsoft Agent Character Editor.

For states, the value can be one of the following:

"Gesturing"	To retrieve all **Gesturing** state animations.
"GesturingDown"	To retrieve **GesturingDown** animations.
"GesturingLeft"	To retrieve **GesturingLeft** animations.
"GesturingRight"	To retrieve **GesturingRight** animations.
"GesturingUp"	To retrieve **GesturingUp** animations.

"Hiding"	To retrieve the **Hiding** state animations.
"Hearing"	To retrieve the **Hearing** state animations.
"Idling"	To retrieve all **Idling** state animations.
"IdlingLevel1"	To retrieve all **IdlingLevel1** animations.
"IdlingLevel2"	To retrieve all **IdlingLevel2** animations.
"IdlingLevel3"	To retrieve all **IdlingLevel3** animations.
"Listening"	To retrieve the **Listening** state animations.
"Moving"	To retrieve all **Moving** state animations.
"MovingDown"	To retrieve all **Moving** animations.
"MovingLeft"	To retrieve all **MovingLeft** animations.
"MovingRight"	To retrieve all **MovingRight** animations.
"MovingUp"	To retrieve all **MovingUp** animations.
"Showing"	To retrieve the **Showing** state animations.
"Speaking"	To retrieve the **Speaking** state animations.

For .WAV files, set *bszName* to the URL or file specification for the .WAV file. If the specification is not complete, it is interpreted as being relative to the specification used in the **Load** method.

bQueue   A Boolean specifying whether the server queues the **Prepare** request. TRUE queues the request and causes any animation request that follows it to wait until the animation data it specifies is loaded. FALSE retrieves the animation data asynchronously.

pdwReqID   Address of a variable that receives the **Prepare** request ID.

You can specify multiple animations and states by separating them with commas. However, you cannot mix types in the same **Prepare** statement.

IAgentCharacter::SetDescription

```
HRESULT SetDescription(
   BSTR bszDescription    // character description
);
```

Sets the description of the character.

- Returns S_OK to indicate that the operation was successful.

<table>
<tr><td>bszDescription</td><td>A BSTR that sets the description for the character. A character's default description is defined when it is compiled with the Microsoft Agent Character Editor. The description setting is optional and may not be supplied for all characters. You can change the character's description using IAgentCharacter::SetDescription; however, this value is not persistent (stored permanently). The character's description reverts to its default setting whenever the character is first loaded by a client.</td></tr>
</table>

See also   **IAgentCharacter::GetDescription**

IAgentCharacter::SetIdleOn

```
HRESULT SetIdleOn(
    long bOn  // idle processing flag
);
```

Sets automatic idle processing for a character.

- Returns S_OK to indicate that the operation was successful.

bOn   Idle processing flag. If this parameter is TRUE, the Microsoft Agent automatically plays **Idling** state animations.

The server automatically sets a time out after the last animation played for a character. When this timer's interval is complete, the server begins the **Idling** states for a character, playing its associated **Idling** animations at regular intervals. If you want to manage the **Idling** state animations yourself, set the property to FALSE.

See also   **IAgentCharacter::GetIdleOn**

IAgentCharacter::SetName

```
HRESULT SetName(
    BSTR bszName  // character name
);
```

Sets the name of the character.

- Returns S_OK to indicate that the operation was successful.

bszName   A BSTR that sets the character's name. A character's default name is defined when it is compiled with the Microsoft Agent Character Editor. You can change it using **IAgentCharacter::- SetName**; however, this changes the character name for all current clients of the character. This property is not persistent (stored permanently). The character's name reverts to its default name whenever the character is first loaded by a client.

The server uses the character's name setting in parts of the Microsoft Agent's interface, such as the Commands Window title when the character is input-active and in the Microsoft Agent taskbar pop-up menu.

See also   **IAgentCharacter::GetName**

IAgentCharacter::SetPosition

```
HRESULT SetPosition(
  long lLeft, // screen coordinate of the left edge of character
  long lTop   // screen coordinate of the top edge of character
);
```

Sets the position of the character's animation frame.

- Returns S_OK to indicate that the operation was successful.

lLeft   Screen coordinate of the character animation frame's left edge in pixels, relative to the screen origin (upper left).

lTop   Screen coordinate of the character animation frame's top edge in pixels, relative to the screen origin (upper left).

Even though the character appears in an irregularly shaped region window, the location of the character is based on its rectangular animation frame.

Note Unlike the **MoveTo** method, this function is not queued.

See also   **IAgent::GetPosition**

IAgentCharacter::SetSize

```
HRESULT SetSize(
  long * lWidth,  // width of the character frame
  long * lHeight  // height of the character frame
);
```

Sets the size of the character's animation frame.

- Returns S_OK to indicate that the operation was successful.

lWidth   The width of the character's animation frame in pixels.

lHeight   The height of the character's animation frame in pixels.

Changing the character's frame size scales the character to the size set with this method.

Even though the character appears in an irregularly shaped region window, the location of the character is based on its rectangular animation frame.

See also   **IAgentCharacter::GetSize**

IAgentCharacter::SetSoundEffectsOn

```
HRESULT SetSoundEffectsOn(
   long bOn  // character sound effects setting
);
```

Determines whether the character's sound effects are played.

- Returns S_OK to indicate that the operation was successful.

bOn   Sound effects setting. If this parameter is TRUE, the sound effects for animations are played when the animation plays; if FALSE, sound effects are not played.

This setting determines whether sound effects compiled as a part of the character are played when you play an associated animation. The setting is subject to the user's global sound effects setting in **IAgentAudioOutput-Properties::GetUsingSoundEffects**.

See also   **IAgentCharacter::GetSoundEffectsOn,
IAgentAudioOutputProperties::GetUsingSoundEffects**

IAgentCharacter::Show

```
HRESULT Show(
   long bFast,     // play Showing state animation flag
   long * pdwReqID // address of request ID
);
```

Displays a character.

- Returns S_OK to indicate that the operation was successful. When the function returns, *pdwReqID* contains the ID of the request.

bFast   Showing state animation flag. If this parameter is TRUE, the **Showing** state animation plays after making the character visible; if FALSE, the animation does not play.

pdwReqID   Address of a variable that receives the **Show** request ID.

Avoid setting the *bFast* parameter to TRUE without playing an animation beforehand, otherwise, the character frame may be displayed, but have no image to display. In particular, note that that if you call **MoveTo** when the character is not visible, it does not play any animation. Therefore, if you call the **Show** method with *bFast* set to TRUE, no image will be displayed. Similarly, if you call **Hide** then **Show** with *bFast* set to TRUE, there will be no visible image.

When using the HTTP protocol to access character and animation data, use the **Prepare** method to ensure the availability of the **Showing** state animation before calling this method.

See also   **IAgentCharacter::Hide**

IAgentCharacter::Speak

```
HRESULT Speak(
    BSTR bszText,     // text to speak
    BSTR bszURL,      // URL of a file to speak
    long * pdwReqID   // address of a request ID
);
```

Speaks the

- Returns S_OK to indicate that the operation was successful.

bszText   The text the character is to speak.

bszURL   The URL (or file specification) of a sound file to use for spoken output. This can be a standard sound file (.WAV) or linguistically enhanced sound file (.LWV).

pdwReqID   Address of a variable that receives the **Speak** request ID.

To use this method with a character configured to speak using a text-to-speech (TTS) engine; simply provide the *bszText* parameter. You can include vertical bar characters (|) in the *bszText* parameter to designate alternative strings, so that each time the server processes the method, it randomly choose a different string. Support of TTS output is defined when the character is compiled using the Microsoft Agent Character Editor.

If you want to use sound file output for the character, specify the location for the file in the *bszURL* parameter. When using the HTTP protocol to download a sound file, use the **Prepare** method to ensure the availability of the file before using this method. You can use the *bszText* parameter to specify the words that appear in the character's word balloon. If you specify a linguistically enhanced sound file (.LWV) for the *bszURL* parameter and do not specify text, the *bszText* parameter uses the text stored in the file.

The **Speak** method uses the last animation played to determine which speaking animation to play. For example, if you precede the **Speak** command with a **Play** "GestureRight", the server will play **GestureRight** and then the **GestureRight** speaking animation.

If you call **Speak** and the audio channel is busy, the character's audio output will not be heard, but the text will display in the word balloon. The word balloon's **Enabled** property must also be TRUE for the text to display.

See also   **IAgentCharacter::Play**, **IAgentBalloon::Enabled**, **IAgentCharacter::Prepare**

IAgentCharacter::Stop

```
HRESULT Stop(
   long dwReqID  // request ID
);
```

Stops the specified animation (request) and removes it from the character's animation queue.

- Returns S_OK to indicate that the operation was successful.

dwReqID   The ID of the request to stop.

Stop can also be used to halt any queued **Prepare** calls.

See also   **IAgentCharacter::Prepare**, **IAgentCharacter::StopAll**

IAgentCharacter::StopAll

```
HRESULT StopAll();
   long lType,  // request type
```

Stops all animations (requests) and removes them from the character's animation queue.

lType   A bit field that indicates the types of requests to stop (and remove from the character's queue), comprised from the following:

const unsigned long **STOP_TYPE_ALL = 0xFFFFFFFF;**	Stops all animation requests, including non-queued **Prepare** requests.
const unsigned long **STOP_TYPE_PLAY = 0x00000001;**	Stops all **Play** requests.
const unsigned long **STOP_TYPE_MOVE = 0x00000002;**	Stops all **Move** requests.
const unsigned long **STOP_TYPE_SPEAK = 0x00000004;**	Stops all **Speak** requests.
const unsigned long **STOP_TYPE_PREPARE = 0x00000008;**	Stops all queued **Prepare** requests.
const unsigned long **STOP_TYPE_NONQUEUED-** **PREPARE = 0x00000010;**	Stops all non-queued **Prepare** requests.
const unsigned long **STOP_TYPE_VISIBLE = 0x00000020;**	Stops all **Hide** or **Show** requests.

See also   **IAgentCharacter::Stop**

IAgentCharacter::Wait

```
HRESULT Wait(
    long dwReqID,    // request ID
    long * pdwReqID  // address of request ID
);
```

Holds the character's animation queue at the specified animation (request) until another request for another character completes.

- Returns S_OK to indicate that the operation was successful.

dwReqID   The ID of the request to wait for.

pdwReqID   Address of a variable that receives the **Wait** request ID.

Use this method only when you support multiple (simultaneous) characters and want to sequence their interaction (as a single client). (For a single character, each animation request is played sequentially—after the previous request completes.) If you have two characters and want one character's animation request to wait until the other character's animation completes, set the **Wait** method to the other character's animation request ID.

IAgentCommands

The Microsoft Agent server maintains a list of commands that are currently available to the user. This list includes commands that the server defines for general interaction, such as Hide and Microsoft Agent Properties, the list of available (but non-input-active) clients, and the commands defined by the current active client. The first two sets of commands are global commands; that is, they are available at any time, regardless of the input-active client. Client-defined commands are available only when that client is input-active.

Retrieve an **IAgentCommands** interface by querying the **IAgentCharacter** interface for **IAgentCommands**. Each Microsoft Agent client application can define a collection of commands called a **Commands** collection. To add a **Command** to the collection, use the **Add** or **Insert** method. Although you can specify a **Command's** properties using **IAgentCommand** methods, for optimum code performance, specify all of a **Command's** properties in the **IAgentCommands::Add** or **IAgentCommands::Insert** methods when initially setting the properties for a new **Command**. You can use the **IAgentCommand** methods to query or change the property settings.

For each **Command** in the **Commands** collection, you can determine whether the command appears on the character's pop-up menu, in the Commands Window, in both, or in neither. For example, if you want a command to appear on the pop-up menu for the character, set the command's **Caption** and **Visible** properties. To display the command in the **Commands** Window, set the command's **Caption** and **Voice** properties.

A user can access the individual commands in your Commands collection only when your client application is input-active. Therefore, you will typically want to set the **Caption** and **Voice** properties for the **Commands** collection object as well as for the commands in the collection, because this places an entry for your **Commands** collection on a character's pop-up menu and in the Commands Window. When the user switches to your client by choosing its entry, the server automatically makes your client input-active and makes the **Commands** in its collection available. This enables the server to present and accept only the **Commands** that apply to the current input-active client's context. It also serves to avoid **Command**-name collisions between clients.

When a character's pop-up menu is displayed, changes to the properties of a **Commands** collection or the commands in its collection do not appear until the user redisplays the menu. However, when open, the Commands Window does display changes as they happen.

IAgentCommands defines an interface that allows applications to add, remove, set, and query properties for a **Commands** collection. A **Commands** collection can appear as a command in both the pop-up menu and the Commands Window for a character. To make the **Commands** collection appear, you must set its **Caption** property. The following table summarizes how the properties of a **Commands** collection affect its presentation.

Caption Property	Voice Property	Visible Property	Appears in Character's Pop-up Menu	Appears in Commands Window
Yes	Yes	True	Yes	Yes
Yes	Yes	False	No	Yes
Yes	No	True	Yes	No
Yes	No	False	No	No
No	Yes	True	No	No[*]
No	Yes	False	No	No[*]
No	No	True	No	No
No	No	False	No	No

[*]*The command is still voice-accessible. If the client is input-active and has **Commands** in its collection, "(command undefined)" appears in the Commands Window.*

IAgentCommands Methods in Vtable Order	Description
GetCommand	Retrieves a **Command** object from the **Commands** collection.
GetCount	Returns the value of the number of **Commands** in a **Commands** collection.
SetCaption	Sets the value of the **Caption** property for a **Commands** collection.
GetCaption	Returns the value of the **Caption** property of a **Commands** collection.
SetVoice	Sets the value of the **Voice** property for a **Commands** collection.
GetVoice	Returns the value of the **Voice** property of a **Commands** collection.

(continued)

IAgentCommands Methods in Vtable Order	Description
SetVisible	Sets the value of the **Visible** property for a **Commands** collection.
GetVisible	Returns the value of the **Visible** property of a **Commands** collection.
Add	Adds a **Command** object to a **Commands** collection.
Insert	Inserts a **Command** object in a **Commands** collection.
Remove	Removes a **Command** object in a **Commands** collection.
RemoveAll	Removes all **Command** objects from a **Commands** collection.

IAgentCommands::Add

```
HRESULT Add(
    BSTR bszCaption,    // Caption setting for Command
    BSTR bszVoice,      // Voice setting for Command
    long bEnabled,      // Enabled setting for Command
    long bVisible,      // Visible setting for Command
    long * pdwID        // address for variable for ID
);
```

Adds a **Command** to a **Commands** collection.

- Returns S_OK to indicate that the operation was successful.

bszCaption   A BSTR that specifies the value of the **Caption** text displayed for a **Command** in a **Commands** collection.

bszVoice   A BSTR that specifies the value of the **Voice** text setting for a **Command** in a **Commands** collection.

bEnabled   A Boolean expression that specifies the **Enabled** setting for a **Command** in a **Commands** collection. If the parameter is TRUE, the **Command** is enabled and can be selected; if FALSE, the **Command** is disabled.

bVisible	A Boolean expression that specifies the **Visible** setting for a **Command** in a **Commands** collection. If the parameter is TRUE, the **Command** will be visible in the character's pop-up menu (if the **Caption** property is also set).
pdwID	Address of a variable that receives the ID for the added **Command**.

See also   **IAgentCommand::SetCaption, IAgentCommand::SetEnabled, IAgentCommand::SetVisible, IAgentCommand::SetVoice, IAgentCommands::Insert, IAgentCommands::Remove, IAgentCommands::RemoveAll**

IAgentCommands::GetCaption

```
HRESULT GetCaption(
   BSTR * pbszCaption   // address of Caption text for Commands
);                      // collection
```

Retrieves the **Caption** for a **Commands** collection.

- Returns S_OK to indicate that the operation was successful.

pbszCaption   The address of a BSTR that receives the value of the **Caption** text setting displayed for a **Commands** collection.

See also   **IAgentCommands::SetCaption, IAgentCommands::GetVisible, IAgentCommands::GetVoice**

IAgentCommands::GetCommand

```
HRESULT GetCommand(
   long dwCommandID,          // Command ID
   IUnknown ** ppunkCommand   // address of IUnknown interface
);
```

Retrieves a **Command** object from the **Commands** collection.

- Returns S_OK to indicate that the operation was successful.

dwCommandID   The ID of a Command object in the **Commands** collection.

IUnknown   The address of the **IUnknown** interface for the **Command** object.

See also   **IAgentCommand**

IAgentCommands::GetCount

```
HRESULT GetCount(
    long * pdwCount   // address of count of commands
);
```

Retrieves the number of **Command** objects in a **Commands** collection.

- Returns S_OK to indicate that the operation was successful.

pdwCount   Address of a variable that receives the number of **Commands** in a **Commands** collection.

pdwCount includes only the number of **Commands** you define in your **Commands** collection. Server or other client entries are not included.

IAgentCommands::GetVisible

```
HRESULT GetVisible(
    long * pbVisible   // address of Visible setting for Commands
);                     // collection
```

Retrieves the value of the **Visible** property for a **Commands** collection.

- Returns S_OK to indicate that the operation was successful.

pbVisible   The address of a variable that receives the value of the **Visible** property for a **Commands** collection.

See also   **IAgentCommands::SetVisible, IAgentCommands::SetCaption**

IAgentCommands::GetVoice

```
HRESULT GetVoice(
    BSTR * pbszVoice   // address of Voice setting for Commands
);                     // collection
```

Retrieves the value of the **Voice** property for a **Commands** collection.

- Returns S_OK to indicate that the operation was successful.

pbszVoice   The address of a BSTR that receives the value of the **Voice** text setting for a **Commands** collection.

See also   **IAgentCommands::SetVoice, IAgentCommands::GetCaption, IAgentCommands::GetVisible**

IAgentCommands::Insert

```
HRESULT Insert(
    BSTR bszCaption,    // Caption setting for Command
    BSTR bszVoice,      // Voice setting for Command
    long bEnabled,      // Enabled setting for Command
    long bVisible,      // Visible setting for Command
    long dwRefID,       // reference Command for insertion
    long dBefore,       // insertion position flag
    long * pdwID        // address for variable for Command ID
);
```

Inserts a **Command** object in a **Commands** collection.

- Returns S_OK to indicate that the operation was successful.

bszCaption	A BSTR that specifies the value of the **Caption** text displayed for the **Command**.
bszVoice	A BSTR that specifies the value of the **Voice** text setting for a **Command**.
bEnabled	A Boolean expression that specifies the **Enabled** setting for a **Command**. If the parameter is TRUE, the **Command** is enabled and can be selected; if FALSE, the **Command** is disabled.
bVisible	A Boolean expression that specifies the **Visible** setting for a **Command**. If the parameter is TRUE, the **Command** will be visible in the character's pop-up menu (if the **Caption** property is also set).
dwRefID	The ID of a **Command** used as a reference for the relative insertion of the new **Command**.
dBefore	A Boolean expression that specifies where to place the **Command**. If this parameter is TRUE, the new **Command** is inserted before the referenced **Command**; if FALSE, the new **Command** is placed after the referenced **Command**.
pdwID	Address of a variable that receives the ID for the inserted **Command**.

See also   **IAgentCommand::Add, IAgentCommands::Remove, IAgentCommands::RemoveAll**

IAgentCommands::Remove

```
HRESULT Remove(
    long dwID  // Command ID
);
```

Removes the specified **Command** from a **Commands** collection.

- Returns S_OK to indicate that the operation was successful.

dwID   The ID of a **Command** to remove from the **Commands** collection.

Removing a **Command** from a **Commands** collection also removes it from the pop-up menu and the Commands Window when your application is input-active.

See also   **IAgentCommands::Add**, **IAgentCommands::Insert**,
IAgentCommands::RemoveAll

IAgentCommands::RemoveAll

```
HRESULT Remove();
```

Removes all **Commands** from a **Commands** collection.

- Returns S_OK to indicate that the operation was successful.

Removing all **Commands** from a **Commands** collection also removes them from the pop-up menu and the Commands Window when your application is input-active. **RemoveAll** does not remove server or other client's entries.

See also   **IAgentCommands::Add**, **IAgentCommands::Insert**,
IAgentCommands::Remove

IAgentCommands::SetCaption

```
HRESULT SetCaption(
    BSTR bszCaption  // Caption setting for Commands collection
);
```

Sets the **Caption** text displayed for a **Commands** collection.

- Returns S_OK to indicate that the operation was successful.

bszCaption   A BSTR that specifies the value for the **Caption** property for
a **Commands** collection.

A **Commands** collection with its **Caption** property set and its **Visible** property set to TRUE appears in the character's pop-up menu. If its **Voice** property is also set, it appears in the Commands Window. If you define commands for a **Commands** collection that have their **Caption**, **Enabled**, and **Voice** properties set, you typically also define **Caption** and **Voice** settings for the associated **Commands** collection. If the **Commands** collection has no **Voice** or no **Caption** setting and is currently input-active, but the **Commands** in its collection have **Caption** and **Voice** settings, the **Commands** appear in the **Commands** Window tree view under "(undefined command)" when your client application becomes input-active.

See also   **IAgentCommands::GetCaption, IAgentCommands::SetVisible, IAgentCommands::SetVoice**

IAgentCommands::SetVisible

```
HRESULT SetVisible(
   long bVisible  // the Visible setting for Commands collection
);
```

Sets the value of the **Visible** property for a **Commands** collection.

- Returns S_OK to indicate that the operation was successful.

bVisible   A Boolean value that determines the **Visible** property of a **Commands** collection. TRUE sets the **Commands** collection's **Caption** to be visible when the character's pop-up menu is displayed; FALSE does not display it.

A **Commands** collection must have its **Caption** property set and its **Visible** property set to TRUE to appear on the character's pop-up menu. The **Visible** property must also be set to TRUE for commands in the collection to appear when your client application is input-active.

See also   **IAgentCommands::GetVisible, IAgent::SetCaption**

IAgentCommands::SetVoice

```
HRESULT SetVoice(
   BSTR bszVoice  // the Voice setting for Command collection
);
```

Sets the **Voice** text property for a **Command**.

- Returns S_OK to indicate that the operation was successful.

bszVoice   A BSTR that specifies the value for the **Voice** text property of a **Commands** collection.

A **Commands** collection must have its **Voice** text property set to be voice-accessible. It also must have its **Caption** property set to appear in the Commands Window and its **Visible** property set to TRUE to appear on the character's pop-up menu.

The BSTR expression you supply can include square bracket characters ([ ]) to indicate optional words and vertical bar characters (I) to indicate alternative strings. Alternates must be enclosed in parentheses. For example, "(hello [there] I hi)" tells the speech engine to accept "hello," "hello there," or "hi" for the command. Remember to include appropriate spaces between words you include in brackets or parentheses as well as other text. Remember to include appropriate spaces between the text that's in brackets or parentheses and the text that's not in brackets or parentheses.

You can also use an ellipsis (...) to support *word spotting*, that is, telling the speech recognition engine to ignore words spoken in this position in the phrase (sometimes called *garbage* words). When you use ellipses, the speech engine recognizes only specific words in the string regardless of when spoken with adjacent words or phrases. For example, if you set this property to "...check mail..." the speech recognition engine will match phrases like "please check mail" or "check mail please" to this command. Ellipses can be used anywhere within a string. However, be careful using this technique as voice settings with ellipses may increase the potential of unwanted matches.

When defining the words and grammar for your command, always make sure that you include at least one word that is required; that is, avoid supplying only optional words. In addition, make sure that the word includes only pronounceable words and letters. For numbers, it is better to spell out the word rather than using the numeric representation. Also, omit any punctuation or symbols. For example, instead of "the #1 $10 pizza!", use "the number one ten dollar pizza". Including non-pronounceable characters or symbols for one command may cause the speech engine to fail to compile the grammar for all your commands. Finally, make your voice parameter as distinct as reasonably possible from other voice commands you define. The greater the similarity between the voice grammar for commands, the more likely the speech engine will make a recognition error. You can also use the confidence scores to better distinguish between two commands that may have similar or similar-sounding voice grammar.

The operation of this property depends on the state of Microsoft Agent server's speech recognition state. For example, if speech recognition is disabled or not installed, this function has no immediate effect. If speech recognition is enabled during a session, however, the command will become accessible when its client application is input-active.

See also   **IAgentCommands::GetVoice**, **IAgentCommands::SetCaption**, **IAgentCommands::SetVisible**

IAgentCommand

A **Command** object is an item in a **Commands** collection. The server provides the user access to your commands your client application becomes input active. To retrieve a **Command**, call **IAgentCommands::GetCommand**.

IAgentCommand defines an interface that allows applications to set and query properties for **Command** objects that can appear in a character's pop-up menu and in the Commands Window. A **Command** object is an item in a **Commands** collection. The server provides the user access to your commands when your client application becomes input active.

A **Command** may appear in either or both the character's pop-up menu and the Commands Window. To appear in the pop-up menu, it must have a **Caption** and have the **Visible** property set to TRUE. The **Visible** property for its **Commands** collection object must also be set to TRUE for the command to appear in the pop-up menu when your client application is input-active. To appear in the Commands Window, a **Command** must have its **Caption** and **Voice** properties set.

A character's pop-up menu entries do not change while the menu is displayed. If you add or remove Commands or change their properties while the character's popup menu is displayed, the menu displays those changes when redisplayed. However, the Commands Window does display changes as you make them.

The following table summarizes how the properties of a command affect its presentation.

Caption Property	Voice Property	Visible Property	Enabled Property	Appears in Character's Pop-up Menu	Appears in Commands Window
Yes	Yes	True	True	Normal	Yes
Yes	Yes	True	False	Disabled	No
Yes	Yes	False	True	Does not appear	Yes
Yes	Yes	False	False	Does not appear	No
Yes	No	True	True	Normal	No
Yes	No	True	False	Disabled	No
Yes	No	False	True	Does not appear	No
Yes	No	False	False	Does not appear	No
No	Yes	True	True	Does not appear	No*
No	Yes	True	False	Does not appear	No
No	Yes	False	True	Does not appear	No*
No	Yes	False	False	Does not appear	No
No	No	True	True	Does not appear	No
No	No	True	False	Does not appear	No
No	No	False	True	Does not appear	No
No	No	False	False	Does not appear	No

The command is still voice-accessible.

Generally, if you define a **Command** with a **Voice** setting, you also define **Caption** and **Voice** settings for its associated **Commands** collection. If the **Commands** collection for a set of commands has no **Voice** or no **Caption** setting and is currently input-active, but the **Commands** have **Caption** and **Voice** settings, the **Commands** appear in the Commands Window tree view under "(undefined command)" when your client application becomes input-active.

When the server receives input that matches one of the **Command** objects you defined for your **Commands** collection, it sends a **IAgentNotifySink::-Command** event, and passes back the ID of the command as an attribute of the **IAgentUserInput** object. You can then use conditional statements to match and process the command.

IAgentCommand

Methods in Vtable Order	Description
SetCaption	Sets the value for the **Caption** for a **Command** object.
GetCaption	Returns the value of the **Caption** property of a **Command** object.
SetVoice	Sets the value for the **Voice** text for a **Command** object.
GetVoice	Returns the value of the **Caption** property of a **Command** object.
SetEnabled	Sets the value of the **Enabled** property for a **Command** object.
GetEnabled	Returns the value of the **Enabled** property of a **Command** object.
SetVisible	Sets the value of the **Visible** property for a **Command** object.
GetVisible	Returns the value of the **Visible** property of a **Command** object.
SetConfidenceThreshold	Sets the value of the **Confidence** property for a **Command** object.
GetConfidenceThreshold	Returns the value of the **Confidence** property of a **Command** object.
SetConfidenceText	Sets the value of the **ConfidenceText** property for a **Command** object.
GetConfidenceText	Returns the value of the **ConfidenceText** property of a **Command** object.
GetID	Returns the ID of a **Command** object.

IAgentCommand::GetCaption

```
HRESULT GetCaption(
   BSTR * pbszCaption  // address of Caption for Command
);
```

Retrieves the **Caption** for a **Command**.

- Returns S_OK to indicate that the operation was successful.

pbszCaption   The address of a BSTR that receives the value of the **Caption** text displayed for a **Command**.

See also   **IAgentCommand::SetCaption, IAgentCommand::SetEnabled, IAgentCommand::SetVisible, IAgentCommand::SetVoice, IAgentCommands::Add, IAgentCommands::Insert**

IAgentCommand::GetConfidenceText

```
HRESULT GetConfidenceText(
   BSTR * pbszTipText  // address of ConfidenceText setting for Command
);
```

Retrieves the Listening Tip text previously set for a **Command**.

- Returns S_OK to indicate that the operation was successful.

pbszTipText   The address of a BSTR that receives the value of the Listening Tip text for a **Command**.

See also   **IAgentCommand::SetConfidenceThreshold, IAgentCommand::GetConfidenceThreshold, IAgentCommand::SetConfidenceText, IAgentUserInput::GetItemConfidence**

IAgentCommand::GetConfidenceThreshold

```
HRESULT GetConfidenceThreshold(
   long * plConfidenceThreshold  // address of ConfidenceThreshold
);                               // setting for Command
```

Retrieves the value of the **ConfidenceThreshold** property for a **Command**.

- Returns S_OK to indicate that the operation was successful.

plConfidenceThreshold   The address of a variable that receives the value of the **ConfidenceThreshold** property for a Command.

See also   **IAgentCommand::SetConfidenceThreshold, IAgentCommand::SetConfidenceText, IAgentUserInput::GetItemConfidence**

IAgentCommand::GetEnabled

```
HRESULT GetEnabled(
   long * pbEnabled   // address of Enabled setting for Command
);
```

Retrieves the value of the **Enabled** property for a **Command**.

- Returns S_OK to indicate that the operation was successful.

pbEnabled   The address of a variable that receives TRUE if the **Command** is enabled, or FALSE if it is disabled. A disabled **Command** cannot be selected.

See also   **IAgentCommand::SetCaption, IAgent::SetVisible, IAgentCommand::SetVoice, IAgentCommands::Add, IAgentCommands::Insert**

IAgentCommand::GetID

```
HRESULT GetID(
   long * pdwID   // address of ID for Command
);
```

Retrieves the ID for a **Command**.

- Returns S_OK to indicate that the operation was successful.

pdwID   The address of a variable that receives the ID of a **Command**.

See also   **IAgentCommands::Add, IAgentCommands::Insert, IAgentCommands::Remove**

IAgentCommand::GetVisible

```
HRESULT GetVisible(
   long * pbVisible   // address of Visible setting for Command
);
```

Retrieves the value of the **Visible** property for a **Command**.

- Returns S_OK to indicate that the operation was successful.

pbVisible   The address of a variable that receives the **Visible** property for a **Command**.

See also   **IAgentCommand::SetVisible, IAgent::SetCaption, IAgentCommands::Add, IAgentCommands::Insert**

IAgentCommand::GetVoice

```
HRESULT GetVoice(
   BSTR * pbszVoice  // address of Voice setting for Command
);
```

Retrieves the value of the **Voice** text property for a **Command**.

- Returns S_OK to indicate that the operation was successful.

pbszVoice   The address of a BSTR that receives the **Voice** text property for a **Command**.

A **Command** with its **Voice** property set and its **Enabled** property set to TRUE will be voice-accessible. If its **Caption** property is also set it appears in the Commands Window. If its **Visible** property is set to TRUE, it appears in the character's pop-up menu.

See also   **IAgentCommand::SetVoice,
IAgentCommands::Add, IAgentCommands::Insert**

IAgentCommand::SetCaption

```
HRESULT SetCaption(
   BSTR bszCaption  // Caption setting for Command
);
```

Sets the **Caption** text displayed for a **Command**.

- Returns S_OK to indicate that the operation was successful.

bszCaption   A BSTR that specifies the text for the **Caption** property for a **Command**.

A **Command** with its **Caption** property set and its **Visible** property set to TRUE appears in the character's pop-up menu. If its **Voice** property is also set, it appears in the Commands Window. To make it accessible, you must also set its **Enabled** property to TRUE.

See also   **IAgentCommand::GetCaption, IAgentCommand::SetEnabled,
IAgentCommand::SetVisible, IAgentCommand::SetVoice,
IAgentCommands::Add, IAgentCommands::Insert**

IAgentCommand::SetConfidenceThreshold

```
HRESULT SetConfidenceThreshold(
   long lConfidence  // Confidence setting for Command
);
```

Sets the value of the **Confidence** property for a **Command**.

- Returns S_OK to indicate that the operation was successful.

lConfidence   The value for the **Confidence** property of a **Command**.

If the confidence value returned of the best match returned in the **Command** event does not exceed the value set for the **ConfidenceThreshold** property, the text supplied in **SetConfidenceText** is displayed in the Listening Tip.

See also   **IAgentCommand::GetConfidenceThreshold**,
IAgentCommand::SetConfidenceText,
IAgentUserInput::GetItemConfidence

IAgentCommand::SetConfidenceText

```
HRESULT SetConfidenceText(
   BSTR bszTipText  // ConfidenceText setting for Command
);
```

Sets the value of the Listening Tip text for a **Command**.

- Returns S_OK to indicate that the operation was successful.

bszTipText   A BSTR that specifies the text for the **ConfidenceText** property of a **Command**.

If the confidence value returned of the best match returned in the **Command** event does not exceed the value set for the **ConfidenceThreshold** property, the text supplied in *bszTipText* is displayed in the Listening Tip.

See also   **IAgentCommand::SetConfidenceThreshold**,
IAgentCommand::GetConfidenceThreshold,
IAgentCommand::GetConfidenceText,
IAgentUserInput::GetItemConfidence

IAgentCommand::SetEnabled

```
HRESULT SetEnabled(
   long bEnabled  // Enabled setting for Command
);
```

Sets the **Enabled** property for a **Command**.

- Returns S_OK to indicate that the operation was successful.

bEnabled   A Boolean value that sets the value of the **Enabled** setting of a **Command**. TRUE enables the **Command**; FALSE disables it. A disabled **Command** cannot be selected.

A **Command** must have its **Enabled** property set to TRUE to be selectable. It also must have its **Caption** property set and its **Visible** property set to TRUE to appear in the character's pop-up menu. To make the **Command** appear in the **Commands** Window, you must set its **Voice** property.

See also   **IAgentCommand::GetCaption, IAgentCommand::SetVoice, IAgentCommands::Add, IAgentCommands::Insert**

IAgentCommand::SetVisible

```
HRESULT SetVisible(
    long bVisible   // Visible setting for Command
);
```

Sets the value of the **Visible** property for a **Command**.

- Returns S_OK to indicate that the operation was successful.

bVisible   A Boolean value that determines the **Visible** property of a **Command**. TRUE shows the **Command**; FALSE hides it.

A **Command** must have its **Visible** property set to TRUE and its **Caption** property set to appear in the character's pop-up menu.

See also   **IAgentCommand::GetVisible, IAgent::SetCaption, IAgentCommands::Add, IAgentCommands::Insert**

IAgentCommand::SetVoice

```
HRESULT SetVoice(
    BSTR bszVoice   // voice text setting for Command
);
```

Sets the **Voice** property for a **Command**.

- Returns S_OK to indicate that the operation was successful.

bszVoice   A BSTR that specifies the text for the **Voice** property of a **Command**.

A **Command** must have its **Voice** property and **Enabled** property set to be voice-accessible. It also must have its **Caption** property set to appear in the Commands Window.

The BSTR expression you supply can include square bracket characters ([ ]) to indicate optional words and vertical bar characters (|) to indicate alternative strings. Alternates must be enclosed in parentheses. For example, "(hello [there] | hi)" tells the speech engine to accept "hello," "hello there," or "hi" for the command. Remember to include appropriate spaces between the text that's in brackets or parentheses and the text that's not in brackets or parentheses.

You can also use an ellipsis (…) to support *word spotting*, that is, telling the speech recognition engine to ignore words spoken in this position in the phrase (sometimes called *garbage* words). Therefore, the speech engine recognizes only specific words in the string regardless of when spoken with adjacent words or phrases. For example, if you set this property to "…check mail…" the speech recognition engine will match phrases like "please check mail" or "check mail please" to this command. Ellipses can be used anywhere within a string. However, be careful using this technique, because voice settings with ellipses may increase the potential of unwanted matches.

When defining the words and grammar for your command, always make sure that you include at least one word that is required; that is, avoid supplying only optional words. In addition, make sure that the word includes only pronounceable words and letters. For numbers, it is better to spell out the word rather than using the numeric representation. Also, omit any punctuation or symbols. For example, instead of "the #1 $10 pizza!", use "the number one ten dollar pizza". Including non-pronounceable characters or symbols for one command may cause the speech engine to fail to compile the grammar for all your commands. Finally, make your voice parameter as distinct as reasonably possible from other voice commands you define. The greater the similarity between the voice grammar for commands, the more likely the speech engine will make a recognition error. You can also use the confidence scores to better distinguish between two commands that may have similar or similar-sounding voice grammar.

The operation of this property depends on the state of Microsoft Agent server's speech recognition state. For example, if speech recognition is disabled or not installed, this function has no immediate effect. If speech recognition is enabled during a session, however, the command will become accessible when its client application is input-active.

See also   **IAgentCommand::GetVoice, IAgentCommand::SetCaption, IAgentCommand::SetEnabled, IAgentCommands::Add, IAgentCommands::Insert**

IAgentUserInput

When a **Command** event occurs, the Microsoft Agent server returns information through the **UserInput** object. **IAgentUserInput** defines an interface that allows applications to query these values.

IAgentUserInput Methods in Vtable Order	Description
GetCount	Returns the number of command alternatives returned in a **Command** event.
GetItemId	Returns the ID for a specific **Command** alternative.
GetItemConfidence	Returns the value of the **Confidence** property for a specific **Command** alternative.
GetItemText	Returns the value of **Voice** text for a specific **Command** alternative.
GetAllItemData	Returns the data for all **Command** alternatives.

IAgentUserInput::GetAllItemData

```
HRESULT GetAllItemData(
    VARIANT * pdwItemIndices,    // address of variable for alternative IDs
    VARIANT * plConfidences,     // address of variable for confidence scores
    VARIANT * pbszText           // address of variable for voice text
);
```

Retrieves the data for all **Command** alternatives passed to an **IAgentNotifySink::Command** callback.

- Returns S_OK to indicate that the operation was successful.

pdwItemIndices   Address of a variable that receives the IDs of **Commands** passed to the **IAgentNotifySink::Command** callback.

plConfidences   Address of a variable that receives the confidence scores for **Command** alternatives passed to the **IAgentNotifySink::Command** callback.

pbszText   Address of a variable that receives the voice text for **Command** alternatives passed to the **IAgentNotifySink::Command** callback.

If voice input was not the source for the **Command**, for example, if the user selected the command from the character's pop-up menu, the Microsoft Agent server returns the ID of the **Command** selected, with a confidence score of 100 and voice text as NULL. The other alternatives return as NULL with confidence scores of zero (0) and voice text as NULL.

See also   **IAgentUserInput::GetItemConfidence**, **IAgentUserInput::GetItemText**,
                    IAgentUserInput::GetItemID

IAgentUserInput::GetCount

```
HRESULT GetCount(
    long * pdwCount  // address of a variable for number of alternatives
);
```

Retrieves the number of **Command** alternatives passed to an **IAgentNotify-Sink::Command** callback.

- Returns S_OK to indicate that the operation was successful.

pdwCount   Address of a variable that receives the count of **Commands** alternatives identified by the server.

If voice input was not the source for the command, for example, if the user selected the command from the character's pop-up menu, **GetCount** returns 1. If **GetCount** returns zero (0), the speech recognition engine detected spoken input but determined that there was no matching command.

IAgentUserInput::GetItemConfidence

```
HRESULT GetItemConfidence(
    long dwItemIndex,    // index of Command alternative
    long * plConfidence  // address of confidence value for Command
);
```

Retrieves the confidence value for a **Command** passed to an **IAgentNotifySink::Command** callback.

- Returns S_OK to indicate that the operation was successful.

dwItemIndex   The index of a **Command** alternative passed to the **IAgentNotifySink::Command** callback.

plConfidence   Address of a variable that receives the confidence score for a **Command** alternative passed to the **IAgentNotifySink::-Command** callback.

If voice input was not the source for the command, for example, if the user selected the command from the character's pop-up menu, the Microsoft Agent server returns the confidence value of the best match as 100 and the confidence values for all other alternatives as zero (0).

See also   **IAgentUserInput::GetItemID**, **IAgentUserInput::GetAllItemData**,
                    IAgentUserInput::GetItemText

IAgentUserInput::GetItemID

```
HRESULT GetItemID(
    long dwItemIndex,     // index of Command alternative
    long * pdwCommandID    // address of a variable for number of
);                        // alternatives
```

Retrieves the identifier of a **Command** alternative passed to an **IAgent-NotifySink::Command** callback.

- Returns S_OK to indicate that the operation was successful.

dwItemIndex   The index of the **Command** alternative passed to the **IAgentNotifySink::Command** callback.

pdwCommandID   Address of a variable that receives the ID of a **Command**.

If voice input triggers the **IAgentNotifySink::Command** callback, the server returns the IDs for any matching **Commands** defined by your application.

See also   **IAgentUserInput::GetItemConfidence, IAgentUserInput::GetItemText, IAgentUserInput::GetAllItemData**

IAgentUserInput::GetItemText

```
HRESULT GetItemText(
    Long dwItemIndex,     // index of Command alternative
    BSTR * pbszText        // address of voice text for Command
);
```

Retrieves the voice text for a **Command** alternative passed to the **IAgentNotifySink::Command** callback.

- Returns S_OK to indicate that the operation was successful.

dwItemIndex   The index of a **Command** alternative passed to the **IAgentNotifySink::Command** callback.

pbszText   Address of a BSTR that receives the value of the voice text for the **Command**.

If voice input was not the source for the command, for example, if the user selected the command from the character's pop-up menu, the server returns NULL for the **Command**'s voice text.

See also   **IAgentUserInput::GetItemConfidence, IAgentUserInput::GetItemID, IAgentUserInput::GetAllItemData**

IAgentCommandWindow

IAgentCommandWindow defines an interface that allows applications to set and query the properties of the Commands Window. The Commands Window is a shared resource primarily designed for allowing users to view voice-enabled commands. If speech recognition is disabled or not installed, the Commands Window is not accessible. Attempting to set or query its properties will result in an error.

IAgentCommandWindow Methods in Vtable Order	Description
SetVisible	Sets the value of the **Visible** property of the Commands Window.
GetVisible	Returns the value of the **Visible** property of the Commands Window.
GetPosition	Returns the position of the Commands Window.
GetSize	Returns the size of the Commands Window.

IAgentCommandWindow::GetPosition

```
HRESULT GetPosition(
   long * plLeft,   // address of variable for left-edge of Commands
                    // Window
   long * plTop     // address of variable for top-edge of Commands
);                  // Window
```

Retrieves the Commands Windows' position.

- Returns S_OK to indicate that the operation was successful.

plLeft   Address of a variable that receives the screen coordinate of the left edge of the Commands Window in pixels, relative to the screen origin (upper left).

plTop   Address of a variable that receives the screen coordinate of the top edge of the Commands Window in pixels, relative to the screen origin (upper left).

See also   **IAgentCommandWindow::GetSize**

IAgentCommandWindow::GetSize

```
HRESULT GetSize(
   long * plWidth,  // address of variable for Commands Window width
   long * plHeight  // address of variable for Commands Window height
);
```

Retrieves the current size of the Commands Window.

- Returns S_OK to indicate that the operation was successful.

plWidth   Address of a variable that receives the width of the Commands
              Window in pixels, relative to the screen origin (upper left).

plHeight   Address of a variable that receives the height of the Commands
              Window in pixels, relative to the screen origin (upper left).

See also   **IAgentCommandWindow::GetPosition**

IAgentCommandWindow::GetVisible

```
HRESULT GetVisible(
   long * pbVisible  // address of variable for Visible setting for
);                   // Commands Window
```

Determines whether the Commands Window is visible or hidden.

- Returns S_OK to indicate that the operation was successful.

pbVisible   Address of a variable that receives TRUE if the Commands
              Window is visible, or FALSE if hidden.

See also   **IAgentCommandWindow::SetVisible**

IAgentCommandWindow::SetVisible

```
HRESULT SetVisible(
   long bVisible  // Commands Window Visible setting
);
```

Set the **Visible** property for the Commands Window.

- Returns S_OK to indicate that the operation was successful.

bVisible   **Visible** property setting. A value of TRUE displays the Commands
              Window; FALSE hides it.

The user can override this property.

See also   **IAgentCommandWindow::GetVisible**

IAgentSpeechInputProperties

IAgentSpeechInputProperties provides access to the speech recognition properties maintained by the server. Most of the properties are read-only for client applications, but the user can change them in the Microsoft Agent property sheet. The Microsoft Agent server only returns values if a compatible speech engine has been installed and is enabled. Querying these properties attempts to start the speech engine.

IAgentSpeechInputProperties Methods in Vtable Order	Description
GetInstalled	Returns whether a compatible speech recognition engine has been installed.
GetEnabled	Returns whether the speech recognition engine is enabled.
GetHotKey	Returns the current key assignment of the listening hot key.
GetLCID	Returns the locale (language) ID of the selected speech recognition engine.
GetEngine	Returns the ID of the selected speech recognition engine.
SetEngine	Sets the ID for the selected speech recognition engine.
GetListeningTip	Returns whether the Listening Tip is enabled.

IAgentSpeechInputProperties::GetEnabled

```
HRESULT GetEnabled(
   long * pbEnabled  // address of variable for speech recognition
);                   // engine Enabled setting
```

Retrieves a value indicating whether the installed speech recognition engine is enabled.

- Returns S_OK to indicate that the operation was successful.

pbEnabled   Address of a variable that receives TRUE if the speech engine is currently enabled and FALSE if disabled.

If **GetInstalled** returns FALSE, querying this setting returns an error.

See also   **IAgentSpeechInput::GetInstalled**

IAgentSpeechInputProperties::GetEngine

```
HRESULT GetEngine(
    BSTR * pbszEngine  // address of variable for speech engine mode ID
);
```

Retrieves the mode ID for the current selected speech recognition engine.

- Returns S_OK to indicate that the operation was successful.

pbszEngine   Address of a BSTR that receives a string representation of the CLSID for the selected speech recognition engine.

If **GetInstalled** and **GetEnabled** return FALSE, querying this setting returns an error.

See also   **IAgentSpeechInput::SetEngine**

IAgentSpeechInputProperties::GetHotKey

```
HRESULT GetHotKey(
    BSTR * pbszHotCharKey   // address of variable for listening hotkey
);
```

Retrieves the current keyboard assignment for the speech input listening hot key.

- Returns S_OK to indicate that the operation was successful.

pbszHotCharKey   Address of a BSTR that receives the current hot key setting used to open the audio channel for speech input.

If **GetInstalled** and **GetEnabled** return FALSE, querying this setting raises an error.

See also   **IAgentSpeechInput::GetEnabled**, **IAgentSpeechInput::GetInstalled**

IAgentSpeechInputProperties::GetInstalled

```
HRESULT GetInstalled(
   long * pbInstalled    // address of variable for speech recognition
);                       // engine installation flag
```

Retrieves a value indicating whether a speech recognition engine has been installed.

- Returns S_OK to indicate that the operation was successful.

pbInstalled   Address of a variable that receives TRUE if a compatible speech recognition engine has been installed and FALSE if no engine is installed.

If **GetInstalled** and **GetEnabled** return FALSE, querying any other speech input properties returns an error.

See also   **IAgentSpeechInput::GetEnabled**

IAgentSpeechInputProperties::GetLCID

```
HRESULT GetLCID(
   LCID * plcidCurrent   // address of variable for locale ID
);
```

Retrieves the current setting for the locale ID.

- Returns S_OK to indicate that the operation was successful.

plcidCurrent   Address of LCID that receives the current locale setting. The locale setting determines the language of the speech recognition engine.

If **GetInstalled** and **GetEnabled** return FALSE, querying this setting returns an error.

See also   **IAgentSpeechInput::GetEnabled, IAgentSpeechInput::GetInstalled**

IAgentSpeechInputProperties::GetListeningTip

```
HRESULT GetListeningTip(
   long * pbListeningTip  // address of variable for listening
);                        // tip flag
```

Retrieves a value indicating whether the Listening Tip is enabled for display.

- Returns S_OK to indicate that the operation was successful.

pbInstalled   Address of a variable that receives TRUE if the Listening Tip is enabled for display, or FALSE if the Listening Tip is disabled.

If **GetInstalled** and **GetEnabled** return FALSE, querying any other speech input properties returns an error.

See also   **IAgentSpeechInput::GetEnabled**, **IAgentSpeechInput::GetInstalled**

IAgentSpeechInputProperties::SetEngine

```
HRESULT SetEngine(
    BSTR bszEngine  // speech engine mode ID
);
```

Sets the selected speech recognition engine.

- Returns S_OK to indicate that the operation was successful.

bszEngine   A BSTR that contains a string representation of the CLSID for the desired speech recognition mode (engine).

If **GetInstalled** and **GetEnabled** return FALSE, setting this property returns an error.

See also   **IAgentSpeechInput::GetEngine**

IAgentAudioOutputProperties

IAgentAudioOutputProperties provides access to audio output properties maintained by the Microsoft Agent server. The properties are read-only, but the user can change them in the Microsoft Agent property sheet.

IAgentAudioOutputProperties Methods	Description
GetEnabled	Returns whether audio output is enabled.
GetUsingSoundEffects	Returns whether sound-effect output is enabled.

IAgentAudioOutputProperties::GetEnabled

```
HRESULT GetEnabled(
   long * pbEnabled   // address of variable for audio output Enabled
);                    // setting
```

Retrieves a value indicating whether character speech output is enabled.

- Returns S_OK to indicate that the operation was successful.

pbEnabled   Address of a variable that receives TRUE if the speech output is currently enabled and FALSE if disabled.

Because this setting affects spoken output (TTS and sound file) for all characters, only the user can change this property in the Microsoft Agent property sheet.

IAgentAudioOutputProperties::GetUsingSoundEffects

```
HRESULT GetUsingSoundEffects(
   long * pbUsingSoundEffects   // address of variable sound effects
);                              // output setting
```

Retrieves a value indicating whether sound effects output is enabled.

- Returns S_OK to indicate that the operation was successful.

pbUsingSoundEffects   Address of a variable that receives TRUE if the sound effects output is currently enabled and FALSE if disabled.

Sound effects for a character's animation are assigned in the Microsoft Agent Character Editor. Because this setting affects sound effects output for all characters, only the user can change this property in the Microsoft Agent property sheet.

IAgentPropertySheet

IAgentPropertySheet defines an interface that allows applications to set and query properties for the Microsoft Agent property sheet (window).

IAgentPropertySheet Methods in Vtable Order	Description
GetVisible	Returns whether the Microsoft Agent property sheet is visible.
SetVisible	Sets the **Visible** property of the Microsoft Agent property sheet.
GetPosition	Returns the position of the Microsoft Agent property sheet.
GetSize	Returns the size of the Microsoft Agent property sheet.
GetPage	Returns the current page for the Microsoft Agent property sheet.
SetPage	Sets the current page for the Microsoft Agent property sheet.

IAgentPropertySheet::GetPage

```
HRESULT GetPage(
    BSTR * pbszPage  // address of variable for current property page
);
```

Retrieves the current page of the Microsoft Agent property sheet.

- Returns S_OK to indicate that the operation was successful.

pbszPage   Address of a variable that receives the current page of the property sheet (last viewed page if the window is not open). The parameter can be one of the following:

"Speech"   The Speech Recognition page.

"Output"   The Output page.

"Copyright"   The Copyright page.

See also   **IAgentPropertySheet::SetPage**

IAgentPropertySheet::GetPosition

```
HRESULT GetPosition(
    long * plLeft,  // address of variable for left edge
    long * plTop    // address of variable for top edge
);
```

Retrieves the Microsoft Agent's property sheet window position.

- Returns S_OK to indicate that the operation was successful.

plLeft   Address of a variable that receives the screen coordinate of the left edge of the property sheet in pixels, relative to the screen origin (upper left).

plTop   Address of a variable that receives the screen coordinate of the top edge of the property sheet in pixels, relative to the screen origin (upper left).

See also   **IAgentPropertySheet::GetSize**

IAgentPropertySheet::GetSize

```
HRESULT GetSize(
   long * plWidth,   // address of variable for property sheet width
   long * plHeight   // address of variable for property sheet height
);
```

Retrieves the size of the Microsoft Agent property sheet window.

- Returns S_OK to indicate that the operation was successful.

plWidth   Address of a variable that receives the width of the property sheet in pixels, relative to the screen origin (upper left).

plHeight   Address of a variable that receives the height of the property sheet in pixels, relative to the screen origin (upper left).

See also   **IAgentPropertySheet::GetPosition**

IAgentPropertySheet::GetVisible

```
HRESULT GetVisible(
   long * pbVisible   // address of variable for property sheet
);                    // Visible setting
```

Determines whether the Microsoft Agent property sheet is visible or hidden.

- Returns S_OK to indicate that the operation was successful.

pbVisible   Address of a variable that receives TRUE if the property sheet is visible and FALSE if hidden.

See also   **IAgentPropertySheet::SetVisible**

IAgentPropertySheet::SetPage

```
HRESULT SetPage(
   BSTR bszPage  // current property page
);
```

Sets the current page of the Microsoft Agent property sheet.

- Returns S_OK to indicate that the operation was successful.

bszPage   A BSTR that sets the current page of the property. The parameter can be one of the following:

"Speech"   The Speech Recognition page.
"Output"   The Output page.
"Copyright" The Copyright page.

See also   **IAgentPropertySheet::GetPage**

IAgentPropertySheet::SetVisible

```
HRESULT SetVisible(
   long bVisible  // property sheet Visible setting
);
```

Sets the **Visible** property for the Microsoft Agent property sheet.

- Returns S_OK to indicate that the operation was successful.

bVisible   Visible property setting. A value of TRUE displays the property sheet; a value of FALSE hides it.

See also   **IAgentPropertySheet::GetVisible**

IAgentBalloon

IAgentBalloon defines an interface that allows applications to query properties for the Microsoft Agent word balloon.

Initial defaults for a character's word balloon are set in the Microsoft Agent Character Editor, but once the application is running, the user may override the Enabled and font properties. If a user changes the balloon's properties, the change affects all characters.

IAgentBalloon Methods in Vtable Order	Description
GetEnabled	Returns whether the word balloon is enabled.
GetNumLines	Returns the number of lines displayed in the word balloon.
GetNumCharsPerLine	Returns the average number of characters per line displayed in the word balloon.
GetFontName	Returns the name of the font displayed in the word balloon.
GetFontSize	Returns the size of the font displayed in the word balloon.
GetFontBold	Returns whether the font displayed in the word balloon is bold.
GetFontItalic	Returns whether the font displayed in the word balloon is italic.
GetFontStrkethru	Returns whether the font displayed in the word balloon is displayed as strikethrough.
GetFontUnderline	Returns whether the font displayed in the word balloon is underlined.
GetForeColor	Returns the foreground color displayed in the word balloon.
GetBackColor	Returns the background color displayed in the word balloon.
GetBorderColor	Returns the border color displayed in the word balloon.
SetVisible	Sets the word balloon to be visible.
GetVisible	Returns the visibility setting for the word balloon.
SetFontName	Sets the font used in the word balloon.
SetFontSize	Sets the font size used in the word balloon.
SetFontCharSet	Sets the character set used in the word balloon.
GetFontCharSet	Returns the character set used in the word balloon.

IAgentBalloon::GetBackColor

```
HRESULT GetBackColor(
   long * plBGColor   // address of variable for background color
);                    // displayed in word balloon
```

Retrieves the value for the background color displayed in a word balloon.

- Returns S_OK to indicate that the operation was successful.

plBGColor   The address of a variable that receives the color setting for the balloon background.

The background color used in a character word balloon is defined in the Microsoft Agent Character Editor. It cannot be changed by an application. However, the user can change the background color of the word balloons for all characters through the Microsoft Agent property sheet.

See also   **IAgentBalloon::GetForeColor**

IAgentBalloon::GetBorderColor

```
HRESULT GetBorderColor (
   long * plBorderColor   // address of variable for border color
);                        // displayed for word balloon
```

Retrieves the value for the border color displayed for a word balloon.

- Returns S_OK to indicate that the operation was successful.

plBorderColor   The address of a variable that receives the color setting for the balloon border.

The border color for a character word balloon is defined in the Microsoft Agent Character Editor. It cannot be changed by an application. However, the user can change the border color of the word balloons for all characters through the Microsoft Agent property sheet.

See also   **IAgentBalloon::GetBackColor, IAgentBalloon::GetForeColor**

IAgentBalloon::GetEnabled

```
HRESULT GetEnabled(
   long * pbEnabled   // address of variable for Enabled setting
);                    // for word balloon
```

Retrieves the value of the **Enabled** property for a word balloon.

- Returns S_OK to indicate that the operation was successful.

pbEnabled   The address of a variable that receives TRUE when the word balloon is enabled and FALSE when it is disabled.

The Microsoft Agent server automatically displays the word balloon for spoken output, unless it is disabled. The word balloon can be disabled for a character in the Microsoft Agent Character Editor, or for all characters by the user, in the Microsoft Agent property sheet. If the user disables the word balloon, the client cannot restore it.

IAgentBalloon::GetFontBold

```
HRESULT GetFontBold(
   long * pbFontBold    // address of variable for bold setting for
);                      // font displayed in word balloon
```

Indicates whether the font used in a word balloon is bold.

- Returns S_OK to indicate that the operation was successful.

pbFontBold   The address of a value that receives TRUE if the font is bold and FALSE if not bold.

The font style used in a character word balloon is defined in the Microsoft Agent Character Editor. It cannot be changed by an application. However, the user can override the font settings for all characters through the Microsoft Agent property sheet.

IAgentBalloon::GetFontCharSet

```
HRESULT GetFontCharSet(
   short * psFontCharSet   // character set displayed in word balloon
);
```

Indicates the character set of the font displayed in a word balloon.

- Returns S_OK to indicate that the operation was successful.

psFontCharSet   The address of a value that receives the font's character set. The following are some common settings for value:

0   Standard Windows® characters (ANSI).

1   Default character set.

2   The symbol character set.

128   Double-byte character set (DBCS) unique to the Japanese version of Windows.

129   Double-byte character set (DBCS) unique to the Korean version of Windows.

134   Double-byte character set (DBCS) unique to the Simplified Chinese version of Windows.

136   Double-byte character set (DBCS) unique to the Traditional Chinese version of Windows.

255   Extended characters normally displayed by DOS applications.

For other character set values, consult the Microsoft Win32® documentation.

The default character set used in a character's word balloon is defined in the Microsoft Agent Character Editor. You can change it using **IAgentBalloon::-SetFontCharSet**. However, the user can override the character set setting for all characters using the Microsoft Agent property sheet.

See also   **IAgentBalloon::SetFontCharSet**

IAgentBalloon::GetFontItalic

```
HRESULT GetFontItalic(
   long * pbFontItalic  // address of variable for italic setting for
);                      // font displayed in word balloon
```

Indicates whether the font used in a word balloon is italic.

■ Returns S_OK to indicate that the operation was successful.

pbFontItalic   The address of a value that receives TRUE if the font is italic and FALSE if not italic.

The font style used in a character's word balloon is defined in the Microsoft Agent Character Editor. It cannot be changed by an application. However, the user can override the font settings for all characters through the Microsoft Agent property sheet.

IAgentBalloon::GetFontName

```
HRESULT GetFontName(
   BSTR * pbszFontName   // address of variable for font displayed
);                       // in word balloon
```

Retrieves the value for the font displayed in a word balloon.

- Returns S_OK to indicate that the operation was successful.

pbszFontName   The address of a BSTR that receives the font name
displayed in a word balloon.

The default font used in a character word balloon is defined in the Microsoft Agent Character Editor. You can change it with **IAgentBalloon::SetFontName**. The user can override the font setting for all characters using the Microsoft Agent property sheet.

IAgentBalloon::GetFontSize

```
HRESULT GetFontSize(
   long * plFontSize   // address of variable for font size
);                     // for font displayed in word balloon
```

Retrieves the value for the size of the font displayed in a word balloon.

- Returns S_OK to indicate that the operation was successful.

plFontSize   The address of a value that receives the size of the font.

The default font size used in a character word balloon is defined in the Microsoft Agent Character Editor. You can change it with **IAgentBalloon::SetFontSize**. However, the user can override also the font size settings for all characters using the Microsoft Agent property sheet.

IAgentBalloon::GetFontStrikethru

```
HRESULT GetFontStrikethru(
   long * pbFontStrikethru   // address of variable for strikethrough
);                           // setting for font displayed in word balloon
```

Indicates whether the font used in a word balloon has the strikethrough style set.

- Returns S_OK to indicate that the operation was successful.

pbFontStrikethru   The address of a value that receives TRUE if the font strikethrough style is set and FALSE if not.

The font style used in a character word balloon is defined in the Microsoft Agent Character Editor. It cannot be changed by an application. However, the user can override the font settings for all characters using the Microsoft Agent property sheet.

IAgentBalloon::GetFontUnderline

```
HRESULT GetFontUnderline(
    long * pbFontUnderline   // address of variable for underline setting
);                           // for font displayed in word balloon
```

Indicates whether the font used in a word balloon has the underline style set.

- Returns S_OK to indicate that the operation was successful.

pbFontUnderline   The address of a value that receives TRUE if the font underline style is set and FALSE if not.

The font style used in a character word balloon is defined in the Microsoft Agent Character Editor. It cannot be changed by an application. However, the user can override the font settings for all characters using the Microsoft Agent property sheet.

IAgentBalloon::GetForeColor

```
HRESULT GetForeColor(
    long * plFGColor // address of variable for foreground color
);                   // displayed in word balloon
```

Retrieves the value for the foreground color displayed in a word balloon.

- Returns S_OK to indicate that the operation was successful.

plFGColor   The address of a variable that receives the color setting for the balloon foreground.

The foreground color used in a character word balloon is defined in the Microsoft Agent Character Editor. It cannot be changed by an application. However, the user can override the foreground color of the word balloons for all characters through the Microsoft Agent property sheet.

See also   **IAgentBalloon::GetBackColor**

IAgentBalloon::GetNumCharsPerLine

```
HRESULT GetNumCharsPerLine(
    long * plCharsPerLine  // address of variable for characters per
);                         // line displayed in word balloon
```

Retrieves the value for the average number of characters per line displayed in a word balloon.

- Returns S_OK to indicate that the operation was successful.

pbCharsPerLine   The address of a variable that receives the number of characters per line.

The Microsoft Agent server automatically scrolls the lines displayed for spoken output in the word balloon. The average number of characters per line for a character's word balloon is defined in the Microsoft Agent Character Editor. It cannot be changed by an application.

See also   **IAgentBalloon::GetNumLines**

IAgentBalloon::GetNumLines

```
HRESULT GetNumLines(
    long * pbcLines  // address of variable for number of lines
);                   // displayed in word balloon
```

Retrieves the value of the number of lines displayed in a word balloon.

- Returns S_OK to indicate that the operation was successful.

pbcLines   The address of a variable that receives the number of lines displayed.

The Microsoft Agent server automatically scrolls the lines displayed for spoken output in the word balloon. The number of lines for a character word balloon is defined in the Microsoft Agent Character Editor. It cannot be changed by an application.

See also   **IAgentBalloon::GetNumCharsPerLine**

IAgentBalloon::GetVisible

```
HRESULT GetVisible(
    long * pbVisible  // address of variable for word balloon
);                    // Visible setting
```

Determines whether the word balloon is visible or hidden.

- Returns S_OK to indicate that the operation was successful.

pbVisible   Address of a variable that receives TRUE if the word balloon is visible and FALSE if hidden.

See also   **IAgentBalloon::SetVisible**

IAgentBalloon::SetFontCharSet

```
HRESULT SetFontCharSet(
    short sFontCharSet  // character set displayed in word balloon
);
```

Sets the character set of the font displayed in the word balloon.

- Returns S_OK to indicate that the operation was successful.

sFontCharSet   The character set of the font. The following are some common settings for value:

0	Standard Windows characters (ANSI).
1	Default character set.
2	The symbol character set.
128	Double-byte character set (DBCS) unique to the Japanese version of Windows.
129	Double-byte character set (DBCS) unique to the Korean version of Windows.
134	Double-byte character set (DBCS) unique to the Simplified Chinese version of Windows.
136	Double-byte character set (DBCS) unique to the Traditional Chinese version of Windows.
255	Extended characters normally displayed by DOS applications.

For other character set values, consult the Microsoft Win32 documentation.

The default character set used in a character's word balloon is defined in the Microsoft Agent Character Editor. You can change it with **IAgentBalloon::-SetFontCharSet**. However, the user can override the character set setting for all characters using the Microsoft Agent property sheet.

See also   **IAgentBalloon::GetFontCharSet**

IAgentBalloon::SetFontName

```
HRESULT SetFontName(
    BSTR bszFontName  // font displayed in word balloon
);
```

Sets the font displayed in the word balloon.

- Returns S_OK to indicate that the operation was successful.

bszFontName   A BSTR that sets the font displayed in the word balloon.

The default font used in a character's word balloon is defined in the Microsoft Agent Character Editor. You can change it with **IAgentBalloon::SetFont-Name**. However, the user can override the font setting for all characters using the Microsoft Agent property sheet.

See also   **IAgentBalloon::GetVisible**

IAgentBalloon::SetFontSize

```
HRESULT SetFontSize(
    long lFontSize  // font size displayed in word balloon
);
```

Sets the size of the font displayed in the word balloon.

- Returns S_OK to indicate that the operation was successful.

lFontSize   The size of the font.

The default font size used in a character's word balloon is defined in the Microsoft Agent Character Editor. You can change it with **IAgentBalloon::-SetFontSize**. However, the user can override the font size setting for all characters using the Microsoft Agent property sheet.

See also   **IAgentBalloon::GetFontSize**

IAgentBalloon::SetVisible

```
HRESULT SetVisible(
    long bVisible  // word balloon Visible setting
);
```

Sets the **Visible** property for the word balloon.

- Returns S_OK to indicate that the operation was successful.

bVisible   Visible property setting. A value of TRUE displays the word balloon; a value of FALSE hides it.

See also   **IAgentBalloon::GetVisibleEvents**

Microsoft Agent provides several events for tracking user interaction and server states. This section describes the event methods exposed by the **IAgentNotifySink** interface.

Events

IAgentNotifySink Methods in Vtable Order	Description
Command	Occurs when the server processes a client-defined command.
ActivateInputState	Occurs when a character becomes or ceases to be input-active.
Restart	Occurs when the server restarts.
Shutdown	Occurs when the user exits the server.
VisibleState	Occurs when the character's Visible state changes.
Click	Occurs when a character is clicked.
DblClick	Occurs when a character is double-clicked.
DragStart	Occurs when a user starts dragging a character.
DragComplete	Occurs when a user stops dragging a character.
RequestStart	Occurs when the server begins processing a **Request** object.
RequestComplete	Occurs when the server completes processing a **Request** object.
Bookmark	Occurs when the server processes a bookmark.
Idle	Occurs when the server starts or ends idle processing.
Move	Occurs when a character has been moved.
Size	Occurs when a character has been resized.
BalloonVisibleState	Occurs when the visibility state of a character's word balloon changes.

IAgentNotifySink::ActivateInputState

```
HRESULT ActivateInputState(
    long dwCharID,    // character ID
    long bActivated   // input activation flag
);
```

Notifies a client application that a character's input active state changed.

- No return value.

dwCharID   Identifier of the character whose input activation state changed.

bActivated   Input active flag. This Boolean value is TRUE if the character referred to by *dwCharID* became input active; and FALSE if the character lost its input active state.

See also   **IAgentCharacter::SetInputActive, IAgentCharacter::GetInputActive**

IAgentNotifySink:: BalloonVisibleState

```
HRESULT BalloonVisibleState(
    long dwCharID,    // character ID
    long bVisible     // visibility flag
);
```

Notifies a client application when the visibility state of the character's word balloon changes.

- No return value.

dwCharID   Identifier of the character whose word balloon's visibility state has changed.

bVisible   Visibility flag. This Boolean value is TRUE when character's word balloon becomes visible; and FALSE when it becomes hidden.

This event is sent to all clients of the character.

IAgentNotifySink::Bookmark

```
HRESULT Bookmark(
    long dwBookMarkID  // bookmark ID
);
```

Notifies a client application when its bookmark completes.

- No return value.

dwBookMarkID   Identifier of the bookmark that resulted in triggering the event.

When you include bookmark tags in a **Speak** method, you can track when they occur with this event.

See also   **IAgentCharacter::Speak**, Speech Output Tags

IAgentNotifySink::Click

```
HRESULT Click(
    long dwCharID,    // character ID
    short fwKeys,     // mouse button and modifier key state
    long x,           // x coordinate of mouse pointer
    long y            // y coordinate of mouse pointer
);
```

Notifies a client application when the user clicks a character.

- No return value.

dwCharID   Identifier of the clicked character.

fwKeys   A parameter that indicates the mouse button and modifier key state. The parameter can return any combination of the following:

0x0001	Left Button
0x0010	Middle Button
0x0002	Right Button
0x0004	Shift Key Down
0x0008	Control Key Down
0x0020	Alt Key Down

x   The x-coordinate of the mouse pointer in pixels, relative to the screen origin (upper left).

y   The y-coordinate of the mouse pointer in pixels, relative to the screen origin (upper left).

IAgentNotifySink::Command

```
HRESULT Command(
    long dwCommandID,          // Command ID of the best match
    IUnknown * punkUserInput   // address of IAgentUserInput object
);
```

Notifies a client application that a Command was selected by the user.

- No return value.

dwCommandID   Identifier of the best match command alternative.

punkUserInput   Address of the IUnknown interface for the **IAgentUserInput** object.

Use QueryInterface to retrieve the **IAgentUserInput** interface.

See also   **IAgentUserInput**

IAgentNotifySink::DblClick

```
HRESULT DblClick(
    long dwCharID,    // character ID
    short fwKeys,     // mouse button and modifier key state
    long x,           // x coordinate of mouse pointer
    long y            // y coordinate of mouse pointer
);
```

Notifies a client application when the user double-clicks a character.

- No return value.

dwCharID   Identifier of the double-clicked character.

fwKeys   A parameter that indicates the mouse button and modifier key state. The parameter can return any combination of the following:

0x0001	Left Button
0x0010	Middle Button
0x0002	Right Button
0x0004	Shift Key Down
0x0008	Control Key Down
0x0020	Alt Key Down

x   The x-coordinate of the mouse pointer in pixels, relative to the screen origin (upper left).

y   The y-coordinate of the mouse pointer in pixels, relative to the screen origin (upper left).

IAgentNotifySink::DragComplete

```
HRESULT DragComplete(
    long dwCharID,   // character ID
    short fwKeys,    // mouse button and modifier key state
    long x,          // x-coordinate of mouse pointer
    long y           // y-coordinate of mouse pointer
);
```

Notifies a client application when the user stops dragging a character.

- No return value.

dwCharID   Identifier of the dragged character.

fwKeys   A parameter that indicates the mouse button and modifier key state. The parameter can return any combination of the following:

0x0001	Left Button
0x0010	Middle Button
0x0002	Right Button
0x0004	Shift Key Down
0x0008	Control Key Down
0x0020	Alt Key Down

x   The x-coordinate of the mouse pointer in pixels, relative to the screen origin (upper left).

y   The y-coordinate of the mouse pointer in pixels, relative to the screen origin (upper left).

IAgentNotifySink::DragStart

```
HRESULT DragStart(
    long dwCharID,   // character ID
    short fwKeys,    // mouse button and modifier key state
    long x,          // x-coordinate of mouse pointer
    long y           // y-coordinate of mouse pointer
);
```

Notifies a client application when the user starts dragging a character.

- No return value.

dwCharID   Identifier of the dragged character.

fwKeys   A parameter that indicates the mouse button and modifier key state. The parameter can return any combination of the following:

0x0001	Left Button
0x0010	Middle Button
0x0002	Right Button
0x0004	Shift Key Down
0x0008	Control Key Down
0x0020	Alt Key Down

x   The x-coordinate of the mouse pointer in pixels, relative to the screen origin (upper left).

y   The y-coordinate of the mouse pointer in pixels, relative to the screen origin (upper left).

IAgentNotifySink::Idle

```
HRESULT Idle(
    long dwCharID,  // character ID
    long bStart     // start flag
);
```

Notifies a client application when a character's **Idling** state has changed.

- No return value.

dwCharID   Identifier of the request that started.

bStart   Start flag. This Boolean value is TRUE when the character begins idling and FALSE when it stops idling.

This event enables you to track when the Microsoft Agent server starts or stops idle processing for a character.

See also   **IAgentCharacter::GetIdleOn, IAgentCharacter::SetIdleOn**

IAgentNotifySink:: Move

```
HRESULT Move(
    long dwCharID,  // character ID
    long x,         // x-coordinate of new location
    long y,         // y-coordinate of new location
    long dwCause    // cause of move state
);
```

Notifies a client application when the character has been moved.

- No return value.

dwCharID   Identifier of the character that has been moved.

x   The x-coordinate of the new position in pixels, relative to the screen origin (upper left). The location of a character is based on the upper left corner of its animation frame.

y   The y-coordinate of the new position in pixels, relative to the screen origin (upper left). The location of a character is based on the upper left corner of its animation frame.

dwCause   The cause of the character move. The parameter may be one of the following:

const unsigned short NeverMoved = 0;	Character has not been moved.
const unsigned short UserMoved = 1;	User dragged the character.
const unsigned short ProgramMoved = 2;	Your application moved the character.
const unsigned short OtherProgram-Moved = 3;	Another application moved the character.

This event is sent to all clients of the character.

See also   **IAgentCharacter::GetMoveCause, IAgentCharacter::MoveTo**

IAgentNotifySink::RequestComplete

```
HRESULT RequestComplete(
    long dwRequestID,  // request ID
    long hrStatus      // status code
);
```

Notifies a client application when a request completes.

- No return value.

dwRequestID   Identifier of the request that started.

hrStatus   Status code. This parameters returns the status code for the request.

This event enables you to track when a queued method completes.

See also

**IAgentNotifySink::RequestStart, IAgent::Load,
IAgentCharacter::GestureAt, IAgentCharacter::Hide,
IAgentCharacter::Interrupt, IAgentCharacter::MoveTo,
IAgentCharacter::Prepare, IAgentCharacter::Play,
IAgentCharacter::Show, IAgentCharacter::Speak,
IAgentCharacter::Wait**

IAgentNotifySink::RequestStart

```
HRESULT RequestStart(
   long dwRequestID  // request ID
);
```

Notifies a client application when a request begins.

- No return value.

dwRequestID   Identifier of the request that started.

This event enables you to track when a queued request begins.

See also

**IAgentNotifySink::RequestComplete, IAgent::Load,
IAgentCharacter::GestureAt, IAgentCharacter::Hide,
IAgentCharacter::Interrupt, IAgentCharacter::MoveTo,
IAgentCharacter::Prepare, IAgentCharacter::Play,
IAgentCharacter::Show, IAgentCharacter::Speak,
IAgentCharacter::Wait**

IAgentNotifySink::Restart

```
HRESULT Restart();
```

Notifies a client application that the Microsoft Agent server restarted.

- No return value.

See also

IAgentNotifySink::Shutdown

IAgentNotifySink::Shutdown

```
HRESULT Shutdown();
```

Notifies a client application that the Microsoft Agent server shut down.

- No return value.

This event fires only when the user explicitly chooses the Exit command on the pop-up menu of the Microsoft Agent taskbar icon. Requests sent after the server shuts down will fail.

See also   **IAgentNotifySink::Restart**

IAgentNotifySink:: Size

```
HRESULT Size(
   long dwCharID,  // character ID
   long lWidth,    // new width
   long lHeight,   // new height
);
```

Notifies a client application when the character has been resized.

- No return value.

dwCharID   Identifier of the character that has been resized.

lWidth   The width of the character's animation frame in pixels.

lHeight   The height of the character's animation frame in pixels.

This event is sent to all clients of the character.

See also   **IAgentCharacter::GetSize**, **IAgentCharacter::SetSize**

IAgentNotifySink::VisibleState

```
HRESULT VisibleState(
   long dwCharID,  // character ID
   long bVisible,  // visibility flag
   long dwCause,   // cause of visible state
);
```

Notifies a client application when the visibility state of the character changes.

- No return value.

dwCharID   Identifier of the character whose visibility state is changed.

bVisible   Visibility flag. This Boolean value is TRUE when character becomes visible and FALSE when the character becomes hidden.

dwCause   Cause of last change to the character's visibility state. The parameter may be one of the following:

const unsigned short NeverShown = 0;	Character has not been shown.
const unsigned short UserHid = 1;	User hid the character.
const unsigned short UserShowed = 2;	User showed the character.
const unsigned short ProgramHid = 3;	Your application hid the character.
const unsigned short ProgramShowed = 4;	Your application showed the character.
const unsigned short OtherProgramHid = 5;	Another application hid the character.
const unsigned short OtherProgramShowed = 6;	Another application showed the character.

See also   **IAgentCharacter::GetVisible**, **IAgentCharacter::SetVisible**, **IAgentCharacter::GetVisibilityCause**

C H A P T E R   6

Designing Characters for Microsoft Agent

This chapter provides information that can help you design and develop a character for use with Microsoft Agent. It includes conceptual and technical information on character, image, and animation design; the size, use of color, and types of images you need to create; suggested animations; speaking animations; and agent states. The final section of the chapter describes effective animation principles you can use to create visually convincing animated characters.

Characters

Human communication is fundamentally social. Microsoft Agent allows you to leverage this aspect of interaction using animated characters. Users will expect a character to conform to the same social, though not necessarily physical, rules they use when interacting with other people, even when they understand that the character is synthetic. To the extent you create characters that meet their expectations, users will find your characters more believable and likable. Therefore, how you design a character can have a dramatic effect on its success.

When designing a character, first consider the profile of your target audience and what appeals to them as well as what tasks they do. Similarly, consider how well your character's design matches its purpose in addition to the application it supports. For example, a dog character may work well for a retrieval or security application, depending on the character's overall appearance. Often the success is also in the details. Research has shown that roundness of eyes and shapes of ears in a character can generate very different reactions to an animal character.

Also consider your character's basic personality type: dominant or submissive, emotional or reserved, sophisticated or down-to-earth; or perhaps you want to adapt its personality based on user interaction. For example, you can provide a control that enables a user to adjust whether the character volunteers more information or waits to be asked. The former would be more outgoing than the latter.

The name you supply for your character can infer a particular type of personality. For example, "Max" and "Linus" may convey very different personalities. The Microsoft Agent Character Editor enables you to set your character's name and include a short description. These attributes can be queried at run time.

In addition, decide whether you plan to use a synthetic voice (using a text-to-speech engine) or recorded voice (.WAV file). This decision may depend on the type of character you use, the languages you plan to support, and what you want the character to be able to say. For example, a synthesized voice enables your character to say almost anything. Programming what your character will say is easy and quick: You just supply the text the character will speak. However, using a computer-generated speech engine requires some extra overhead for initial installation and will be language-specific. Further, most synthesized voices sound computer-generated, not matching the clarity and prosody of most human speech. It may be difficult to simulate a voice that matches your character, particularly if you use a character that already has an established identity or one that has a very distinctive voice. In such a case, you may want to use recorded speech files for your output. Microsoft Agent supports lip-syncing for recorded speech output. Although audio files provide a natural voice and are easier to implement in other languages, they must be copied or downloaded to local machines. Recorded speech files also limit your character to the vocabulary contained in them. Regardless of whether you choose synthetic and recorded speech output, keep in mind that a voice carries with it additional social information as to the gender, age, and personality of the speaker.

You can also decide to use the word balloon for output and the default settings for the balloon's font and color. Note, however, that the user can change the font and color attributes. In addition, you cannot assume that the word balloon's state remains constant because the user can turn the balloon off.

Animations

A character's animations reflect its personality and behavior. The number and types of animations you create for a character depend on what your character does and how it responds to different situations.

Like traditional animations, digital animations involve creating a series of slightly differing images that, when displayed sequentially, provide the illusion of action. Creating high-quality animation images may require a skilled animator, but the style and presentation of the character you create also affect quality. Two-dimensional characters with simple shapes and features can sometimes be as effective as (or more effective than) highly rendered characters. It is not necessary to create a realistic image to portray an effective character. Many popular cartoon characters are not realistic in their presentation, yet they are effective because the animator understands how to convey action and emotion. The last section of this chapter provides general information about fundamental animation design principles.

Frames

Each animation you create for a Microsoft Agent character is composed of a timed sequence of frames. Each frame in the animation is composed of one or more bitmap images. Images can be as small as you need them or as large as the frame itself.

Animation details such as eye blinking or finger movement can be included as additional images for the frame. You can overlay several images to create a composite, and vary their position in the layers. This technique enables you to reuse images in multiple frames and vary the details that change. For example, if you want to have a character wave its hand, for each frame you could use a base image with everything but the hand and overlay the base image with a different hand image. Similarly, if you want to make the character blink, you can overlay a different set of eyes over a base image for each frame. Images can also be offset from the base image. However, only the part of the image that exists within the frame's size will be displayed.

You can have as many frames in an animation as you wish; however, a typical animation averages about 14 frames so that it plays for no more than 6 seconds. This modest length of time ensures that your character appears responsive to user input. In addition, the greater the number of frames, the larger your animation file. For downloaded Web-based characters, keep the size of your animation file as small as possible while still providing a reasonably-sized set of frames, so that the character's animation does not appear jerky.

Image Design

You can use any graphics or animation tool to create images for animation frames, provided that you store the final images in the Windows bitmap (.BMP) format. When the images are created, use the Microsoft Agent Character Editor to assemble, sequence, and time the images, supply other character information, and compile all the information into a final character file.

Character images must be designed to a 256-color palette, preserving the 20 standard Windows system colors in their standard position in the palette (the first ten and last ten positions). That means that your character's color palette can use the standard system colors and up to 236 other colors. When defining your palette, include any props your character uses in the animation. If your character's palette places colors in the system color positions, those character colors will be overwritten with the system colors when Microsoft Agent creates the palette.

The larger the number of colors you use in a character's color palette, the greater the possibility that part of your character's colors may get remapped for systems configured to an 8-bit (256-color) setting. Consider also the palette usage of the application in which the character will be used. It's best to avoid having the character remap the colors of its host application and vice-versa. Similarly, if you plan to support multiple characters displayed at the same time, you'll probably want to maintain a consistent palette for those characters. You might consider using only the standard system colors in your character if you target users with an 8-bit color configuration. However, this still may not prevent remapping of your character's color if another application extensively redefines the color palette. On systems set to higher color resolutions, color palette remapping should not be a problem because the system manages the color palettes automatically.

Using a larger number of colors in an image can also increase the overall size of your animation file. The number of colors and frequency of variation may determine how well your character file compresses. For example, a two-dimensional character that uses only a few colors will compress better than a three-dimensional, shaded character.

You must use the same color palette for your entire character file. You cannot change the palette for different animations. If you attempt to support 8-bit color configurations, consider using the same palette for your application and any other characters you plan to support.

The 11th position in the palette is defined by default as the transparency (or alpha) color, although you can also set the color using the Microsoft Agent Character Editor. The Microsoft Agent animation services render transparent any pixels in this color, so use the color in your images only where you want transparency.

Carefully consider the shape of your character, because it can affect animation performance. To display the character, the animation services create a region window based on the overall image. Small irregular areas often require more region data and may reduce the animation performance of your character. Therefore, when possible, avoid gaps or single-pixel elements and details.

Avoid anti-aliasing the outside edge of your character. Although anti-aliasing is a good technique to reduce jagged edges, it is based on adjacent colors. Because your character may appear on top of a variety of colors, anti-aliasing the outside edge may make your character appear poorly against other backgrounds. However, you can use anti-aliasing on the inside details of your character without encountering this problem.

Frame Size

Frame size should typically be no larger than 128 x 128 pixels. Although characters can be larger or smaller in either dimension, the Microsoft Agent Character Editor uses this as its display size, and scales character images if you define a larger frame size. The 128 x 128 frame size makes reasonable tradeoffs with the space the character will occupy on the screen. Your application can scale a character at run time.

Frame Duration

You can use the Microsoft Agent Character Editor to set how long each frame of animation will display before moving to the next frame. Set the duration of each frame to at least 10 hundredths of a second (10 frames per second); anything less might not be perceptible on some systems. You can also set the duration longer, but avoid unnatural pauses in the action.

The Microsoft Agent Character Editor also supports branching from one frame in an animation to another, based on probability percentages that you supply. For any given frame, you can define up to three different branches. Branching enables you to create animations that vary when they are played and animations that loop. However, be careful when using branching as it may create problems when trying to play one animation after another. For example, if you play a looping or branching animation, it could continue indefinitely unless you use a **Stop** method. If you are uncertain, avoid branching.

Frames that don't have images and are set to zero duration do not appear when included in an animation. You can use this feature to create frames that support branching without being visible. However, a frame that does not have images yet has a duration greater than zero will be displayed. Therefore, avoid including empty frames in your animation, because the user may not be able to distinguish an empty frame from when the character is hidden.

Frame Transition

When designing an animation, consider how to smoothly transition from and to the animation. For example, if you create an animation in which the character gestures right, and another in which the character gestures left, you want the character to animate smoothly from one position to the other. Although you could build this into either animation, a better solution is to define a neutral or transitional position from which the character starts and returns. Animating to the neutral position can be incorporated as part of each animation or as a separate animation. In the Microsoft Agent Character Editor, you can specify a complementary **Return** animation for each animation for your character. The **Return** animation should typically be no more than 2-4 frames so the character can quickly transition to the neutral position.

For example, using a "gesturing right, then gesturing left" scenario, you can create a **GestureRight** animation, starting with a frame where the character appears in a neutral position, and add frames with images that extend the character's hand to the right. Then create its **Return** animation: a complementary animation with images that return the character to its neutral position. You can assign this as the **Return** animation for the **GestureRight** animation. Next, create the **GestureLeft** animation that starts from the neutral position and extends the character's arm to the left. Finally, create a complementary **Return** animation for this animation as well. A **Return** animation typically begins with an image that follows the last image of the preceding animation.

Starting and returning to the same neutral position, either within an animation or by using a **Return** animation, enables you to play any animation in any order. The Microsoft Agent animation services automatically play your designated **Return** animation in many situations. For example, the services play the designated **Return** animation before playing your character's **Idling** state animations. It is a good idea to define and assign **Return** animations if your animations do not already end in the neutral position.

If you want to provide your own transitions between specific animations; for example, because you always play them in a well-defined order, you can avoid defining **Return** animations. However, it is still a good idea to begin and end the sequence of animations from the neutral position.

Suggested Animations

The following table lists the animations defined for the Microsoft Agent sample characters and can be used as a guide for designing your own characters. How you plan to use a character determines the names and number of animations you support for a character. Appendix A describes the animations available for the standard Microsoft Agents included on the CD-ROM.

An asterisk after an animation indicates a speaking animation that includes mouth overlay images for the last frame of the animation.

Animation	Example of Use	Example Animation
Acknowledge	When the character acknowledges the user's request.	Character nods or flashes "OK" hand gesture. Note that this animation should return the character to its neutral position.
Alert *	When the character is waiting for instructions, typically played after the user turns on listening mode.	Character faces front, breathing, blinking occasionally, but clearly awaiting instruction.
AlertReturn	When the character completes coming to the alert position.	Character returns to its neutral position.
Announce *	When the character has found information for the user.	Character gestures by raising eyebrows and hand or opens an envelope.
AnnounceReturn	When the character completes telling the user about the information it has found.	Character returns to its neutral position.
Appearing	When the character starts up or returns after being summoned.	Character pops up in a puff of smoke, beams in, or walks on-screen.
Confused *	When the character doesn't understand what to do.	Character scratches head.

Animation	Example of Use	Example Animation
ConfusedReturn	When the character returns from the **Confused** animation.	Character returns to neutral position.
Congratulate *	When the character or user completes a task (a stronger form of the **Acknowledge** animation.)	Character performs congratulatory gesture, conveys "YES!"
CongratulateReturn	When the character completes a **Congratulate** animation.	Character returns to neutral position.
Decline *	When the character cannot do or declines the user's request.	Character shakes head, conveys "no can do."
DeclineReturn	When the character completes the **Decline** animation.	Character returns to neutral position.
DontRecognize *	When the character didn't recognize the user's request.	Character holds hand to ear.
DontRecognizeReturn	When the character completes the **DontRecognize** animation.	Character returns to neutral position.
Explain *	When the character explains something to the user.	Character gestures as if explaining something.
ExplainReturn	When the character completes the **Explain** animation.	Character returns to neutral position.
GestureDown *	When the character needs to point to something below it.	Character points down.
GestureDownReturn	When the character completes gesturing down.	Character returns to neutral position.
GestureLeft *	When the character needs to point to something at its left.	Character points with left hand.
GestureLeftReturn	When the character is finished gesturing left.	Character returns to neutral position.

Animation	Example of Use	Example Animation
GestureRight *	When the character needs to point to something at its right.	Character points with right hand or morphs into an arrow pointing right.
GestureRightReturn	When the character is finished gesturing right.	Character returns to neutral position.
GestureUp *	When the character needs to point to something above it.	Character points up.
GestureUpReturn	When the character is finished gesturing up.	Character returns to neutral position.
GetAttention	When the character needs to notify the user about something important.	Character waves hands or jumps up and down.
GetAttentionReturn	When the character completes the **GetAttention** animation.	Character returns to neutral position.
GlanceDown	When character wants to subtly direct attention below.	Character looks briefly downward and returns to neutral position.
GlanceLeft	When character wants to subtly direct attention to the left.	Character looks briefly to the left and returns to neutral position.
GlanceRight	When character wants to subtly direct attention to the right.	Character looks briefly to the right and returns to neutral position.
GlanceUp	When character wants to subtly direct attention upward.	Character looks briefly upward and returns to neutral position.
Greet *	When the user starts up the system.	Character smiles and waves.
GreetReturn	When the character completes the greeting.	Character returns to neutral position.
Hear	When the character hears the start of an spoken utterance (actively listening).	Character leans forward and nods, or turns head showing response to speech input.
Hide	When the user dismisses the character.	Character removes self from screen.

Animation	Example of Use	Example Animation
Idle1	When the character has no task and the user is not interacting with the character.	Character blinks or looks around, remaining in or returning to the neutral position.
Idle2	When the character has been idle for some time.	Character yawns or reads magazine remaining in or returning to the neutral position.
Idle3	When the character has been idle for a long time.	Character sleeps or puts on headphones to listen to music.
Idle3Return	When the character transitions out of the Idling Level 3 state.	Character returns to its neutral position.
LookDown	When the character needs to look down.	Character looks down.
LookDownReturn	When the character completes looking down.	Character returns to its neutral position.
LookLeft	When the character needs to look left.	Character looks to the left.
LookLeftReturn	When the character completes looking left.	Character returns to its neutral position.
LookRight	When the character needs to look right.	Character looks to the right.
LookRightReturn	When the character completes looking right.	Character returns to its neutral position.
LookUp	When the character needs to look up.	Character looks up.
LookUpReturn	When the character completes looking up.	Character returns to its neutral position.
MoveDown	When the character prepares to move down.	Character transitions to a walking/flying down position.
MoveDownReturn	When the character completes moving down.	Character returns to its neutral position.
MoveLeft	When the character prepares to move left.	Character transitions to a walking/flying left position.

Animation	Example of Use	Example Animation
MoveLeftReturn	When the character completes moving left.	Character returns to its neutral position.
MoveRight	When the character prepares to move right.	Character transitions to a walking/flying right position.
MoveRightReturn	When the character completes moving right.	Character returns to its neutral position.
MoveUp	When the character prepares to move up.	Character transitions to a walking/flying up position.
MoveUpReturn	When the character completes moving up.	Character returns to its neutral position.
Pleased *	When the character is pleased with the user's request or choice.	Character smiles.
PleasedReturn	When the character completes the **Pleased** animation.	Character returns to neutral position.
Processing	When the character is busy processing a task.	Character scribbles on pad of paper. Note: This animation loops to some intermediate frame that occurs after the character moves to an appropriate position.
ProcessingReturn	When the character completes the **Processing** animation.	Character returns to its neutral position.
Read *	When the character reads something to the user.	Character displays book or paper, reads, and looks back at user.
ReadContinued *	When the character reads further to the user.	Character reads again, then looks back at user.
ReadReturn	When the character completes the **Read** animation.	Character returns to its neutral position.
Reading	When the character reads something but cannot accept input.	Character reads from a piece of paper. Note: This animation loops.

Animation	Example of Use	Example Animation
ReadingReturn	When the character completes the **Reading** animation.	Character returns to its neutral position.
RestPose *	When the character speaks from its neutral position.	Character stands with relaxed but attentive posture.
Sad *	When the character is disappointed with the user's choice.	Character frowns or looks disappointed.
SadReturn	When the character completes the **Sad** animation.	Character returns to neutral position.
Searching	When character is searching for user-specified information.	Character shuffles through file drawer or other container looking for something.
		Note: This animation loops to some intermediate frame(s) that occurs after the character moves to an appropriate position.
SearchingReturn	When the character completes the **Search** animation.	Character returns to its neutral position.
Show	When the character starts up or returns after being summoned.	Character pops up in a puff of smoke, beams in, or walks on-screen.
StartListening *	When the character is listening.	Character puts hand to ear.
StartListeningReturn	When the character completes the **StartListening** animation.	Character returns to neutral position.
StopListening *	When the character stops listening.	Character puts hands over ears.
StopListeningReturn	When the character completes the animation.	Character returns to neutral position.
Suggest *	When the character has a tip or suggestion for the user.	Light bulb appears next to character.
SuggestReturn	When the character completes the **Suggest** animation.	Character returns to its neutral position.

Animation	Example of Use	Example Animation
Surprised *	When the character is surprised by the user's action or choice.	Character widens eyes, opens mouth.
SurprisedReturn	When the character completes the **Surprised** animation.	Character returns to its neutral position.
Think *	When the character is thinking about something.	Character looks up and holds hand on head.
ThinkReturn	When the character completes the **Think** animation.	Character returns to its neutral position.
Uncertain *	When the character needs the user to confirm a request.	Character looks quizzical, conveys ("are you sure?")
UncertainReturn	When the character completes the **Uncertain** animation.	Character returns to its neutral position.
Wave *	When the user chooses to shut down the server or system.	Character waves goodbye or hello.
WaveReturn	When the character completes the **Wave** animation.	Character returns to neutral position.
Write *	When the character is listening for instructions from the user.	Character displays paper, writes, and looks back at user.
WriteContinued *	When the character continues listening for instructions from the user.	Character writes on a piece of paper and looks back at user.
WriteReturn	When the character completes the **Write** animation.	Character returns to its neutral position.
Writing	When the character writes out information for the user.	Character writes on piece of paper. Note: This animation loops.
WritingReturn	When the character completes the **Writing** animation.	Character returns to its neutral position.

Speaking Animation

Supply mouth images for each animation during which you want the character to be able to speak, unless your character's design has no animated mouth or indication of spoken output. In general, mouth movement is very important. A character may appear less intelligent, likable, or honest if its mouth does not move reasonably synced with its speech. Mouth images allow your character to lip-sync to spoken output. You define mouth images separately and as Windows bitmap files. They must match the same color palette as the other images in your animation.

The Microsoft Agent animation services display mouth animation frames on top of the last frame of an animation, also called the *speaking frame* of the animation. For example, when the character speaks in the **GestureRight** animation, the animation services overlay the mouth animation frames on the last frame of **GestureRight**. A character cannot speak while animating, so you only supply mouth images for only the last frame of an animation. In addition, the speaking frame must be the end frame of an animation, so a character cannot speak in a looping animation.

Typically, you would supply the mouth images in the same size as the frame (and base image), but include only the area that animates as part of the mouth movement, and render the rest of the image in the transparent color. Design the image so that it matches the image in the speaking frame when overlaid on top of it. To have it match correctly, it is likely you'll need to create a separate set of mouth images for every animation in which the character speaks.

A mouth image can include more than the mouth itself, such as the chin or other parts of the character's body while it speaks. However, if you move a hand or leg, note that it may appear to move randomly because the mouth overlay displayed will be based on the current phoneme of a spoken phrase. In addition, the server clips the mouth image to the speaking frame image's outline. Design your mouth overlay image to remain within the outline of its base speaking frame image, because the server uses the base image to create the window boundary for the character.

The Microsoft Agent Character Editor enables you to define seven basic mouth positions that correspond to common phoneme mouth shapes shown in the following table:

Mouth Animation Images

Mouth Position	Sample Image	Representation
Closed		Normal mouth closed shape.
		Also used for phonemes such as "m" as in "mom," "b" as in "bob," "f" as in "fife."
Open-wide 1		Mouth is slightly open, at full width.
		Used for phonemes such as "g" as in "gag," "l" as in "lull," "ear" as in "hear."
Open-wide 2		Mouth is partially open, at full width.
		Used for phonemes such as "n" as in "nun," "d" as in "dad," "t" as in "tot."
Open-wide 3		Mouth is open, at full width.
		Used for phonemes such as "u" as in "hut," "ea" as in "head," "ur" as in "hurt."
Open-wide 4		Mouth is completely open, at full width.
		Used for phonemes such as "a" as in "hat," "ow" as in "how."
Open-medium		Mouth is open at half width.
		Used for phonemes such as "oy" as in "ahoy," "o" as in "hot."
Open-narrow		Mouth is open at narrow width.
		Used for phonemes such as "o" as in "hoop", "o" as in "hope," "w" as in "wet."

Agent States

The Microsoft Agent animation services automatically play certain animations for you. For example, when you use **MoveTo** or **GestureAt** commands, the animation services play an appropriate animation. Similarly, after the idle time out, the services automatically play animations. To support these states, you can define appropriate animations and then assign them to the states. You can still play any animation you define directly using the **Play** method, even if you assign it to a state.

You can assign multiple animations to the same state, and the animation services will randomly choose one of your animations. This enables your character to exhibit far more natural variety in its behavior.

Although animations that you assign to states can include branching frames, avoid looping animations (animations that branch forever). Otherwise, you will have to use the **Stop** method before you can play another animation.

It's important to define and assign at least one animation for each state that occurs for the character. If you do not supply these animations and state assignments, your character may not appear to behave appropriately to the user. However, if a state does not occur for a particular character, you need not assign an animation to that state. For example, if your host application never calls the **MoveTo** method, you can skip creating and assigning **Moving** state animations.

State	Example of Use
GesturingDown	When the **GestureAt** animation method is processed.
GesturingLeft	When the **GestureAt** animation method is processed.
GesturingRight	When the **GestureAt** animation method is processed.
GesturingUp	When the **GestureAt** animation method is processed.
Hearing	When the beginning of spoken input is detected.
Hiding	When the user or the application hides the character.
IdlingLevel1	When the character begins the **Idling** state.
IdlingLevel2	When the character begins the second **Idling** level state.
IdlingLevel3	When the character begins the final **Idling** level state.
Listening	When the character starts listening (the user first presses the speech input hot key).
MovingDown	When the **MoveTo** animation method is processed.

State	Example of Use
MovingLeft	When the **MoveTo** animation method is processed.
MovingRight	When the **MoveTo** animation method is processed.
MovingUp	When the **MoveTo** animation method is processed.
Showing	When the user or the application shows the character.
Speaking	When the **Speak** animation method is processed.

The Hearing and Listening States

The animation you assign to the **Listening** state plays when the user presses the push-to-talk hot key for speech input. Create and assign a short animation that makes the character look attentive. Similarly, define its **Return** animation to have a short duration so that the character plays its **Hearing** state animation when the user speaks. A **Hearing** state animation should also be brief, and designed to let the user know that the character is actively listening to what the user says. Head tilts or other slight gestures are appropriate. To provide natural variability, provide several **Hearing** state animations.

The Gesturing States

You need to create and assign **Gesturing** state animations only if you plan to use the **GestureAt** method. **Gesturing** state animations play when Microsoft Agent processes a call to the **GestureAt** method. If you define mouth overlays for your **Gesturing** state animations, the character can speak as it gestures.

The animation services determine the character's location and its relation to the location of the coordinates specified in the method, and play an appropriate animation. Gesturing direction is always with respect to the character; for example, **GestureRight** should be a gesture to the character's right.

The Showing and Hiding States

The **Showing** and **Hiding** states play the assigned animations when the user or the host application requests to show or hide the character. These states also appropriately set the character frame's **Visible** state. When defining animations for these states, keep in mind that a character can appear or depart at any screen location. Because the user can show or hide any character, always support at least one animation for these states.

Animations that you assign to the **Showing** state typically end with a frame containing the character's neutral position image. Conversely, **Hiding** state animations typically begin with the neutral position. **Showing** and **Hiding** state animations can include an empty frame at the beginning or end, respectively, to provide a transition from the character's current state.

The Idling States

The **Idling** states are progressive. The animation services begin using the Level 1 assignments for the first idle period, and use the Level 2 animations for the second. After this, the idle cycle progresses to the Level 3 assigned animations and remains in this state until canceled, such as when a new animation request begins.

Design animations for the **Idling** states to communicate the state of the character, but not to distract the user. The animations should appropriately reflect the responsiveness of the character in subtle but clear ways. For example, glancing around or blinking are good animations to assign to the **IdlingLevel1** state. Reading animations work well for the **IdlingLevel2** state. Sleeping or listening to music with headphones are good examples of animations to assign to the **IdlingLevel3** state. Animations that include many or large movements are not well suited for idle animations because they draw the user's attention. Because **Idling** state animations are played frequently, provide several **Idling** state animations, especially for the **IdlingLevel1** and **IdlingLevel2** states.

Note that an application can turn off the automatic idle processing for a character and manage the character's **Idling** state itself. The Agent **Idling** states are designed to help you avoid any situation where the character has no animation to play. A character image that does not change after a brief period of time is like an application displaying a wait pointer for a long time, which detracts from the sense of believability and interactivity. Maintaining the illusion does not take much: sometimes just an animated blink, visible breath, or body shift.

The Speaking State

The animation services use the **Speaking** state when a speaking animation cannot be found for the current animation. Assign a simple speaking animation to this state. For example, you can use a single frame consisting of the character's neutral positon with mouth overlays.

The Moving States

The **Moving** states play when an application calls the **MoveTo** method. The animation services determine which animation to play based on the character's current location and the specified coordinates. Movement direction is based on the character's position. Therefore, the animation you assign to the **MovingLeft** animation should be based on the character's left. If you don't use the **MoveTo** method, you can skip creating and assigning an animation.

Moving state animations should animate the character into its moving position. The last frame of this animation is displayed as the character's frame is moved on the screen. There is no support for animating the character while its frame moves.

Animation Principles

Effective animation design requires more than simply rendering a character. Successful animators follow a variety of principles and techniques to create "believable" characters.

Squash and Stretch

There should be a degree of distortion as an animated object moves. The amount of deformation that occurs reflects the rigidity of that object. Flattening or elongating a part of a character's body as it moves helps you convey the nature and composition of the character.

Anticipation

Anticipation sets the stage for an upcoming action. Without anticipatory actions, body movements look abrupt, rigid, and unnatural. This principle is based on how a body moves in the real world. Movement in one direction often begins with movement in the opposite direction. Legs contract before a jump. To exhale, you first inhale. Anticipatory action also has an important role in communicating the nature of both the character and the action and helps your audience prepare for the action. A key aspect of creating a believable character involves demonstrating that the character's actions stem from a purposeful intent. Anticipation helps communicate the character's motivation to the audience.

Timing

Timing defines the nature of an action. The speed that a head moves from left to right conveys whether a character is casually looking around or giving a negative response. Timing also helps convey the weight and size of an object. Larger objects tend to take longer to accelerate and decelerate than smaller ones. In addition, the pacing of a character's movements affects how it draws attention. In a normal scenario, rapid motion draws the eye, while in a frenetic environment, stationary or slow movements may have the same effect.

Staging

The background and props a character uses can also convey its mood or purpose. Staging also includes what the character wears, lighting effects, viewing angle, and the presence of other characters. These elements all contribute to reinforcing a character's personality, objectives, and actions. Effective staging involves understanding how to direct the eye to where you want to communicate.

Follow-Through and Overlapping Action

Just as a golfer's follow-through communicates the result of the swing, the transition from one action to the next is important in communicating the relationship between the actions. Actions rarely come to a sudden and complete stop. So, too, follow-through and overlapping actions allow you to establish the flow of the character's motion. You can typically implement this by varying the speed at which different parts of a body move, allowing movement beyond the primary aspect of the motion. For example, the fingers of a hand typically follow the movement of the wrist in a hand gesture. This principle also emphasizes that actions should not come to a complete stop, but smoothly blend into other actions.

Slow In-and-Out

Slow In-and-Out refers to moving a character smoothly from one pose to another. The character begins and ends actions slowly. You accomplish this by the number, timing, and location of "in-between" frames. The more in-between frames you include, the slower and smoother the transition.

Arcs

Living objects in nature rarely move in a perfectly straight line. As a result, arcs or curved paths for movement provide more natural effects. Arcs also convey speed of motion. The slower the motion, the higher the arc, and the faster the motion, the flatter the arc.

Exaggeration

Good animators often exaggerate the shape, color, emotion, or actions of a character. Making aspects of the motion "larger than life" more clearly communicates the idea of the action to the audience. For example, a character's arms may stretch to the point that they appear elastic. However, exaggeration must be balanced. If used in some situations and not others, the exaggerated action may appear unrealistic and may be interpreted by the user as having a particular meaning. Similarly, if you exaggerate one aspect of an image, consider what other aspects should be exaggerated to match.

Secondary Action

Animation requires more than the mechanistic creation of in-between images from one pose to the next. A primary action is typically supported by secondary actions. Secondary actions can enhance the presentation, but should not detract from or dominate the main action. Facial expressions can often be used as secondary actions to body movement. Richness comes from adding elements that support the main idea.

Solid Drawing

Creating an animated character involves more than creating a series of images. Effective animation design considers how the character looks in different positions and from different angles. Even characters rendered as two-dimensional images become more realistic and believable if considered conceptually in three dimensions. Avoid *twins*: mirroring the position the face, arms, and legs on both sides of the body. This results in a wooden, unnatural presentation. Body movement is rarely symmetrical, but involves overall balancing of posture or reactions.

Appeal

Successful implementation depends on how well you understand your audience. Your character's overall image and personality should appeal to your target audience; appeal does not require photo-realism. A character's personality can be conveyed—no matter how simple its shape—by using gestures, posture, and other mannerisms. A common assignment of beginning animators is to create a variety of expressions for a flour sack or small rug. Characters with simple shapes are often more effective than complex ones. Consider, for example, that many popular characters have only three fingers and a thumb.

CHAPTER 7

Using the Microsoft Agent Character Editor

The Microsoft Agent Character Editor enables you to compile character animations for use with Microsoft Agent. You can define animations by importing Windows bitmap images, setting their duration, and optionally including branching, sound effects, and speaking overlays. For information about designing a character's animation, see Chapter 6, "Designing Characters for Microsoft Agent."

With the Agent Character Editor you can define the character's name and description as well as output options, including text-to-speech (TTS), synthesized voice output, pop-up menu support, and the character's word balloon design.

Installing the Agent Character Editor

To install the Microsoft Agent Character Editor, open its self-extracting cabinet file as described on the accompanying CD-ROM. This will automatically install the appropriate files on your system. If you are downloading the Agent Character Editor from the Microsoft Web site, the downloading software gives you the option to save the file and open it or open it automatically as soon as the download completes.

If you plan to use a TTS engine for your character's output, you need to install that engine before you begin creating your character. A special version of the Lernout & Hauspie TruVoice text-to-speech engine (American English language) is also included on the CD-ROM. You can use and distribute this

engine as part of a Microsoft Agent application, subject to the conditions described in the End User Licensing Agreement that displays when you install
the engine. If you plan to use another TTS engine, contact that vendor to confirm their support for Microsoft Agent and for information on their licensing
provisions for use and redistribution.

Starting the Agent Character Editor

To run the Agent Character Editor, choose the Agent Character Editor option
from the Windows Taskbar's Start menu, or double-click the Microsoft Agent
Character Editor icon on your desktop. The Editor's window will open, displaying its menus, a toolbar with frequently used commands, a tree listing the
components that make up a character's definition, and a set of tabbed pages
that change based on your selection in the component tree.

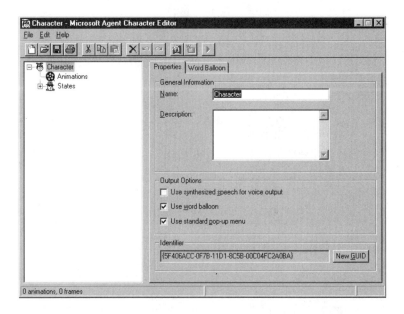

FIGURE 7-1. Microsoft Agent Character Editor window

To access fields in the window from the keyboard, you can use the TAB
key and SHIFT+TAB to navigate between controls, or use the access key
(ALT+*underlined letter*) to move to a specific control. Once the Editor completes starting up, you can begin creating a new character definition or load
an existing character definition.

The status bar displays information about commands or toolbar buttons when you move the pointer over them. It also displays summary information about your character animation data and status information when you build a character.

Defining a New Character

To define a new character, run the Agent Character Editor. If you have an existing character file loaded, choose the New command from the File menu or the New button on the toolbar. This action selects the Character icon in the tree and displays its property pages on the right side of the window. The following sections describe how to set your character's properties and how to create animations for the character.

Setting Your Character's Properties

To begin defining a character, provide the character's name by entering it in the Name text box (32 characters maximum). Because Microsoft Agent uses the name to allow users to access the character, specify a user-friendly name. Supply a name that can be pronounced using conventional spelling, or you may disable speech input for the character. You can also specify a short optional description (256 characters) for your character in the Description text box. The server exposes what you enter in the Description text box to client applications.

For your character's spoken output, Microsoft Agent provides the choice of a synthesized, text-to-speech (TTS) voice or a voice that uses recorded sound files. If you want to use a synthesized voice, check the Use Synthesized Speech For Voice Output option. This will add a Voice page for selecting the characteristics of the voice. Choose the Voice page and use the controls on it page to select a voice, speed, and pitch of any compatible TTS engines you have installed. The range of the voice parameters you can select depends on TTS engines. If you have not yet installed a TTS engine, the Voice ID list will be empty. You must have a TTS engine installed before you define your character's voice settings in the Agent Character Editor.

If you plan to use a TTS engine for your character's output, you must also install that engine on the user's system. For more information on how to install the Lernout & Hauspie TruVoice engine on a user's system from a Web script, see Chapter 4, "Programming The Microsoft Agent Control."

If you are using another TTS engine, check with the vendor for appropriate installation information. If you select a voice based on a particular TTS engine, but the user has a different TTS engine installed, the server attempts to fit the voice based on the characteristics you defined in the Agent Character Editor.

If you plan to use recorded sound files (.WAV files) for your character's spoken output, do not check the Use Synthesized Speech For Voice Output option. Instead, you will need to record the spoken output audio files separately and load them from your application code.

The Use Word Balloon on the character's Properties page enables you to determine whether you want to support this feature for your character. Once defined, it cannot be changed through the Microsoft Agent programming interface.

When the Use Word Balloon option is checked, you can access the Word Balloon page. The options on the Word Balloon page enable you to change the default characteristics of your word balloon. The Characters Per Line setting enables you to define the width of the balloon based on the average number of characters per line. You can set the default height based on either a fixed number of lines you want to display at once or automatically sized to the text you supply in the **Speak** method. You can also set whether the balloon automatically hides after a **Speak** method is completed and whether the balloon automatically displays or "paces" words to the character's speech output speed setting.

The Word Balloon page also enables you to set the default font for the character's word balloon and the balloon's display colors. However, be aware that users can override your word balloon font settings using the Microsoft Agent property sheet.

Each character requires a unique identifier (GUID). The server uses the identifier to differentiate characters. When you create a new character, the Editor automatically creates a new identifier for your character. You need to change a character's identifier only if you copied the character definition file of another character or if you intentionally want to differentiate a character from a former version. To change a character's identifier, click the New GUID button and the Editor will generate a new identifier.

Creating Animations

To begin creating animations for your character, select the Animations icon in the tree. This displays the Properties page with the default settings for all animations. You can alter the frame size, the default frame duration, and color palette settings on the Properties page. The animation frame height and width must remain constant throughout the entire character definition (that is, for all of that character's animations). Although you can change the frame size from its default setting (128 x 128 pixels), images displayed in the Editor will be scaled to fit default display size. If you change the default frame setting, you can display the frame's full, non-scaled size by choosing Open Frame Window from the Edit menu.

By default, the Editor uses the first bitmap image you load to set your character's default color palette, and sets the color in the 11th palette position as your transparency color. However, you can change these settings using the buttons in the Palette Information group. Your character's color palette must not remap the standard system colors. The Editor will automatically reserve the system's color palette when displaying images. In addition, make sure all your animation images use the same color palette and transparency color. If they do not, you may see color remapping of your images when you load them into the Editor.

Once you have determined your global animation settings, you can begin creating animations. To create a new animation, choose New Animation from the Edit menu or the New Animation button on the toolbar. This adds a new animation icon in the tree under the Animations icon and assigns the new icon a default name. You can rename your animation by typing in the Animation Name field. Note that animation names within a character definition must be unique. Also, avoid using characters in the name that are not valid characters for file names.

Every animation is composed of frames. To create a new frame for your animation, choose New Frame from either the Edit menu or the toolbar. This adds a new frame icon to the tree under your animation icon, and displays three tabbed pages. The General page includes controls that enable you to load and adjust an image for your frame. It also includes a display area for the frame's appearance.

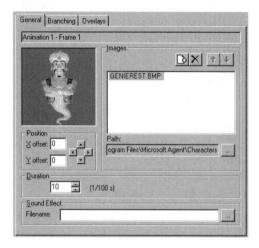

FIGURE 7-2. The Frame Image display and controls

A frame can contain one or more images. To define an image for a frame, click the Add Image File button just above the Images list box. The Select Image Files dialog box displays, which allows you to select a bitmap image file.

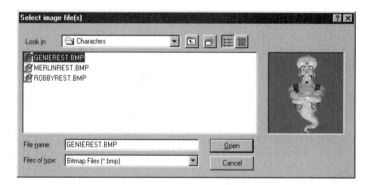

FIGURE 7-3. The Select Image Files dialog box

Select the file you want to load, choose Open, and the image appears in the frame display on the General page. The Editor accepts images stored as 1-bit (monochrome), 4-bit, or 8-bit Windows bitmap format, or as GIF format.

You can use the four arrow buttons beneath the image in the Position box to adjust the image's appearance within the frame. If the image is larger than your frame's size, only the portion of the image that appears within the frame will display. If you increase the frame size, the image may be scaled to fit within the display area of the Editor.

You can also display a frame by choosing Open Frame Window from the Edit menu. This displays the current frame in a separate window without scaling the images loaded into the frame. This window's initial size is based on your frame's height and width settings. You can resize it smaller, but not larger. The Frame Window reflects the changes you make using the controls in the Editor and also allows you view the frame while viewing its other property pages.

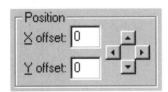

FIGURE 7-4. Image Position controls

You can compose a frame from multiple images. Each time you select the Add Image button and choose another image, the image gets added to the list and to the image display area. You can also add multiple images by selecting more than one file. Press SHIFT or CTRL while you click in the Select Image Files dialog box, and then choose Open. The Move Up and Move Down buttons above the Images list box move a selected image in the display order (z-order) for the frame. You can also move images by dragging them within the list. Selecting an image in the list and clicking the Delete button removes an image. To change an image you have loaded to another image file, you can click the file name to edit it directly or use the Ellipsis (…) button to bring up the Select Image Files dialog box and select a different file.

FIGURE 7-5. The Ellipsis button

You can use the Duration text box to set the duration for the frame; that is, how long the frame will be displayed. If a frame has no image and zero duration, the frame will not be displayed when the animation plays.

You can also specify a sound effect file to play when the frame is displayed. If you plan to load the character from a Web server, you may want to compress the sound effect file to minimize load time. You can then specify the compressed sound file in the Agent Character Editor. In addition, avoid using a sound effect with a duration longer than the duration of your animation and especially avoid a sound effect that loops, because the Microsoft Agent animation services do not send an animation complete event until the sound completes. Also avoid specifying a sound effect for any animation you assign to the **Listening** or **Hearing** states, because this interferes with speech input. Finally, while you can include more than one sound effect in an animation, avoid placing them so they overlap, because this may affect the timing of the animation. Also, keep in mind that sound effects may play at different rates based on the user's hardware.

To add frames to your animation, choose the New Frame command again and follow the same procedure. As an option, you can also load multiple images and automatically generate new frames for them. To use this feature, choose New Frames From Images from the Edit menu. The frames will be created in alphabetic order based on the image file names. When you are finished defining all frames for your animation, you can choose the New Animation command again to begin a new animation.

There are other ways to add frames to animations and move frames within or between animations. You can select another frame (from the same or another animation) and choose Cut or Copy, then select the animation or a frame in that animation and choose Paste. You can also drag a frame from one animation to another. If you drag within an animation, the action moves the frame. If you drag to another animation, it copies the frame. Dragging to a preceding frame in the same animation inserts the frame before the frame to which you drag. Dragging to a following frame places it after the frame to which you drag. If you drag a frame using the right mouse button, releasing the button displays a pop-up menu with your transfer choices.

You can also create an animation by copying an existing animation (select the animation and choose Copy), and selecting the Animations icon or another animation icon and choosing Paste. The Editor automatically creates a new name for the animation, although you can change the name.

Branching

When you create a frame, you can also define which frame plays next. By default, the next frame played in the animation sequence is always the next frame in the z-order. However, by choosing the Branching page, you can set the probability for up to three other frames that the server may play. Enter the probability percentage and the target frame number in the appropriate fields. You can specify branching even for frames that don't have images and have their duration set to zero. This enables you to branch without first displaying a particular image.

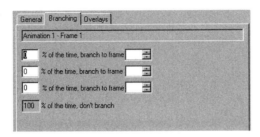

FIGURE 7-6. The Branching page

You can use the branching feature to create animations that will loop indefinitely. However, note that when a looping animation plays, other animations in the character's queue will not play until an event—such as a user pressing the push-to-talk key or the client application calling the **Stop** method—halts the looping animation. Therefore, carefully consider the context in which the animation will be used before creating a looping animation.

Previewing an Animation

You can preview your animation in the Agent Character Editor by choosing the Preview command on the Edit menu or the Preview button on the toolbar. This plays your animation, including any branches and sound effects, starting from the current selected frame. It resets to the current selected frame when the animation completes. To play your entire animation, go to the tree view, select the animation's icon or first frame of the animation, and choose the Preview command. The Editor animates your frames on the General page. To stop the preview before it ends, choose the Stop Preview command. The Preview command automatically changes to Stop Preview while the preview plays.

Assigning Speaking Overlays

You can define a character so that it speaks during the last frame of its animation. On this frame, choose the Overlay page. This page enables you to load and assign mouth image files to the standard mouth positions supported by Microsoft Agent. Click the Add Image button and select the image from the dialog box. You can also select multiple images, and the Editor will load and assign the images starting with the mouth position you selected. Click the Move Up and Move Down buttons or drag an entry to change an image assignment in the list. Click the Delete button to remove an image. You can also edit the pathname of an assigned file by clicking its entry in the list and retyping its file name, or by choosing the Ellipsis (…) button to display the Select Image Files dialog box.

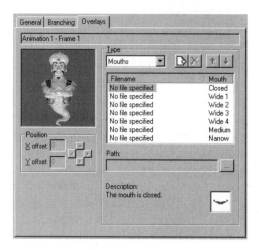

FIGURE 7-7. The Overlay page image controls

Assigning a Return Animation

To create a smooth transition from one animation to the next, design your animation sequences to begin and end with a neutral image. For more information, see Chapter 6, "Designing Characters for Microsoft Agent." However, this does not mean that every animation must end at the neutral position. You can animate a character through a sequence of frames, have it speak during the last frame, and create a separate, complementary animation that returns the character to the neutral position. This complementary animation is called a **Return** animation. Define a **Return** animation like any other animation. To assign the **Return** animation, select an animation in the tree, and select the **Return** animation you created from the **Return** Animation drop-down list on the Properties page.

Creating and assigning a **Return** animation has an added benefit: When the server gets a request to play another animation, it will attempt to play the **Return** animation for the last animation it played, if a **Return** animation is assigned. This ensures a smooth transition. If an animation begins and ends at the neutral position, you don't need to define a **Return** animation. Similarly, if you intend to handle transitions from one animation to another yourself, you may not need to assign a **Return** animation.

Assigning Animations to States

The Microsoft Agent animation services automatically play animations when the hosting client application uses certain methods. For example, when an application calls the **MoveTo** and **GestureAt** methods, the server automatically determines where the character is displayed and plays an appropriate animation. Similarly, Microsoft Agent automatically plays **Idle** animations when the user has not interacted with the character for several seconds. These conditions when the server automatically plays animations on an application's behalf are called *states*. However, for the server to know which animation to play, you must assign animations to these states.

To define a state, create the appropriate animation, expand the States entry in the tree view of the Editor window, and select the State icon. The list of animations you have created appear in a list box on the right side of the window. Check the animation you want to assign to this state. Note that you can assign more than one animation to the same state. This allows the server to randomly select different animations for the state. Assigning an animation to a state does not prevent an animation from playing that animation directly.

You can also assign an animation to a state by selecting the animation's entry in the tree. The Assign To State list box on the Properties page lists the states. Select the check box of the state to which you're assigning the animation.

Saving Your Character Definition

You can save your character's definition file by choosing the Save command on the File menu or the Save Character Definition button on the toolbar. If you want to save the character definition file with a new name, choose the Save As command on the File menu. The Editor saves a character's editable definition as an Agent Character Definition (.ACD) file. You can also edit this self-documenting text file format with most text editors and word processing applications.

Printing Your Character Definition

To print your character's definition, choose the Print command on the File menu or the Print button on the toolbar. To set the properties for your printed output, choose the Page Setup command and choose your settings before selecting the Print command.

Building A Character

When you are done creating your animations, the character and images must be compiled into a special format that Microsoft Agent uses to load this data. To build a character, select the Build Character command on the File menu or from the toolbar. If you have unsaved edits in your character definition file, the Editor saves the definition file before displaying the Build Character dialog box.

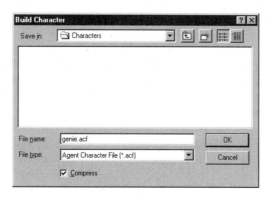

FIGURE 7-8. The Build Character dialog box

The Agent Character Editor will automatically propose a file name based on your character definition file name. The Build Character dialog box also includes a drop-down list so you can choose between building the character as a single storage file (.ACS) or as multiple files. If you choose the latter, the Editor builds an .ACF file that includes character's data and an .AAF file for each animation you created. If you plan to install and access a character stored on the same machine as your client application, you would typically choose the single structured file format. This format provides easy and efficient installation of and access to the character. However, if the character will be accessed from a Web server using the HTTP protocol, build your character using the .ACF (individual) file format. This latter file structure allows a Web page script to load individual animation files, storing the data in the user's browser file cache. It provides more efficient access over the Web because animation data can be downloaded as needed rather than requiring the user to wait for the entire set of animations to download at one time. In addition, because the character's data is stored in the browser cache, the file space can be automatically reclaimed.

Although you can also download character data (either as a single structured file or multiple files) from a Web server and install elsewhere on a user's machine, such a method requires security provisions for downloading and installation. As a result, Microsoft Agent does not include support for downloadable installation of a character except to the browser's cache. However, you can still support this scenario by creating your own installation control and distribute it following appropriate security conventions. For more information, see the Microsoft Internet Client Software Development Kit (available at http://msdn/sdk/inetsdk).

The Compress option enables you to set whether the character data is compressed. Typically, you will want to set this option to compact your character data, although building a character with the compacted data takes longer.

Once you build a character, subsequent builds will be faster if you build the character to the same directory location. The character editor automatically verifies and copies those files that have not changed, and recompiles any data that has been edited.

Editing an Existing Character

To edit an existing character, choose Open on the File menu, select the character's definition file (.ACD) in the resulting dialog box, and choose Open. The file will load into the Editor. Note that you cannot load compiled character files (.ACS, .ACF, or .AAF) with the Editor.

Because the character's definition file (.ACD) is a text file, you can also edit a character's definition by opening the file with a text editor or word processing program. However, when completing your changes, make sure to save the file in its original format before loading it into the character editor for compilation.

Storing Additional Data in Your Character Definition

You can also store your own data as part of your character. You can use this capability to include special information about your character or other data. Once compiled with the character editor, this information can be accessed at run time when the character is loaded by using the **ExtraData** property.

To define your own data as part of the character's definition, you must load the character's definition file (.ACD) into a text editor. Then in the

DefineCharacter section of the file (between the DefineCharacter and EndCharacter tags), add an entry using the following syntax:

ExtraData = "*string*"

The string you supply should appear between two double-quotes and can include any characters other than double quotes, provided that the programming language you use to read the data at run time supports them. You can only include a single ExtraData entry, but the string you supply with it can be of any length.

To compile this data with your character, save the file in the original text format and load the character definition file into the character editor. Then build the character following the normal conventions. You can access the data at run time using the **ExtraData** property.

Microsoft Agent Character Editor Command Reference

The File Menu

New

Resets the Agent Character Editor for creating a new character definition. If an existing character is loaded and has unsaved edits, the Editor displays a message to determine whether to save or discard unsaved changes.

Open

Displays the Open File dialog box, enabling you to open an existing character definition file for editing. If an existing character is loaded and has unsaved edits to a file, the Editor displays a message to determine whether to save or discard unsaved changes.

Save

Saves the character definition. If the character definition does not exist (has not been named), the Editor displays the Save As dialog box for input of the file name.

Save As

Displays the Save As dialog box, enabling you to enter a new name for the character definition file.

Print

Displays the Print dialog box, enabling you to choose a printing option and to print the character definition file.

Build Character

Displays the Build Character dialog box, which includes options for defining how to build a character's data and animation files for use with Microsoft Agent.

Page Setup

Displays the Page Setup dialog box that enables you to set the printing options for the character definition file.

Most Recently Open Files

Keeps track of the recent character definition files you opened. Choosing a file automatically opens that file for editing. If an existing character is loaded and has unsaved edits to a file, the Editor displays a message to determine whether to save or discard unsaved changes.

Exit

Quits the Agent Character Editor. If an existing character is loaded and has unsaved edits to a file, the Editor displays a message to determine whether to save or discard unsaved changes.

The Edit Menu

Undo

Removes a change made in the Editor.

Redo

Reverses an undo action in the Editor.

Cut

Removes the selected item from the Editor and places it on the Windows Clipboard.

Copy

Copies the selected item in the Editor to the Windows Clipboard.

Paste

Copies data from the current Windows Clipboard to the selected location.

Delete

Removes the selected item from the Editor.

New Animation

Creates a new animation object in the Editor.

New Frame

Creates a new frame for an animation.

New Frames from Files

Displays the Select Image Files dialog box and creates frames using the selected files.

Preview | Stop Preview

Plays an animation, starting from its selected frame.

Open Frame Window

Displays the current frame and its images in a separate window without scaling the images loaded into the frame.

The Help Menu

Help Topics

Displays the Help Topics dialog box, enabling you to select an Editor help topic.

About Microsoft Editor

Displays a dialog box with copyright and version information for the Editor.

Toolbar buttons

 New

Resets the Editor for creating a new character definition. If an existing character is loaded and has unsaved edits to a file(s), the Editor displays a message to determine whether to save or discard unsaved changes.

 Open

Displays the Open File dialog box, enabling you to open an existing character definition file for editing. If an existing character is loaded and has unsaved edits to a file(s), the Editor displays a message to determine whether to save or discard unsaved changes.

 Save

Saves the character definition. If the character definition does not exist (has not been named), the Editor displays the Save As dialog box for input of the file name.

 Print

Prints the current character definition file open in the Editor.

 Cut

Removes the selected item in the Editor and places it on the Windows Clipboard.

 Copy

Copies the selected item in the Editor to the Windows Clipboard.

 Paste

Copies data from the current Windows Clipboard to the selected location.

 Delete

Removes the selected item from the Editor.

 Undo

Removes a change made in the Editor.

Redo

Reverses an undo action in the Editor.

New Animation

Creates a new animation object in the Editor.

New Frame

Creates a new frame for an animation.

Preview

Plays an animation, starting from its selected frame.

Stop Preview

Stops playing the preview of an animation.

Add Image File

Displays the Select Image File dialog box. Selected images are added to the list.

Move Up

Moves an image up in the ordered (z-ordered) list. In a frame's images list, this moves the image up in the visual z-order.

Move Down

Moves an image down in the ordered (z-ordered) list. In a frame's images list, this moves the image down in the visual z-order.

C H A P T E R   8

Using the Microsoft Linguistic Information Sound Editing Tool

The Microsoft Linguistic Information Sound Editing Tool enables you to generate phoneme and word-break information for enhancing Windows sound (.WAV) files to support high-quality lip-syncing character animation.

You can use linguistically enhanced sound files generated with the sound editor to support lip-syncing Microsoft Agent character output. To do so, simply pass the file as a parameter to the **Speak** method. For further information, see Chapter 4, "Programming the Microsoft Agent Control" or Chapter 5, "Programming the Microsoft Agent Server Interface."

Installing the Sound Editor

The recommended system configuration for using the sound editor is a PC with a Pentium 166, at least 32 Megabytes of RAM, and a Windows compatible sound card. If you want to record spoken input with the tool, you will also need a compatible microphone.

To install the Microsoft Linguistic Sound Editing Tool, follow the instructions on the accompanying CD-ROM. Open its self-extracting installation file. This will automatically install the appropriate files on your system. The installation tool will propose to install itself in the Tools subdirectory of Microsoft Agent. We recommend that you use this location.

The Microsoft Command and Control speech recognition engine (version. 3.0) must also be installed before you can use the sound editor. This normally gets installed with the sound editor, but if it was subsequently uninstalled, you can reinstall it from the CD-ROM. The sound editor can only generate linguistic information based on the language supported by the speech engine. To generate information for other languages, a compatible speech recognition engine for that language must be installed. Contact your speech engine vendor to determine whether they support the Microsoft Linguistic Sound Editing Tool.

Starting the Sound Editor

To run the Microsoft Linguistic Information Sound Editing Tool, choose it from the Start menu or double-click the sound editor's icon. The sound editor's window will open, displaying its menus, a toolbar for frequently used commands, a text box for entering the words the editor uses to process the sound file, and a display area for viewing and editing the audio and linguistic data.

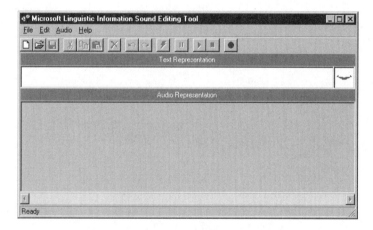

FIGURE 8-1. Microsoft Linguistic Information Sound Editing Tool Window

Once the sound editor starts up, you can begin recording a new sound file or load an existing sound file.

Creating a New Sound File

When you first start the editor, you can create a new sound file by choosing Record on the Audio menu or the Record button on the sound editor's toolbar, and then speaking into the microphone attached to your system. Click the Stop button on the toolbar to stop recording. You can click the Play command on the Audio menu or toolbar to see how Microsoft Agent would process the sound file without linguistic enhancement. To create another new file, choose the New command on the File menu or on the editor's toolbar.

Loading an Existing Sound File

You can also load an existing Windows sound file (.WAV) or linguistically enhanced sound file (.LWV) by choosing the Open command on the File menu or the sound editor toolbar. This displays the Open dialog box. Select a file and click Open to load the file into the editor.

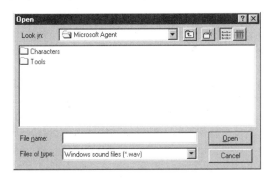

FIGURE 8-2. The Open Dialog Box

Generating Linguistic Information

Once you have recorded a new sound file or loaded an existing sound file, you can generate phonetic and word-break information by entering text that corresponds to your sound file in the Text Representation box. Then choose the Generate Linguistic Info command from the Edit menu or from the toolbar. The sound editor displays a progress message and begins processing your sound file. When it completes generating linguistic information, it displays a mapping of word and phoneme labels for the sound file in boxes in the Audio Representation box. Note that the Generate Linguistic Info command remains disabled until you enter a text representation for your sound file.

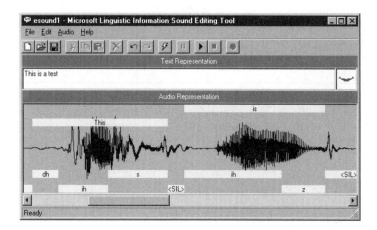

FIGURE 8-3. Word and Phoneme Labels Generated for a Sound File

If the editor doesn't produce an acceptable set of word or phoneme labels, choose the Generate Linguistic Info command again. If the editor does not generate any linguistic information, check your text representation to ensure that all the words are correctly ordered and spelled, and that you don't have any unnecessary spaces around punctuation. Then choose the Generate Linguistic Info command again. You can edit the text representation by selecting text in the Text Representation text box and using the Cut, Copy, and Paste commands on the Edit menu. If you are uncertain of the words the sound file includes, you can play the sound file by choosing Play from the Edit menu or the editor's toolbar. If the editor still fails to produce linguistic labels, try recording your sound file again. A poor quality recording, especially with excessive background noise, is likely to reduce the probability of generating reasonable linguistic information.

To see how the linguistic information could be used for lip-syncing character animation with Microsoft Agent, choose the Play button on the toolbar and the editor will play your sound file, animating a sample mouth image based on the generated label information.

You can change the phoneme label display to show the IPA (International Phonetic Alphabet) assignments by choosing the Phoneme Label Display command on the Edit menu, then the IPA command. This displays the byte value for the phoneme. To change back to the descriptive names, choose the Phoneme Label Display command again, and then choose Name.

Playing a Sound File

You can play standard Windows sound files or linguistically enhanced sound files by choosing the Play command from the Audio menu or the editor's toolbar. The Pause and Stop commands enable you to pause or stop playing the sound file. As you play the file, the sample mouth image animates to show how the lip-sync information could be used by a Microsoft Agent character.

You can also play a selected portion of a sound file by dragging a selection in the Audio Representation or clicking a word or phoneme label, then choosing Play. You can extend an existing selection by pressing SHIFT and clicking or pressing SHIFT and dragging to the new location in the Audio Representation.

Editing Linguistic Information

You can edit a file's linguistic information in several ways. For example, you can adjust a word or phoneme label's boundary by moving the pointer to the edge of the box that defines the range of the label. When the pointer changes to the boundary move pointer, drag left or right. The editor automatically adjusts the adjacent word or phoneme boundary as well.

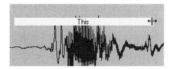

FIGURE 8-4. Adjusting a Word or Phoneme Label Boundary

Adjusting a phoneme label's boundary changes the timing of a phoneme when the audio plays. For characters developed for use with Microsoft Agent, changing the phoneme label boundary may change the timing or duration for a mouth image mapped to that phoneme. Changing the boundary of a word label changes the timing of the word's appearance in the character's word balloon.

You can also replace a phoneme assignment by selecting the phoneme label and choosing Replace Phoneme from the Edit menu, or right-clicking the phoneme label and choosing Replace Phoneme from the pop-up menu. The editor displays the Replace Phoneme dialog box and highlights the label's current phoneme assignment. You can choose a replacement phoneme by selecting one in the IPA list or by choosing another entry in the Name list. If more than one IPA translation is available for that name, choose an item in the IPA list. To enter an IPA designation for a phoneme that may not be directly included in the language, type in its hex value or multiple hex values, concatenated with a plus (+) character. Once you have selected the replacement phoneme information, choose OK, and the editor replaces the phoneme label you selected.

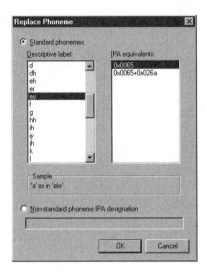

FIGURE 8-5. Replace Phoneme Dialog Box

Similarly, you can replace a word label by clicking the label's box and choosing Replace Word, or by right-clicking the label's box and choosing Replace Word from the pop-up menu. The editor displays the Replace Word dialog box. Enter the replacement word and choose OK.

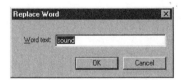

FIGURE 8-6. Replace Word Dialog Box

For characters developed for use with Microsoft Agent, replacing a phoneme label may change the mouth image displayed when the sound file plays. Replacing a word replaces the text that appears in the character's word balloon when the **Speak** method is called.

You can also insert a new phoneme label or word by making a selection in the Audio Representation and choosing Insert Phoneme or Insert Word from the Edit menu, or right-clicking within the selection and choosing the commands from the pop-up menu. These commands bring up dialog boxes similar to the Replace Phoneme and Replace Word dialog boxes, except that the editor inserts the new word or phoneme rather than replacing the existing information.

Finally, you can delete a phoneme or word by selecting its label and choosing Delete Phoneme or Delete Word. This removes its linguistic information from the file.

Saving a Sound File

When you are ready to save your sound file, choose the Save command on the File menu or on the editor's toolbar. The editor displays the Save As dialog box and proposes a name and default file type based on whether you generated linguistic information for the file. If you save the file as a sound file (.WAV), the editor saves just the audio data. If you save the file information as a linguistically enhanced sound file (.LWV), the word and phoneme information are automatically included as part of a modified sound file. Once you have confirmed or edited the name, location, file type, and format, choose the Save button.

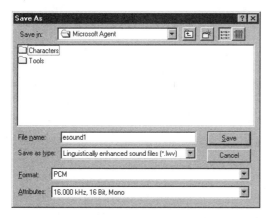

FIGURE 8-7. The Save As Dialog Box

If you want to save a sound file with a new name, different location, or different format, choose the Save As command on the File menu. When the Save As dialog box appears, type in the new file name and click the Save button.

You can also save a portion of the sound file. For example, you may want to save the file without excessive silence at its beginning or end. In the Audio Representation, select the portion of the file you want to save, and choose Save Selection As from the File menu. The command is enabled only when you have a selection in the Audio Representation.

Microsoft Linguistic Information Sound Editing Tool Command Reference

The File Menu

New

Resets the sound editor for creating a new enhanced sound file. If an existing sound file is loaded and has unsaved edits, the sound editor displays a message to determine whether to save or discard unsaved changes.

Open

Displays the Open dialog box, enabling you to open an existing sound file. If an existing sound file is loaded and has unsaved edits, the sound editor displays a message to determine whether to save or discard unsaved changes.

Save

Saves a sound file. If the sound file does not exist (has not been named), the sound editor displays the Save As dialog box for input of the file name.

Save As

Displays the Save As dialog box, enabling you to enter a new name for the sound file.

Save Selection As

Displays the Save Selection As dialog box, enabling you to enter a name for the selected part of the sound file.

Most Recently Open Files

Keeps track of the recent character definition files you opened. Choosing a file automatically opens that file for editing. If an existing character is loaded and has unsaved edits to a file, the sound editor displays a message to determine whether to save or discard unsaved changes.

Exit

Quits the sound editor. If an existing file is loaded and has unsaved edits, the sound editor displays a message to determine whether to save or discard unsaved changes.

The Edit Menu

Undo

Removes a change made in the sound editor.

Redo

Reverses an undo action in the sound editor.

Cut

Removes the selected text and places it on the clipboard.

Copy

Copies the selected text to the clipboard.

Paste

Copies text on the clipboard to the insertion point or selection in the Text Representation text box.

Delete

Removes the selected text.

Select All

Selects the text in the Text Representation text box.

Generate Linguistic Info

Begins generating word-break and phoneme information for a sound file.

Insert Phoneme

Displays the Insert Phoneme dialog box that enables you to insert a selected phoneme label.

Replace Phoneme

Displays the Replace Phoneme dialog box that enables you to replace the selected phoneme label.

Delete Phoneme

Deletes the selected phoneme label.

Insert Word

Displays the Insert Word dialog box that enables you to insert a word label in the Audio Representation.

Replace Word

Displays the Replace Word dialog box that enables you to replace the selected word label in the Audio Representation.

Delete Word

Deletes the selected word label in the Audio Representation.

Phoneme Label Display

Changes the phoneme label display between descriptive names and IPA byte values.

The Audio Menu

Play

Plays the sound file or selected portion of the sound file.

Record

Records a new sound file.

Pause

Pauses the play of the sound file or selected portion of the sound file. Use Play to resume playing.

Stop

Stops recording or playing the sound file or selected portion of the sound file.

The Help Menu

Help Topics

Displays the Help Topics dialog box, enabling you to select a sound editor help topic.

About Microsoft Linguistic Sound Editing Tool

Displays a dialog box with copyright and version information for the sound editor.

Toolbar buttons

New

Resets the sound editor for creating a new sound file. If an existing sound file is loaded and has unsaved edits, the sound editor displays a message to determine whether to save or discard unsaved changes.

Open

Displays the Open File dialog box, enabling you to open an existing sound file. If an existing sound file is loaded and has unsaved edits, the sound editor displays a message to determine whether to save or discard unsaved changes.

Save

Saves the sound file. If the file does not exist (has not been named), the editor displays the Save As dialog box for input of the file name.

Cut

Removes the selected text from the editor and places it on the Windows Clipboard.

 Copy

Copies the selected text in the editor to the Windows Clipboard.

 Paste

Copies text from the current Windows Clipboard to the selected location in the Text Representation text box.

 Delete

Removes the selected text from the sound editor.

 Undo

Removes a change made in the sound editor.

 Redo

Reverses an undo action in the sound editor

 Generate Linguistic Info

Generates phoneme and word labels for the sound file.

 Pause

Pauses playing of the sound file.

 Play

Plays the sound file or selected portion of the sound file.

■ **Stop**

Stops recording or playing the sound file or selected portion of the sound file.

● **Record**

Starts recording a sound file.

C H A P T E R   9

Microsoft Agent Speech Output Tags

The Microsoft Agent services support modifying speech output through special tags inserted in the speech text string. These tags help you change the characteristics of the output expression of the character.

Speech output tags use the following rules of syntax:

- All tags begin and end with a backslash character (\).

- The single backslash character is not enabled *within* a tag. To include a backslash character in a text parameter of a tag, use a double backslash (\\).

- Tags are case-insensitive. For example, \pit\ is the same as \PIT\.

- Tags are whitespace-dependent. For example, \Rst\ is not the same as \ Rst \.

Unless otherwise specified or modified by another tag, the speech output retains the characteristic set by the tag within the text specified in a single **Speak** method. Speech output is automatically reset through the user-defined parameters after a **Speak** method is completed.

Some tags include quoted strings. For some programming languages, such as Visual Basic Scripting Edition (VBScript) and Visual Basic, this means that you may have to use two quote marks to designate the tag's parameter or concatenate a double-quote character as part of the string. The latter is shown in this Visual Basic example:

```
Agent1.Characters("Genie").Speak "This is \map=" + chr(34) + _
   "Spoken text" + chr(34) + "=" + chr(34) + "Balloon text" _
   + chr(34) + "\."
```

For C, C++, and Java programming, precede backslashes and double quotes with a backslash. For example:

```
BSTR bszSpeak = SysAllocString(L"This is \\map=\"Spoken text"=\ _
   "Balloon text\"\\");


pCharacter->Speak(bszSpeak, ......);
```

For foreign languages that support double-byte character set (DBCS) characters, you can use double-byte characters to specify string parameters. However, use single-byte characters for all other parameters and characters that are used to define the tag, including the tag itself.

The following tags are supported:

Chr	**Ctx**	**Emp**	**Lst**	**Map**	**Mrk**
Pau	**Pit**	**Rst**	**Spd**	**Vol**	

The tags are primarily designed for adjusting text-to-speech (TTS)-generated output. Only the **Mrk** and **Map** tags can be used with sound file-based spoken output.

Note Microsoft Agent does not support all the tags documented in the Microsoft Speech SDK. Parameters may also vary depending on the TTS engine installed.

Chr Tag

Description   Sets the character of the voice.

Syntax   **Chr**=*string*\\

Part	Description
string	A string specifying the character of the voice.

"Normal"	(Default) A normal tone of voice.
"Monotone"	A monotone voice.
"Whisper"	A whispered voice.

Remarks   This tag is supported only for TTS-generated output. The range of values for the parameter may vary depending on the installed TTS engine.

Ctx Tag

Description

Sets the context of the output text.

Syntax

Ctx=*string*\\

Part	Description
string	A string specifying the context of the text that follows, which determines how symbols or abbreviations are spoken.

"Address"	Addresses and/or phone numbers.
"Email"	Electronic mail.
"Unknown"	(Default) Context is unknown.

Remarks

This tag is supported only for TTS-generated output. The range of values for the parameter may vary depending on the installed TTS engine.

Emp Tag

Description

Emphasizes the next word spoken. This tag must immediately precede the word.

Syntax

Emp\\

Remarks

This tag is supported only for TTS-generated output. The range of values for the parameter may vary depending on the installed TTS engine.

Lst Tag

Description

Repeats last spoken statement for the character.

Syntax

Lst\\

Remarks

This tag enables a character repeat its last spoken statement. This tag must appear by itself in the **Speak** method; no other text or parameters can be included. When the spoken text is repeated, any other tags included in the original text are repeated, except for bookmarks. Any .WAV and .LWV files included in the text are also repeated.

Map Tag

Description   Maps spoken text to text displayed in the word balloon.

Syntax   **Map**=*"spokentext"*=*"balloontext"*\\

Part	Description
spokentext	A string specifying the text for spoken output.
balloontext	A string specifying the text for word balloon output.

Remarks   This tag enables you to use different spoken text than that displayed in the word balloon.

Mrk Tag

Description   Defines a bookmark in the spoken text.

Syntax   **Mrk**=*number*\\

Part	Description
number	A Long integer value that identifies the bookmark.

Remarks   When the server processes a bookmark, it generates a bookmark event. You must specify a number greater than zero (0) and not equal to 2147483647 or 2147483646.

See also   **Bookmark** event

Pau Tag

Description   Pauses speech for the specified number of milliseconds.

Syntax   **Pau**=*number*\\

Part	Description
number	The number of milliseconds to pause.

Remarks

This tag is supported only for TTS-generated output. The range of values for the parameter may vary depending on the installed TTS engine. The speech engine supplied with Microsoft Agent supports values from 10 (0.01sec) to 2550 (2.55sec).

Pit Tag

Description

Sets the baseline pitch of the output to the specified value in Hertz.

Syntax

\Pit=*number*\

Part	Description
number	The pitch in Hertz.

Remarks

This tag is supported only for TTS-generated output. The range of values for the parameter may vary depending on the installed TTS engine. The speech engine supplied with Microsoft Agent supports values from 50 to 400.

Rst Tag

Description

Resets all tags to the default settings.

Syntax

\Rst\

Spd Tag

Description

Sets the baseline average talking speed of the speech output.

Syntax

\Spd=*number*\

Part	Description
number	Baseline average talking speed, in words per minute.

Remarks

This tag is supported only for TTS-generated output. The range of values for the parameter may vary depending on the installed TTS engine. The speech engine supplied with Microsoft Agent supports values from 50 to 250.

Vol Tag

Description   Sets the baseline speaking volume of the speech output.

Syntax   \Vol=*number*\

Part	Description
number	Baseline speaking volume: 0 is silence and 65535 is maximum volume.

Remarks   The volume setting affects both left and right channels. You cannot set the volume of each channel separately. This tag is supported only for TTS-generated output.

APPENDIX A

Animations for Microsoft Characters

Animations for Genie Character

If accessing these character animations using the HTTP protocol and the control's **Get** or server's **Prepare** method, consider how you will download them. Instead of downloading all the animations at once, you may want to retrieve the **Showing** and **Speaking** state animations first. This will allow you to display the character quickly and have it speak while bringing down other animations asynchronously. In addition, to ensure that character and animation data load successfully, use the **RequestComplete** event. If a load request fails, you can retry loading the data or display an appropriate message.

Animation	Return Animation	Supports Speaking	Assigned to State	Description
Acknowledge	None	No	None	Nods head
Alert	**AlertReturn**	Yes	**Listening**	Straightens and raises eyebrows
AlertReturn	None	No	None	Returns to neutral position
Announce	**AnnounceReturn**	Yes	None	Raises hand
AnnounceReturn	None	No	None	Returns to neutral position
Blink	None	No	**IdlingLevel1**	Blinks eyes
Confused	**ConfusedReturn**	Yes	None	Scratches head
ConfusedReturn	None	No	None	Returns to neutral position

Animation	Return Animation	Supports Speaking	Assigned to State	Description
Congratulate	**CongratulateReturn**	Yes	None	Thumbs-up gesture
CongratulateReturn	None	No	None	Returns to neutral position
Decline	**DeclineReturn**	Yes	None	Raises hands and shakes head
DeclineReturn	None	No	None	Returns to neutral position
DontRecognize	**DontRecognizeReturn**	Yes	None	Holds hand to ear
DontRecognizeReturn	None	No	None	Returns to neutral position
Explain	**ExplainReturn**	Yes	None	Extends arms to side
ExplainReturn	None	No	None	Returns to neutral position
GestureDown	**GestureDownReturn**	Yes	**GesturingDown**	Gestures down
GestureDownReturn	None	No	None	Returns to neutral position
GestureLeft	**GestureLeftReturn**	Yes	**GesturingLeft**	Gestures left
GestureLeftReturn	None	No	None	Returns to neutral position
GestureRight	**GestureRightReturn**	Yes	**GesturingRight**	Gestures right
GestureRightReturn	None	No	None	Returns to neutral position
GestureUp	**GestureUpReturn**	Yes	**GesturingUp**	Gestures up
GestureUpReturn	None	No	None	Returns to neutral position
GetAttention	**GetAttentionReturn**	Yes	None	Waves arms
GetAttentionReturn	None	No	None	Returns to neutral position
GlanceDown	None	No	None	Looks down briefly

Animation	Return Animation	Supports Speaking	Assigned to State	Description
GlanceLeft	None	No	None	Looks left briefly
GlanceRight	None	No	None	Looks right briefly
GlanceUp	None	No	None	Looks up briefly
Greet	**GreetReturn**	Yes	None	Bows
GreetReturn	None	No	None	Returns to neutral position
Hear_1	None	No	**Hearing**	Ears extend
Hear_2	None	No	**Hearing**	Tilts head left
Hear_3	None	No	**Hearing**	Turns head left
Hear_4	None	No	**Hearing**	Turns head right
Hide	None	No	**Hiding**	Disappears
Idle1_1	None	No	**IdlingLevel1**	Takes breath
Idle1_2	None	No	**IdlingLevel1**	Glances left and blinks
Idle1_3	None	No	**IdlingLevel1**	Glance right and blinks
Idle1_4	None	No	**IdlingLevel1**	Glances up to the right and blinks
Idle1_5	None	No	**IdlingLevel1**	Glances down and blinks
Idle1_6	None	No	**IdlingLevel1**	Glances up and blinks
Idle2_1	None	No	**IdlingLevel2**	Blinks and moves wisp
Idle2_2	None	No	**IdlingLevel2**	Reads
Idle2_3	None	No	**IdlingLevel2**	Writes
Idle3_1	**Idle3_1Return**	No	**IdlingLevel3**	Falls asleep
Idle3_1Return	None	No	None	Returns to neutral position
Idle3_2	None	No	**IdlingLevel3**	Yawns

Animation	Return Animation	Supports Speaking	Assigned to State	Description
LookDown	None	No	None	Looks down
LookDownBlink	None	No	None	Looks down and blinks
LookDownReturn	None	No	None	Returns to neutral position
LookLeft	None	No	None	Looks left
LookLeftBlink	None	No	None	Looks left and blinks
LookLeftReturn	None	No	None	Returns to neutral position
LookRight	None	No	None	Looks right
LookRightBlink	None	No	None	Looks right and blinks
LookRightReturn	None	No	None	Returns to neutral position
LookUp	None	No	None	Looks up
LookUpBlink	None	No	None	Looks up and blinks
LookUpReturn	None	No	None	Returns to neutral position
MoveDown	**MoveDownReturn**	No	**MovingDown**	Flies down
MoveDownReturn	None	No	None	Returns to neutral position
MoveLeft	**MoveLeftReturn**	No	**MovingLeft**	Flies left
MoveLeftReturn	None	No	None	Returns to neutral position
MoveRight	**MoveRightReturn**	No	**MovingRight**	Flies right
MoveRightReturn	None	No	None	Returns to neutral position
MoveUp	**MoveUpReturn**	No	**MovingUp**	Flies up
MoveUpReturn	None	No	None	Returns to neutral position

Animation	Return Animation	Supports Speaking	Assigned to State	Description
Pleased	**PleasedReturn**	Yes	None	Clasps hands and smiles
PleasedReturn	None	No	None	Returns to neutral position
Processing	**ProcessingReturn**	No	None	Spins (*looping animation)
ProcessingReturn	None	No	None	Returns to neutral position
Read	None	Yes	None	Takes scroll out of vest, reads and looks up
ReadContinued	None	Yes	None	Reads and looks up
ReadReturn	None	No	None	Returns to neutral position
Reading	**ReadingReturn**	No	None	Reads (*looping animation)
ReadingReturn	None	No	None	Returns to neutral position
RestPose	None	Yes	**Speaking**	Neutral position
Sad	**SadReturn**	Yes	None	Sad expression
SadReturn	None	No	None	Returns to neutral position
Searching	**SearchingReturn**	No	None	Spins and looks through binoculars (*looping animation)
SearchingReturn	None	No	None	Returns to neutral position
Show	None	No	**Showing**	Appears in a puff of smoke
StartListening	**StartListeningReturn**	Yes	None	Puts hand to ear
StartListeningReturn	None	No	None	Returns to neutral position

* If you play a looping animation, you must use **Stop** to clear it before other animations in the character's queue will play.

Animation	Return Animation	Supports Speaking	Assigned to State	Description
StopListening	**StopListeningReturn**	Yes	None	Puts hands to ears
StopListeningReturn	None	No	None	Returns to neutral position
Suggest	**SuggestReturn**	Yes	None	Displays light bulb
SuggestReturn	None	No	None	Returns to neutral position
Surprised	**SurprisedReturn**	Yes	None	Looks surprised
SurprisedReturn	None	No	None	Returns to neutral position
Think	**ThinkReturn**	Yes	None	Looks up with hand on chin
ThinkReturn	None	No	None	Returns to neutral position
Uncertain	**UncertainReturn**	Yes	None	Raises eyebrow with hand on chin
UncertainReturn	None	No	None	Returns to neutral position
Wave	**WaveReturn**	Yes	None	Waves
WaveReturn	None	No	None	Returns to neutral position
Write	None	Yes	None	Takes scroll out of vest, writes and looks up
WriteContinued	None	Yes	None	Writes and looks up
WriteReturn	None	No	None	Returns to neutral position
Writing	**WritingReturn**	No	None	Writes (*looping animation)
WritingReturn	None	No	None	Returns to neutral position

*If you play a looping animation, you must use **Stop** to clear it before other animations in the character's queue will play.

Animations for Robby Character

If accessing these character animations using the HTTP protocol and the control's **Get** or server's **Prepare** method, consider how you will download them. Instead of downloading all the animations at once, you may want to retrieve the **Showing** and **Speaking** state animations first. This will allow you to display the character quickly and have it speak while bringing down other animations asynchronously. In addition, to ensure that character and animation data load successfully, use the **RequestComplete** event. If a load request fails, you can retry loading the data or display an appropriate message.

Animation	Return Animation	Supports Speaking	Assigned to State	Description
Acknowledge	None	No	None	Nods head
Alert	**AlertReturn**	No	**Listening**	Straightens and raises eyebrows
AlertReturn	None	No	None	Returns to neutral position
Announce	**AnnounceReturn**	Yes	None	Prints output and reads
AnnounceReturn	None	No	None	Returns to neutral position
Blink	None	No	**IdlingLevel1**	Blinks eyes
Confused	**ConfusedReturn**	Yes	None	Scratches head
ConfusedReturn	None	No	None	Returns to neutral position
Congratulate	**CongratulateReturn**	Yes	None	Raises then clasps hands and smiles
CongratulateReturn	None	No	None	Returns to neutral position
Decline	**DeclineReturn**	Yes	None	Raises hands and shakes head
DeclineReturn	None	No	None	Returns to neutral position
DontRecognize	**DontRecognizeReturn**	Yes	None	Holds hand to ear

Animation	Return Animation	Supports Speaking	Assigned to State	Description
DontRecognizeReturn	None	No	None	Returns to neutral position
Explain	**ExplainReturn**	Yes	None	Extends arms to side
ExplainReturn	None	No	None	Returns to neutral position
GestureDown	**GestureDownReturn**	Yes	**GesturingDown**	Gestures down
GestureDownReturn	None	No	None	Returns to neutral position
GestureLeft	**GestureLeftReturn**	Yes	**GesturingLeft**	Gestures left
GestureLeftReturn	None	No	None	Returns to neutral position
GestureRight	**GestureRightReturn**	Yes	**GesturingRight**	Gestures right
GestureRightReturn	None	No	None	Returns to neutral position
GestureUp	**GestureUpReturn**	Yes	**GesturingUp**	Gestures up
GestureUpReturn	None	No	None	Returns to neutral position
GetAttention	**GetAttentionReturn**	Yes	None	Raises and shakes arms
GetAttentionReturn	None	No	None	Returns to neutral position
GlanceDown	None	No	None	Looks down briefly
GlanceLeft	None	No	None	Looks left briefly
GlanceRight	None	No	None	Looks right briefly
GlanceUp	None	No	None	Looks up briefly
Greet	**GreetReturn**	Yes	None	Waves
GreetReturn	None	No	None	Returns to neutral position
Hear_1	None	No	**Hearing**	Turns head left

Animation	Return Animation	Supports Speaking	Assigned to State	Description
Hear_2	None	No	Hearing	Turns head right
Hear_3	None	No	Hearing	Tilts head right
Hear_4	None	No	Hearing	Tilts head forward
Hide	None	No	Hiding	Disappears under cap
Idle1_1	None	No	IdlingLevel1	Glances right
Idle1_2	None	No	IdlingLevel1	Glances up to the left
Idle2_1	None	No	IdlingLevel2	Crosses arms
Idle2_2	None	No	IdlingLevel2	Removes head and makes adjustment
Idle3_1	Idle3_1Return	No	IdlingLevel3	Falls asleep
Idle3_1Return	None	No	None	Returns to neutral position
Idle3_2	None	No	IdlingLevel3	Yawns
LookDown	LookDownReturn	No	None	Looks down
LookDownReturn	None	No	None	Returns to neutral position
LookLeft	LookLeftReturn	No	None	Looks left
LookLeftReturn	None	No	None	Returns to neutral position
LookRight	LookRightReturn	No	None	Looks right
LookRightReturn	None	No	None	Returns to neutral position
LookUp	LookUpReturn	No	None	Looks up
LookUpReturn	None	No	None	Returns to neutral position
MoveDown	MoveDownReturn	No	MovingDown	Flies down
MoveDownReturn	None	No	None	Returns to neutral position

Animation	Return Animation	Supports Speaking	Assigned to State	Description
MoveLeft	MoveLeftReturn	No	MovingLeft	Flies left
MoveLeftReturn	None	No	None	Returns to neutral position
MoveRight	MoveRightReturn	No	MovingRight	Flies right
MoveRightReturn	None	No	None	Returns to neutral position
MoveUp	MoveUpReturn	No	MovingUp	Flies up
MoveUpReturn	None	No	None	Returns to neutral position
Pleased	PleasedReturn	Yes	None	Straightens body and smiles
PleasedReturn	None	No	None	Returns to neutral position
Processing	ProcessingReturn	No	None	Presses buttons (*looping animation)
ProcessingReturn	None	No	None	Returns to neutral position
Read	None	Yes	None	Tears off printout, reads and looks up
ReadContinued	None	Yes	None	Reads and looks up
ReadReturn	None	No	None	Returns to neutral position
Reading	ReadingReturn	No	None	Reads (*looping animation)
ReadingReturn	None	No	None	Returns to neutral position
RestPose	None	Yes	Speaking	Neutral position
Sad	SadReturn	Yes	None	Sad expression

*If you play a looping animation, you must use **Stop** to clear it before other animations in the character's queue will play.*

Animation	Return Animation	Supports Speaking	Assigned to State	Description
SadReturn	None	No	None	Returns to neutral position
Searching	SearchingReturn	No	None	Looks through toolbox (*looping animation)
SearchingReturn	None	No	None	Returns to neutral position
Show	None	No	Showing	Appears through door
StartListening	StartListeningReturn	Yes	None	Puts hand to ear
StartListeningReturn	None	No	None	Returns to neutral position
StopListening	StopListeningReturn	Yes	None	Puts hands to ears
StopListeningReturn	None	No	None	Returns to neutral position
Suggest	SuggestReturn	Yes	None	Displays light bulb
SuggestReturn	None	No	None	Returns to neutral position
Surprised	SurprisedReturn	Yes	None	Looks surprised
SurprisedReturn	None	No	None	Returns to neutral position
Think	ThinkReturn	Yes	None	Tilts head and scratches
ThinkReturn	None	No	None	Returns to neutral position
Uncertain	UncertainReturn	Yes	None	Shrugs
UncertainReturn	None	No	None	Returns to neutral position
Wave	WaveReturn	Yes	None	Waves

*If you play a looping animation, you must use **Stop** to clear it before other animations in the character's queue will play.*

Animation	Return Animation	Supports Speaking	Assigned to State	Description
WaveReturn	None	No	None	Returns to neutral position
Write	None	Yes	None	Takes out clipboard, writes and looks up
WriteContinued	None	Yes	None	Writes and looks up
WriteReturn	None	No	None	Returns to neutral position
Writing	**WritingReturn**	No	None	Writes (*looping animation)
WritingReturn	None	No	None	Returns to neutral position

** If you play a looping animation, you must use **Stop** to clear it before other animations in the character's queue will play.*

Animations for Merlin Character

If accessing these character animations using the HTTP protocol and the control's **Get** or server's **Prepare** method, consider how you will download them. Instead of downloading all the animations at once, you may want to retrieve the **Showing** and **Speaking** state animations first. This will allow you to display the character quickly and have it speak while bringing down other animations asynchronously. In addition, to ensure that character and animation data load successfully, use the **RequestComplete** event. If a load request fails, you can retry loading the data or display an appropriate message.

Animation	Return Animation	Supports Speaking	Assigned to State	Description
Acknowledge	None	No	None	Nods head
Alert	**AlertReturn**	Yes	Listening	Straightens and raises eyebrows
AlertReturn	None	No	None	Returns to neutral position

Animation	Return Animation	Supports Speaking	Assigned to State	Description
Announce	AnnounceReturn	Yes	None	Raises trumpet and plays
AnnounceReturn	None	No	None	Returns to neutral position
Blink	None	No	IdlingLevel1	Blinks eyes
Confused	ConfusedReturn	Yes	None	Scratches head
ConfusedReturn	None	No	None	Returns to neutral position
Congratulate	CongratulateReturn	Yes	None	Displays trophy
CongratulateReturn	None	No	None	Returns to neutral position
Congratulate_2	PleasedReturn	Yes	None	Applauds
Decline	DeclineReturn	Yes	None	Raises hands and shakes head
DeclineReturn	None	No	None	Returns to neutral position
DoMagic1	None	Yes	None	Raises magic wand
DoMagic2	DoMagicReturn	No	None	Lowers wand, clouds appear
DoMagicReturn	None	No	None	Returns to neutral position
DontRecognize	DontRecognizeReturn	Yes	None	Holds hand to ear
DontRecognizeReturn	None	No	None	Returns to neutral position
Explain	ExplainReturn	Yes	None	Extends arms to side
ExplainReturn	None	No	None	Returns to neutral position
GestureDown	GestureDownReturn	Yes	GesturingDown	Gestures down
GestureDownReturn	None	No	None	Returns to neutral position
GestureLeft	GestureLeftReturn	Yes	GesturingLeft	Gestures left

Animation	Return Animation	Supports Speaking	Assigned to State	Description
GestureLeftReturn	None	No	None	Returns to neutral position
GestureRight	**GestureRightReturn**	Yes	**GesturingRight**	Gestures right
GestureRightReturn	None	No	None	Returns to neutral position
GestureUp	**GestureUpReturn**	Yes	**GesturingUp**	Gestures up
GestureUpReturn	None	No	None	Returns to neutral position
GetAttention	**GetAttentionReturn**	Yes	None	Leans forward and knocks
GetAttentionReturn	None	No	None	Returns to neutral position
GlanceDown	None	No	None	Looks down briefly
GlanceLeft	None	No	None	Looks left briefly
GlanceRight	None	No	None	Looks right briefly
GlanceUp	None	No	None	Looks up briefly
Greet	**GreetReturn**	Yes	None	Bows
GreetReturn	None	No	None	Returns to neutral position
Hear_1	None	No	**Hearing**	Ears extend
Hear_2	None	No	**Hearing**	Tilts head left
Hear_3	None	No	**Hearing**	Turns head left
Hear_4	None	No	**Hearing**	Turns head right
Hide	None	No	**Hiding**	Disappears under cap
Idle1_1	None	No	**IdlingLevel1**	Takes breath
Idle1_2	None	No	**IdlingLevel1**	Glances left and blinks
Idle1_3	None	No	**IdlingLevel1**	Glances right

Animation	Return Animation	Supports Speaking	Assigned to State	Description
Idle1_4	None	No	**IdlingLevel1**	Glances up to the right and blinks
Idle2_1	None	No	**IdlingLevel2**	Looks at wand and blinks
Idle2_2	None	No	**IdlingLevel2**	Holds hands and blinks
Idle3_1	**Idle3_1Return**	No	**IdlingLevel3**	Falls asleep
Idle3_1Return	None	No	None	Returns to neutral position
Idle3_2	None	No	**IdlingLevel3**	Yawns
LookDown	None	No	None	Looks down
LookDownBlink	None	No	None	Blinks looking down
LookDownReturn	None	No	None	Returns to neutral position
LookLeft	None	No	None	Looks left
LookLeftBlink	None	No	None	Blinks looking left
LookLeftReturn	None	No	None	Returns to neutral position
LookRight	None	No	None	Looks right
LookRightBlink	None	No	None	Blinks looking right
LookRightReturn	None	No	None	Returns to neutral position
LookUp	None	No	None	Looks up
LookUpBlink	None	No	None	Blinks looking up
LookUpReturn	None	No	None	Returns to neutral position
MoveDown	**MoveDownReturn**	No	**MovingDown**	Flies down
MoveDownReturn	None	No	None	Returns to neutral position

Animation	Return Animation	Supports Speaking	Assigned to State	Description
MoveLeft	MoveLeftReturn	No	MovingLeft	Flies left
MoveLeftReturn	None	No	None	Returns to neutral position
MoveRight	MoveRightReturn	No	MovingRight	Flies right
MoveRightReturn	None	No	None	Returns to neutral position
MoveUp	MoveUpReturn	No	MovingUp	Flies up
MoveUpReturn	None	No	None	Returns to neutral position
Pleased	PleasedReturn	Yes	None	Smiles and holds hands together
PleasedReturn	None	No	None	Returns to neutral position
Processing	ProcessingReturn	No	None	Stirs caldron (*looping animation)
ProcessingReturn	None	No	None	Returns to neutral position
Read	None	Yes	None	Opens book, reads and looks up
ReadContinued	None	Yes	None	Reads and looks up
ReadReturn	None	No	None	Returns to neutral position
Reading	ReadingReturn	No	None	Reads (*looping animation)
ReadingReturn	None	No	None	Returns to neutral position
RestPose	None	Yes	Speaking	Neutral position
Sad	SadReturn	Yes	None	Sad expression

* If you play a looping animation, you must use **Stop** to clear it before other animations in the character's queue will play.

Animation	Return Animation	Supports Speaking	Assigned to State	Description
SadReturn	None	No	None	Returns to neutral position
Searching	SearchingReturn	No	None	Looks into crystal ball (*looping animation)
SearchingReturn	None	No	None	Returns to neutral position
Show	None	No	Showing	Appears out of cap
StartListening	StartListeningReturn	Yes	None	Puts hand to ear
StartListeningReturn	None	No	None	Returns to neutral position
StopListening	StopListeningReturn	Yes	None	Puts hands to ears
StopListeningReturn	None	No	None	Returns to neutral position
Suggest	SuggestReturn	Yes	None	Displays light bulb
SuggestReturn	None	No	None	Returns to neutral position
Surprised	SurprisedReturn	Yes	None	Looks surprised
SurprisedReturn	None	No	None	Returns to neutral position
Think	ThinkReturn	Yes	None	Looks up with hand on chin
ThinkReturn	None	No	None	Returns to neutral position
Uncertain	UncertainReturn	Yes	None	Leans forward and raises eyebrow
UncertainReturn	None	No	None	Returns to neutral position
Wave	WaveReturn	Yes	None	Waves

*If you play a looping animation, you must use **Stop** to clear it before other animations in the character's queue will play.*

Animation	Return Animation	Supports Speaking	Assigned to State	Description
WaveReturn	None	No	None	Returns to neutral position
Write	None	Yes	None	Opens book, writes and looks up
WriteContinued	None	Yes	None	Writes and looks up
WriteReturn	None	No	None	Returns to neutral position
Writing	**WritingReturn**	No	None	Writes (*looping animation)
WritingReturn	None	No	None	Returns to neutral position

** If you play a looping animation, you must use **Stop** to clear it before other animations in the character's queue will play.*

A P P E N D I X   B

Troubleshooting Microsoft Agent

If you have difficulty running Microsoft Agent on your machine, please refer to the following list of symptoms and try the suggested steps to isolate and solve the problem. If these suggestions don't resolve the problem, let us know by sending us a bug report by using the Contacting Us option at http://www.microsoft.com/workshop/prog/agent. You can also visit this site for the latest update to this information.

Page Loading or Installation Problems

When I attempt to load a page scripted for Microsoft Agent, nothing happens.

This can occur if one of the following conditions exists:

- Check your browser's security options. Your browser must be set to enable the loading of ActiveX scripts and playing of ActiveX controls.

- If you are accessing pages scripted with Microsoft Agent and using Microsoft Internet Explorer, you must have version 3.0 or later (download the latest version of Internet Explorer). In Microsoft Internet Explorer, open the View menu, choose Options, click the Security tab, and check all the Active Content check boxes.

- A Java applet on the page can also cause this error. To run Microsoft Agent on the same page as a Java applet requires version 2.0 of the Microsoft Java VM. For more information, see Appendix C, "Microsoft Agent Technical FAQ."

When I attempt to load a page scripted for Microsoft Agent, I get the message, "Unable to initialize Microsoft Agent."

This usually occurs when you don't have Microsoft Agent or some other control that page uses installed, and choose No when you are prompted to install the control. Try refreshing the page, though the page may work only if you install all the components it requires.

When I attempt to load a page scripted for Microsoft Agent, I get a scripting error: "Microsoft VBScript Runtime Error, Object required."

One of the following conditions may cause the message to display:

- Your security options for Microsoft Internet Explorer must be set to enable ActiveX controls and plug-ins. Check your browser's security page. In Microsoft Internet Explorer, open the View menu, choose Options, click the Security tab, and make sure the Enable ActiveX Controls And Plug-Ins check box is checked.

- You are running on a dual-boot Windows 95/Windows NT system and you have installed Microsoft Agent on one operating system but are trying to access the page from the other operating system. Although the operating systems may share directories and files, the registry information used by Microsoft Agent is not shared, so you must install Microsoft Agent on the operating system you use to access Web pages scripted with the character.

When I attempt to install Microsoft Agent on Microsoft Windows NT, I get a message indicating that I need to be an administrator.

Because Microsoft Agent writes files to your system directory when it installs, you must have administrator (not user) privileges to install.

When I attempt to install Microsoft Agent on Windows NT 4.0, I get the following error: Process (Regsvr32 /s Progra~1\Micros~2\AgentCtl.dll). Error while creating this file. Cannot find this file.

Installation of Microsoft Agent requires the proper installation of Regsvr32.exe (and other OLE dlls). The best way to ensure that all the correct system files are present is to install Microsoft Internet Explorer 3.02 or later.

When I attempt to load a page scripted for Microsoft Agent using Netscape Navigator (or other Internet browsers), I get errors.

Microsoft Agent is implemented using ActiveX interfaces. You can use it only with a browser (such as Microsoft Internet Explorer) that supports embedding ActiveX objects through script on a page, and only on systems running Microsoft Windows 95 and Windows NT 4.0. If you are not using Microsoft Internet Explorer, check with your browser vendor for further information on ActiveX support.

How do I remove Microsoft Agent from my system?

To uninstall Microsoft Agent, open the Control Panel, then open the Add/Remove Programs object. You should find Microsoft Agent included in the list. Select the entry, then click the Add/Remove button.

The Microsoft Agent uninstall utility removes only the Microsoft Agent services. If you also installed the Lernout & Hauspie TruVoice Text-To-Speech Engine for Microsoft Agent, select this and click the Add/Remove button. In addition, if you also installed Microsoft Command and Control speech recognition engine and you know that no other application uses it, you should select and remove the following entries:

Microsoft Command & Control Engine

Microsoft Speech Lexicon

Microsoft Speech API (3.0)

Speech Input Problems

The character does not respond to voice commands that I used to train it.

Voice training does not teach the character new commands. It does help the speech engine better recognize your voice input. The only way to teach the character new commands is to define voice commands as part of your Web page (application). Consult Chapter 4, "Programming the Microsoft Agent Control" for further information on how to do this.

The character does not respond to voice commands on a sample page.

Not all sample pages support speech input. The Goodbye World sample on the CD-ROM does. To speak to the character, press and hold the Scroll Lock key. If the character does not respond to any of these commands, check the following sections on troubleshooting voice input for additional recommendations.

The character does not respond to my voice input.

This symptom may be caused by a number of problems. Try the following to isolate the problem:

- Verify that your microphone is correctly plugged in. It is a good idea to test it with another sound input application to ensure that it works properly.

- Verify that a compatible speech engine is installed. When running a Microsoft Agent sample page, right-click the Microsoft Agent icon in the taskbar (near the clock display) and choose Microsoft Agent Properties. If the Speech Input page is disabled, a compatible speech engine is not installed. You can install the Microsoft Command and Control speech recognition engine from the CD-ROM.

- Verify that your sound card is compatible with Microsoft Windows 95 or Windows NT.

  The best way to do this is to run the Sound Recorder application that comes with Windows. It can usually be found on the Start menu. Click the Start button, then Programs, then Accessories, then Multimedia, and then Sound Recorder. When the Sound Recorder window displays, click the Record button and talk into your microphone. The line in the window should animate in response to your voice input.

  If the Sound Recorder application doesn't work on your system, contact the sound card manufacturer's technical support department for assistance. Your sound card may not be compatible with Windows or there may be a problem with the software drivers for your sound card.

- Verify that your sound input for speech input is set properly.

  1. Load a page scripted for Microsoft Agent. When the agent icon appears in the taskbar, right-click it and choose Microsoft Agent Properties from the pop-up menu.

  2. When the property sheet displays, select the Speech Input page.

3. Choose the Adjust Microphone button. If this button appears disabled, a compatible speech engine is not installed or the speech engine you installed may not support automatic adjustment.

- Verify that no other application is currently using the audio output device.

- Verify that Microsoft Agent's use of MIDI is not blocking the audio channel. (See "Applications that play MIDI have no audio output when Microsoft Agent is running" in the Output Problems section below.)

- If you followed the steps above but still have problems with speech input, verify that your sound card and driver software is compatible with the speech engine you are using. Check with the technical support for your sound card and your speech engine manufacturer. If you installed the Microsoft Command and Control speech recognition engine, check the troubleshooting information at http://www.research.microsoft.com/stg/sndcard.htm.

The character does not respond to voice input, but I can hear my voice through my speakers when I talk into my microphone.

Your sound card is not set up properly for use with Microsoft Agent. Choose the Adjust Microphone options on the Speech Input page of the Microsoft Agent property sheet. See the previous section for information on how to access this button.

Output Problems

The character doesn't produce any audio output when it speaks.

This symptom could have several causes. Try the following to isolate the problem:

- Verify that your speakers are plugged in and your sound card is compatible with Windows. It is a good idea to test them with another sound application to confirm that audio output is working properly.

- Verify that no other application is currently using the audio output device.

- Verify that the character you are using has been configured for spoken output. (You may need to check with the Web site or application supplier.)

- Verify that your Microsoft Agent settings are enabled for spoken output using the following procedure:

  1. Load a page scripted for Microsoft Agent. When the Microsoft Agent icon appears in the taskbar, right-click on it and choose Microsoft Agent Properties from the pop-up menu.

  2. When the property sheet displays, select the Output page.

  3. Set the Play Spoken Output option and click OK.

- Verify that Microsoft Agent's use of MIDI is not blocking the audio channel (see the topic below, "Applications that play MIDI have no audio output when Microsoft Agent is running").

- If the character uses a text-to-speech (TTS) engine to produce spoken output, verify that you have installed a compatible TTS engine. For example, when installed as an Internet Explorer 4.0 add-on component, only the core components of Microsoft Agent are installed. The core components do not include the Lernout & Hauspie TruVoice Text-To-Speech engine. Without this TTS engine (or compatible SAPI engine), Microsoft Agent sample characters will not produce spoken output. The Lernout & Hauspie TruVoice TTS engine can be found on the accompanying CD-ROM.

Applications that play MIDI have no audio output when Microsoft Agent is running

Microsoft Agent uses MIDI to play a tone when you press the Listening key. This may lock up the audio output channel for sound cards configured to play MIDI through the wave device audio output, causing speech recognition and speech output (and audio output from other applications) to fail. To resolve this conflict, turn off the Play Tone When You Can Speak option in the Microsoft Agent properties using the following procedure:

1. Load a page scripted for Microsoft Agent. When the Microsoft Agent icon appears in the taskbar, right-click on it and choose Microsoft Agent Properties from the pop-up menu.

2. When the property sheet displays, select the Speech Input page.

3. Uncheck the Play Tone When You Can Speak option and click OK.

A P P E N D I X   C

Microsoft Agent Technical FAQ

This appendix contains answers to many questions frequently asked by developers. For the most recent information, check http://www.microsoft.com/workshop/prog/agent/.

General

With the release of Microsoft Agent, will my pages built with previous beta releases still work?

The final commercial release of Microsoft Agent is not compatible with any previous beta releases. You should uninstall any beta releases and update to the final release. Any pages or applications authored for a beta release should also be updated to the final release.

When updating to the final release of Microsoft Agent, the following methods will ensure a clean, reliable installation:

- Uninstall any previous beta release **before** installing the commercial release.

- Do **not** install the beta releases over the commercial release. This will create an unreliable installation.

Can I define my own character?

Yes. You can use any animation rendering package, provided that you can produce your images in a 2-bit (monochrome), 4-bit, or 8-bit color Windows bitmap format. Then you can use the Microsoft Agent Character Editor, available for download at this site, to assemble and compile your animations.

Will Microsoft Agent be available for platforms other than Windows 95 and Windows NT?

We are still investigating the feasibility of and demand for this technology on other platforms.

Will Microsoft Agent be available in other languages?

Microsoft Agent will be available in the following languages in addition to English (US): French, German, Italian, Spanish, Simplified Chinese, Traditional Chinese, Korean, and Japanese. These versions of Microsoft Agent will include only the core services, not the speech input or output components. However, because Microsoft Agent supports the Microsoft SAPI interface, you may be able to use other speech engines. Contact your speech vendor to determine whether they are compatible with the SAPI interfaces required by Microsoft Agent. Availability of Microsoft Agent in other languages has not yet been determined.

Programming/Scripting

When I use Microsoft Visual Basic (or other development tools) for scripting Microsoft Agent, I do not see all the properties and events used in your samples. How do I access them?

Most of the events, methods, and properties supported by the Microsoft Agent control are exposed only at run time. Consult Chapter 4, "Programming the Microsoft Agent Control" for further information.

When I try to host the Microsoft Agent control on the same page as a Java applet, it doesn't seem to work.

This is a problem in the Internet Explorer Java VM that has been addressed in the Microsoft Java 2.0 SDK, which can be downloaded at http://microsoft.com/java/pre-sdk/default.htm. This version of the Java VM is expected to be included in a release of the Internet Explorer later this year.

The Map tag (or some other tag) doesn't seem to work.

Some tags include quoted strings. For some programming languages, such as Visual Basic Scripting Edition (VBScript) and Visual Basic, you may have to use two quote marks to designate the tag's parameter or concatenate a double-quote character as part of the string. The latter is shown in this Visual Basic example:

```
Agent1.Characters("Genie").Speak "This is \map=" + chr(34) + _
    "Spoken text" + chr(34) + "=" + chr(34) + "Balloon text" _
    + chr(34) + "\."
```

For C, C++, and Java programming, precede backslashes and double quotes with a backslash. For example:

```
BSTR bszSpeak = SysAllocString(L"This is \\map=\"Spoken text\ _
    "=\"Balloon text\"\\");


pCharacter->Speak(bszSpeak, ......);
```

Note that Microsoft Agent does not support all the tags specified in the Microsoft Speech API. In addition, support for some parameters may depend on the text-to-speech engine installed. For further information, see Chapter 9, "Microsoft Agent Speech Output Tags".

I seem to get RequestStart and RequestComplete events in my scripts even though I don't set any requests.

This is a problem in Visual Basic Scripting Edition (VBScript) 1.0. It has been addressed in VBScript 2.0, which can be downloaded at http://microsoft.com/msdownload/scripting.htm.

I don't seem to get RequestStart and RequestComplete events in my script (or program).

This could be caused by one of the following problems:

- Your programming language doesn't support ActiveX controls. Check your documentation to ensure that it supports the ActiveX interface and events for ActiveX objects.

- On a scripted Web page, another control has failed to install or load. Check to ensure that all other controls are installed and loading properly without Microsoft Agent.

- On a scripted Web page with frames, you have the <OBJECT> tag for the Microsoft Agent control on one page, and the events scripted on another page. Events are sent only to the page that hosts the control.

I am using the Microsoft Agent control with other ActiveX controls on my Web page, and I don't seem to get any events.

Check to see if the other controls are correctly installed. If another ActiveX control fails to correctly register itself, the Microsoft Agent control may receive its events.

What programming languages can I use to program the Microsoft Agent control?

Microsoft Agent should be supportable from any language that supports the ActiveX interface. It includes code samples for Microsoft Visual Basic, VBScript, JavaScript, C/C++, and Java.

Can I access the parameters returned from Microsoft Agent using JavaScript (JScript)?

Yes, but currently the only way to do this is using the <SCRIPT LANGUAGE ="JScript" FOR="*object*" EVENT="event()"> syntax. Although this syntax is supported for Microsoft Internet Explorer, it is not supported by other browsers, so you may want to avoid using JavaScript/JScript for this part of your page's script.

Can Microsoft Agent be used with speech recognition or speech synthesis (text-to-speech, or TTS) engines other than those supplied by Microsoft?

Yes, provided that the engine supports the Microsoft Speech API (SAPI) interfaces required by Microsoft Agent. Check with the engine supplier. Speech engine suppliers can contact the Microsoft Agent Product Group for details on SAPI requirements.

My page includes HTML Object tags for Microsoft Agent, the Lernout & Hauspie TruVoice TTS engine, and the Microsoft Command and Control speech recognition engine, but not all the components install.

We are investigating why this failure occurs. Typically, the problem can be corrected by refreshing the page. As a general practice, it is best to specify the Microsoft Agent Control <OBJECT> tag first, then the Lernout & Hauspie TruVoice engine, then the Command and Control speech recognition engine.

When I attempt to access the Lernout & Hauspie TruVoice Text-To-Speech Engine modes from the Microsoft Speech SDK tools, I get a message indicating that a password is required.

The text-to-speech engine included with Microsoft Agent does not support direct SAPI access. You can access the engine only by using the interfaces supported by Microsoft Agent. If you want to program the Lernout & Hauspie TruVoice Engine with Microsoft SAPI, contact Lernout & Hauspie.

After calling the MoveTo method, my character seems to freeze even though I have Return animations assigned to Moving state animations.

When you play an animation, the animation services continue to display its last frame until another animation is called. Therefore, you should play another animation after calling **MoveTo**. If you defined a **Return** animation for the **Moving** state animation, the server will play it first.

When running under Internet Explorer 4.0 Preview 1 or 2, events don't fire after Microsoft Agent has been running, or the character leaves behind parts of its animation.

These problems are related to the IE 4.0 Preview 1 and 2. Install the official commercial release of IE 4.0.

I cannot load a character when the URL includes a tilde (~) character.

Microsoft Agent does not accept tilde characters as part of a path.

When I attempt to retry loading a character that failed to load, the call fails with a "Character already loaded" error.

The Microsoft Agent control does not unload a character object (release the reference) when its associated character file fails to load. So if you want to retry loading the character, you must explicitly call Unload before you call Load the second time. If you attempt this from a Web page script, you also need to precede the Unload call with an On Error Resume Next statement, otherwise the Unload call will also fail.

However, you may not need to include code to immediately retry loading a character when the file fails to load. Microsoft Internet Explorer and the Microsoft Agent server component automatically attempt to retry several times, so the chances that retrying immediately will result in a successful load are remote. A better strategy would be to wait (set a timer) a few seconds before you retry.

Licensing

Can I redistribute Microsoft Agent and its characters?

Microsoft Agent can be downloaded directly from the Microsoft site by in-cluding the Microsoft Agent control's CLSID in an HTML <OBJECT> tag on your Web page, which will automatically offer to download and install the control when a user loads the page. Details on licensing and use are included in the Microsoft Agent End User License agreement that displays when Microsoft Agent is installed. This license does not include provisions for re-distribution. Application developers who wish to include Microsoft Agent and any of its components as part of their application must obtain a redistribution license. For more information about redistribution licenses, see Appendix E, "Microsoft Agent Licensing and Redistribution."

Can I redistribute the speech engines that are supplied with Microsoft Agent with my own applications?

The Microsoft Agent license agreement includes a license to use the Micro-soft Command and Control speech recognition engine and the special version of the Lernout & Hauspie TruVoice Text-To-Speech Engine, subject to the same provisions and restrictions as Microsoft Agent, and only when used with Microsoft Agent. For redistribution of these engines, contact the Microsoft Agent Product Group at msagent@microsoft.com. For redistribution of the speech engines only, contact the speech engine vendors directly.

Can I redistribute the Microsoft Agent Character Editor and Microsoft Linguistic Information Sound Editing Tool?

Redistribution of these tools is limited to downloading them from the Microsoft Web site or dispensing them as part of any software development kit Microsoft may provide. For other forms of redistribution, contact the Microsoft Agent Product Group at msagent@microsoft.com.

A P P E N D I X   D

Microsoft Agent Error Codes

Microsoft Agent returns the following error information:

Error Number	Hex Value	Description
–2147213310	0x80042002	Invalid character ID. The specified ID may be misspelled or not yet defined.
–2147213309	0x80042003	Animation not supported. Please verify that the animation name is correct.
–2147213308	0x80042004	No animation for this state. Please verify that an animation has been assigned to this state.
–2147213307	0x80042005	Sound file not found. Please verify that the path and filename are correct.
–2147213306	0x80042006	Command name not found. Please verify that the command name you specified is correct.
–2147213305	0x80042007	Command name already in use. The specified command name has already been defined.
–2147213302	0x8004200A	Character is hidden. The method failed because the character is hidden.
–2147213301	0x8004200B	Character already loaded. Please check for previous Load method calls.
–2147213300	0x8004200C	Invalid balloon access. There was an attempt to access the word balloon, but the character does not support a word balloon.
–2147213299	0x8004200D	Invalid Commands Window access. Display of the Commands Window requires speech recognition support and the speech recognition engine has been disabled or is not installed.

Error Number	Hex Value	Description
–2147213298	0x8004200E	Invalid Get method *Type* parameter. Please verify that the type you specified is supported and spelled correctly.
–2147213296	0x80042010	MoveTo method failed. A character cannot be moved while it is being dragged.
–2147213054	0x80042102	Request object not found. The Request object no longer exists in the character's animation queue.
–2147213053	0x80042103	Invalid use of the Stop method. A character cannot stop another character. Try the Interrupt method.
–2147213052	0x80042104	Invalid use of the Interrupt method. A character cannot interrupt itself.
–2147213051	0x80042105	Invalid use of the Wait method. A character cannot wait for its own requests to complete.
–2147213050	0x80042106	Invalid bookmark. Please make sure that the bookmark specified is not reserved by Microsoft Agent.
–2147213049	0x80042107	Microsoft Agent suspended. Right-click the Microsoft Agent taskbar icon and choose Restart Microsoft Agent.
–2147213048	0x80042108	Request object removed. The specified Request object was removed from the character queue.
–2147213047	0x80042109	Interrupted by Repeat Last Statement. The method request was interrupted because Repeat Last Statement was chosen.
–2147213046	0x8004210A	Interrupted by Listening key. The method request was interrupted because the Listening key was pressed.
–2147213045	0x8004210B	Interrupted by spoken input. The method request was interrupted because of spoken input.
–2147213044	0x8004210C	Interrupted by application. The application interrupted the character's animation queue.
–2147213043	0x8004210D	Interrupted by hiding. The method request was interrupted because the character was hidden.

Error Number	Hex Value	Description
–2147212799	0x80042201	Unable to initialize data provider. The Microsoft Agent Data Provider was not properly initialized.
–2147212798	0x80042202	Character data out of date. The specified character file version is not supported by the installed version of Microsoft Agent. You need to update the character.
–2147212797	0x80042203	Invalid version. The version of Microsoft Agent installed is older than the specified character file. Please verify that you have the correct version of Microsoft Agent installed.
–2147212796	0x80042204	Invalid character file. The specified file is not a Microsoft Agent character file. Please verify that the filename is correct.
–2147212795	0x80042205	Invalid character ID. The specified ID may be misspelled or not yet defined.
–2147212794	0x80042206	Invalid sound file. The specified file is not a valid sound (.WAV) file.
–2147212793	0x80042207	Corrupt sound file. The specified sound file does not have correct data.
–2147212792	0x80042208	Multimedia access failure. There was a problem accessing the system's multimedia component.
–2147212791	0x80042209	Protocol failure. The URL protocol you specified is not supported by Microsoft Agent.
–2147212543	0x80042301	Audio device failure. There was a problem accessing the audio device. Please verify that your sound card and drivers are correctly installed.
–2147212542	0x80042302	No installed speech engine. Microsoft Agent could not find a compatible speech recognition engine.
–2147212541	0x80042303	Speech input failure. The speech recognition engine failed to initialize. Please verify that the speech recognition engine is correctly installed.
–2147212540	0x80042304	Invalid Commands object. There is a problem in the specified Commands object definition.

Error Number	Hex Value	Description
–2147212539	0x80042305	Missing right parenthesis. The text for the Voice property of a command is missing a right parenthesis to specify an alternative.
–2147212538	0x80042306	Missing right square bracket. The text for the Voice property of a command is missing a right square bracket to specify an option.
–2147212537	0x80042307	Missing left parenthesis. The text for the Voice property of a command is missing a left parenthesis for specifying an alternative.
–2147212536	0x80042308	Missing left square bracket. The text for the Voice property of a command is missing a left square bracket to specify an option.
–2147212535	0x80042309	Missing parentheses. The text for the Voice property of a command is missing surrounding parentheses to specify alternatives.
–2147212534	0x8004230A	Speech input mode access failure. There was a problem accessing the speech recognition mode. Please verify that the speech engine is correctly installed.
–2147212533	0x8004230B	Invalid speech input mode. The specified speech recognition input mode could not be found. Please verify that the mode ID is correct.
–2147212532	0x8004230C	Speech disabled. The user has disabled speech recognition. The speech input object's properties are not available.
–2147212287	0x80042401	Audio device failure. There was a problem accessing the audio device. Please verify that your sound card and drivers are correctly installed.
–2147212286	0x80042402	Text-to-speech (TTS) failure. There was a problem initializing the text-to-speech engine.
–2147212285	0x80042403	TTS failure. There was a problem initializing the text-to-speech engine.

Error Number	Hex Value	Description
–2147212284	0x80042404	TTS failure. There was a problem initializing the text-to-speech engine.
–2147212283	0x80042405	TTS failure. There was a problem initializing the text-to-speech engine.
–2147212282	0x80042406	Lip-sync failure. There was a problem in the Microsoft Agent lip-sync component.
–2147212281	0x80042407	Lip-sync failure. There was a problem in the Microsoft Agent lip-sync component.
–2147212280	0x80042408	Lip-sync failure. There was a problem in the Microsoft Agent lip-sync component.
–2147212030	0x80042502	Unable to initialize Microsoft Agent. Make sure that Microsoft Agent is properly installed.
–2147212029	0x80042503	Speech-input language access failure. There was a problem accessing the language of the speech recognition engine.
–2147024894	0x80070001	The system cannot find the file specified.
–2147024883	0x8007000C	The data is invalid.
–2146697214	0x800C0002	Invalid URL. Please verify that the specified URL exists and is correct.
–2146697212	0x800C0004	Server access failure. The attempt to connect with the server failed. Please verify that the server is running and available.
–2146697210	0x800C0006	File not found. The file could not be found at the specified URL. Please make sure the URL is correct.
–2146697205	0x800C000B	Server connection time-out. The connection to the server timed out. Please verify that the server is running and available.
–2146697202	0x800C000E	Server security access failure. There was a security problem when accessing the server.
–2147213297	0x8004200F	Invalid animation. The specified animation may be damaged or has no frames.

A P P E N D I X   E

Microsoft Agent Licensing and Redistribution

The following uses for Microsoft Agent Version 1 are currently royalty-free, subject to the end-user license agreement displayed when Microsoft Agent installation file is run, and do not require a redistribution license:

- You can automatically cause Microsoft Agent to download from the Microsoft site by including the CLSID for Microsoft Agent in an HTML <OBJECT> tag on one of your site's pages.

- You can also automatically cause the Microsoft Command and Control speech recognition engine and the Lernout & Hauspie TruVoice Text-To-Speech Engine for Microsoft Agent to download from the Microsoft site, by including their CLSIDs in an HTML <OBJECT> tag on one of your site's pages, provided that these engines are only downloaded and installed for use with Microsoft Agent.

- You can load Microsoft's designated characters or images from the Microsoft Web site in your script code using the Microsoft Agent **Load** and **Get** (**Prepare**) methods.

However, to add or include Microsoft Agent and any of its components to or with an application, or post Microsoft Agent and any of its components on a server, or distribute Microsoft Agent and any of its components using other electronic media, you must first obtain and submit a redistribution license for Microsoft Agent. The Microsoft Agent character files, the Microsoft Command and Control speech engine, and the Lernout & Hauspie TruVoice Text-To-Speech Engine for Microsoft Agent cannot be redistributed without Microsoft Agent. This license for Microsoft Agent Version 1 is currently royalty-free to redistribute within your organization or to your customers. The license does not include the Microsoft Agent Character Editor or the Microsoft Linguistic Sound Editing Tool.

To request a redistribution license or further information, contact the Microsoft Agent Product Group at msagent@microsoft.com.

Bibliography

Ball, G. et al. "Life-Like Computer Characters: The Persona Project at Microsoft Research." *Software Agents*. Ed. Jeff Bradshaw. Cambridge, MA: MIT Press, 1996.

Bates, J. "The Nature of Character in Interactive Worlds and the Oz." *Technical Report CMU-CS-92-200*. School of Computer Science, Carnegie Mellon University. Pittsburgh, PA. October 1992.

Bates, J., Loyall, A., and Reilly, W. "An Architecture for Action, Emotion, and Social Behavior." In *Proceedings of the Fourth European Workshop on Modeling Autonomous Agents in a Multi-Agent World* (S. Martino al Cimino, Italy, 1992).

Bates, J., Loyall, A., and Reilly, W. "Integrating Reactivity, Goals and Emotions in a Broad Agent." In *Proceedings of the 14th Annual Conference of the Cognitive Science Society* (Indiana, July 1992).

Cassell, J. "Believable Communicating Agents: The Relationship Between Verbal and Nonverbal Behavior in Autonomous Communicating Agents." In *Siggraph '96 Course Notes*. Reading, MA: ACM Press, 1996.

Foner, L. "What's an Agent, Anyway? A Sociological Case Study." *Agents Memo 93-01*. Agents Group. Cambridge, MA: MIT Media Lab, 1993.

Grice, H. "Logic and Conversation." In *Syntax and Semantics 3: Speech Acts*. Ed. P. Cole and J. Morgan. New York: Academic Press, 1975.

Herman, J. *Newstalk: A Speech Interface to a Personalized Information Agent*. MIT Master's Thesis, Program in Media Arts and Sciences. Cambridge, MA. June 1995.

Koda, T. and Maes, P. "Agents with Faces: The Effects of Personification of Agents." In *Proceedings of HCI'96* (London, 1996).

Lassiter, J. "Principles of Traditional Animation Applied to 3-D Computer Animation." In *Proceedings of SIGGRAPH '87*. 35-44. Reading, MA: ACM Press, 1987.

Laurel, B. "Interface Agents: Metaphors with Character." *The Art of Human Computer Interface Design*. Reading, MA: Addison-Wesley, 1990.

Maes, P. "Agents that Reduce Work Overload and Information Overload." In *Communications of the ACM*. 31-40. July 1994.

Marx, M. *Toward Effective Conversational Messaging*. MIT Master's Thesis, Program in Media Arts and Sciences. Cambridge, MA.. June 1995.

Nass, C., Steuer, J., and Tauber, E. "Computers are Social Actors." In *Proceedings of the CHI '94 Conference* (Boston, MA, April 1994). 72-77. Reading, MA: ACM Press, 1994.

Nass, C. and Reeves, B. *The Media Equation: How People Treat Computers, Televisions, and New Media as Real People and Places*. Cambridge University Press, 1996.

Negroponte, N. "Hospital Corners." *The Art of Human-Computer Interface Design*. Ed. Brenda Laurel. Reading, MA: Addison Wesley, 1990.

Oren, T., et al. "Guides: Characterizing the Interface." *The Art of Human-Computer Interface Design*. Ed. Brenda Laurel. Reading, MA: Addison Wesley, 1990.

Parke, F. and Waters, K. *Computer Facial Animation*. Wellesley: AK Peters, 1996.

Perlin, K. and Goldberg, A. "Improv: A System for Scripting Interactive Actors in Virtual Worlds." In *Proceeding of SIGGRAPH 1995* (New Orleans, 1995).

Schmandt, C. *Voice Communication with Computers: Conversational Systems*. New York: Van Nostrand Reinhold, 1994.

Syrdal, A., Bennett, R., and Greenspan, S. *Applied Speech Technology*. Boca Raton: CRC Press, 1995.

Thomas, F., and Johnson, O. *The Illusion of Life.* New York: Abbeville Press, 1981.

Thorisson, K. "Dialogue Control in Social Interface Agents." *InterCHI Adjunct Proceedings* (Amsterdam, Holland, 1993). Reading, MA: ACM Press, 1993.

Creating Personalities for Synthetic Actors: Toward Autonomous Personality Agents. Ed. R. Trappl and Paolo Petta. New York: Springer-Verlag, 1997.

Yankelovich, N., Levow, G., and Marx, M. "Designing Speech Acts: Issues in Speech User Interfaces." In *Proceedings of CHI '95* (Denver, CO, May 1995). 369-376. Reading, MA: ACM Press, 1995.

Yankelovich, N. "How Do Users Know What to Say?" *Interactions*, Vol. III.6. 32-43. November/December, 1996.

The Windows Interface Guidelines for Software Design. Redmond, WA: Microsoft Press, 1995.

Index

IMPORTANT—READ CAREFULLY BEFORE OPENING SOFTWARE PACKET(S). By opening the sealed packet(s) containing the software, you indicate your acceptance of the following Microsoft License Agreement.

MICROSOFT LICENSE AGREEMENT

(Book Companion CD)

This is a legal agreement between you (either an individual or an entity) and Microsoft Corporation. By opening the sealed software packet(s) you are agreeing to be bound by the terms of this agreement. If you do not agree to the terms of this agreement, promptly return the unopened software packet(s) and any accompanying written materials to the place you obtained them for a full refund.

MICROSOFT SOFTWARE LICENSE

1. GRANT OF LICENSE. Microsoft grants to you the right to use one copy of the Microsoft software program included with this book (the "SOFTWARE") on a single terminal connected to a single computer. The SOFTWARE is in "use" on a computer when it is loaded into the temporary memory (i.e., RAM) or installed into the permanent memory (e.g., hard disk, CD-ROM, or other storage device) of that computer. You may not network the SOFTWARE or otherwise use it on more than one computer or computer terminal at the same time.

2. COPYRIGHT. The SOFTWARE is owned by Microsoft or its suppliers and is protected by United States copyright laws and international treaty provisions. Therefore, you must treat the SOFTWARE like any other copyrighted material (e.g., a book or musical recording) except that you may either (a) make one copy of the SOFTWARE solely for backup or archival purposes, or (b) transfer the SOFTWARE to a single hard disk provided you keep the original solely for backup or archival purposes. You may not copy the written materials accompanying the SOFTWARE.

3. OTHER RESTRICTIONS. You may not rent or lease the SOFTWARE, but you may transfer the SOFTWARE and accompanying written materials on a permanent basis provided you retain no copies and the recipient agrees to the terms of this Agreement. You may not reverse engineer, decompile, or disassemble the SOFTWARE. If the SOFTWARE is an update or has been updated, any transfer must include the most recent update and all prior versions.

4. DUAL MEDIA SOFTWARE. If the SOFTWARE package contains more than one kind of disk (3.5", 5.25", and CD-ROM), then you may use only the disks appropriate for your single-user computer. You may not use the other disks on another computer or loan, rent, lease, or transfer them to another user except as part of the permanent transfer (as provided above) of all SOFTWARE and written materials.

5. SAMPLE CODE. If the SOFTWARE includes Sample Code, then Microsoft grants you a royalty-free right to reproduce and distribute the sample code of the SOFTWARE provided that you: (a) distribute the sample code only in conjunction with and as a part of your software product; (b) do not use Microsoft's or its authors' names, logos, or trademarks to market your software product; (c) include the copyright notice that appears on the SOFTWARE on your product label and as a part of the sign-on message for your software product; and (d) agree to indemnify, hold harmless, and defend Microsoft and its authors from and against any claims or lawsuits, including attorneys' fees, that arise or result from the use or distribution of your software product.

DISCLAIMER OF WARRANTY

The SOFTWARE (including instructions for its use) is provided "AS IS" WITHOUT WARRANTY OF ANY KIND. MICROSOFT FURTHER DISCLAIMS ALL IMPLIED WARRANTIES INCLUDING WITHOUT LIMITATION ANY IMPLIED WARRANTIES OF MERCHANTABILITY OR OF FITNESS FOR A PARTICULAR PURPOSE. THE ENTIRE RISK ARISING OUT OF THE USE OR PERFORMANCE OF THE SOFTWARE AND DOCUMENTATION REMAINS WITH YOU.

IN NO EVENT SHALL MICROSOFT, ITS AUTHORS, OR ANYONE ELSE INVOLVED IN THE CREATION, PRODUCTION, OR DELIVERY OF THE SOFTWARE BE LIABLE FOR ANY DAMAGES WHATSOEVER (INCLUDING, WITHOUT LIMITATION, DAMAGES FOR LOSS OF BUSINESS PROFITS, BUSINESS INTERRUPTION, LOSS OF BUSINESS INFORMATION, OR OTHER PECUNIARY LOSS) ARISING OUT OF THE USE OF OR INABILITY TO USE THE SOFTWARE OR DOCUMENTATION, EVEN IF MICROSOFT HAS BEEN ADVISED OF THE POSSIBILITY OF SUCH DAMAGES. BECAUSE SOME STATES/COUNTRIES DO NOT ALLOW THE EXCLUSION OR LIMITATION OF LIABILITY FOR CONSEQUENTIAL OR INCIDENTAL DAMAGES, THE ABOVE LIMITATION MAY NOT APPLY TO YOU.

U.S. GOVERNMENT RESTRICTED RIGHTS

The SOFTWARE and documentation are provided with RESTRICTED RIGHTS. Use, duplication, or disclosure by the Government is subject to restrictions as set forth in subparagraph (c)(1)(ii) of The Rights in Technical Data and Computer Software clause at DFARS 252.227-7013 or subparagraphs (c)(1) and (2) of the Commercial Computer Software — Restricted Rights 48 CFR 52.227-19, as applicable. Manufacturer is Microsoft Corporation, One Microsoft Way, Redmond, WA 98052-6399.

If you acquired this product in the United States, this Agreement is governed by the laws of the State of Washington.

Should you have any questions concerning this Agreement, or if you desire to contact Microsoft Press for any reason, please write: Microsoft Press, One Microsoft Way, Redmond, WA 98052-6399.